First Edition

triumphlearning™

Common Core Coach

English Language Arts 8

Common Core Coach, English Language Arts, First Edition, Grade 8 T107NA ISBN-13: 978-1-61997-435-7
Cover Design: Q2A/Bill Smith **Cover Illustration:** Jing Jing Tsong

Printed in the United States of America. 10 9 8 7 6 5 4 3 2 1

Contents

Common Core State Standards

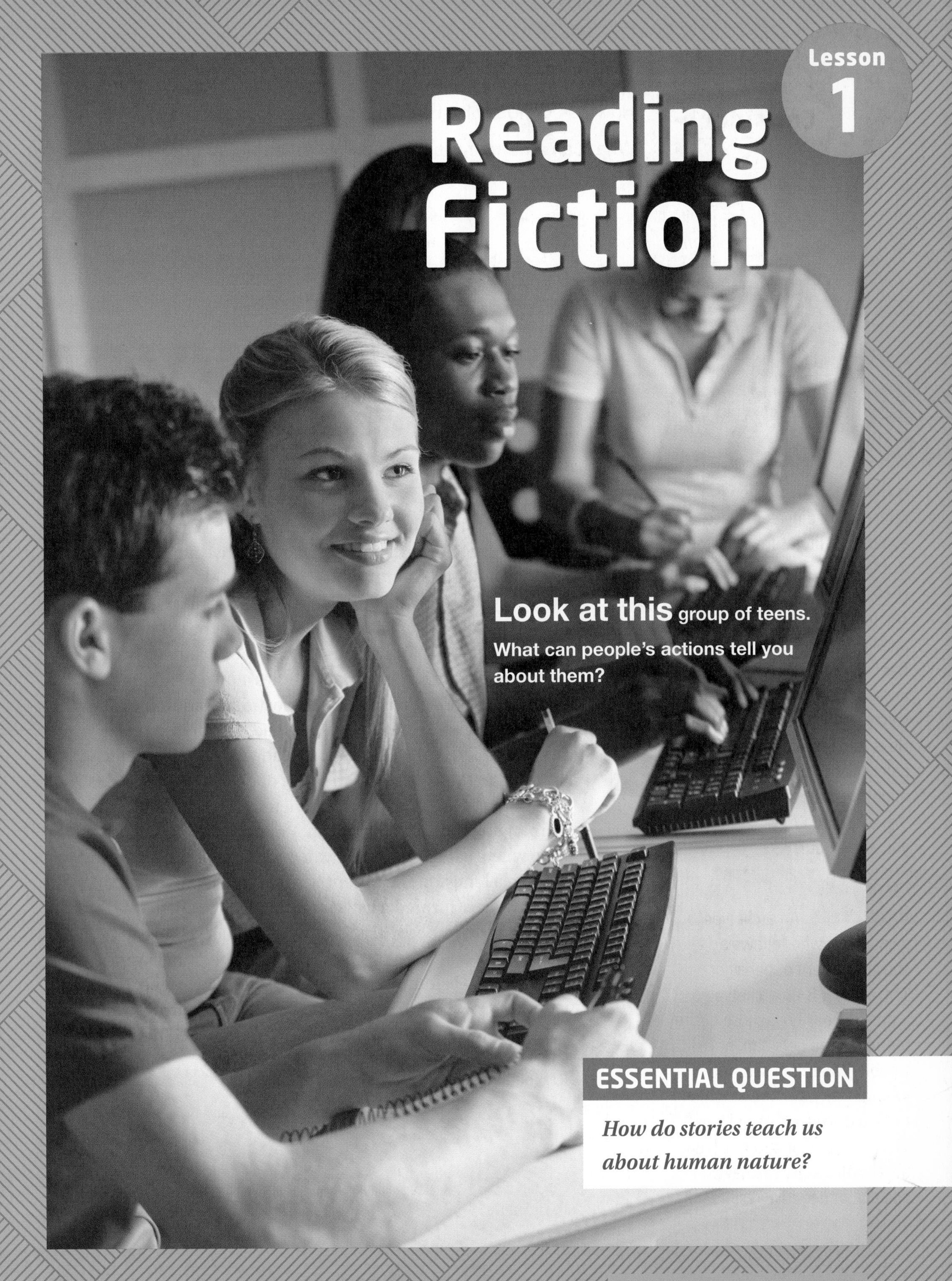

Reading Fiction

Look at this group of teens.

What can people's actions tell you about them?

ESSENTIAL QUESTION

How do stories teach us about human nature?

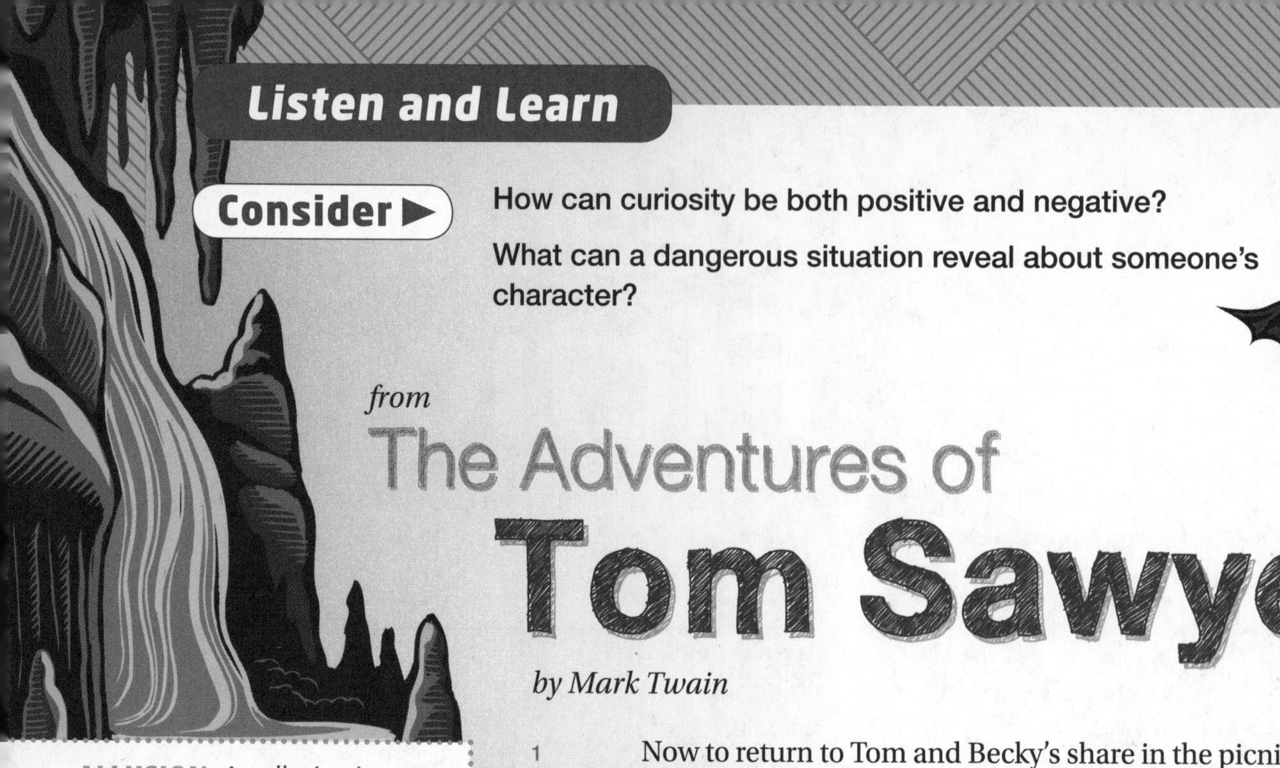

Listen and Learn

Consider ▶ How can curiosity be both positive and negative?

What can a dangerous situation reveal about someone's character?

from

The Adventures of Tom Sawyer

by Mark Twain

1 Now to return to Tom and Becky's share in the picnic. They tripped along the murky aisles with the rest of the company, visiting the familiar wonders of the cave—wonders dubbed with rather over-descriptive names, such as "The Drawing-Room," "The Cathedral," "Aladdin's Palace," and so on. Presently the hide-and-seek frolicking began, and Tom and Becky engaged in it with zeal until the exertion began to grow a trifle wearisome; then they wandered down a sinuous avenue holding their candles aloft and reading the tangled webwork of names, dates, post-office addresses, and mottoes with which the rocky walls had been frescoed[1] (in candle-smoke). Still drifting along and talking, they scarcely noticed that they were now in a part of the cave whose walls were not frescoed. They smoked their own names under an overhanging shelf and moved on. Presently they came to a place where a little stream of water, trickling over a ledge and carrying a limestone sediment with it, had, in the slow-dragging ages, formed a laced and ruffled Niagara in gleaming and imperishable stone. Tom squeezed his small body behind it in order to illuminate it for Becky's gratification. He found that it curtained a sort of steep natural stairway which was enclosed between narrow walls, and at once the ambition to be a discoverer seized him.

[1]**frescoed** refers to a method of wall-painting

ALLUSION An allusion is a reference to a person, place, or event from literature or history. Authors use allusions to provide context or to summarize an idea. The name "Aladdin's Palace" is an allusion to the Middle Eastern folk tale "Aladdin," in which a mischievous boy is tricked by a sorcerer and trapped in a cave. He is freed by a genie, and a palace is built for him. Why might the author have included this allusion? What does it tell you about Tom?

ARCHETYPE An archetype is a character who follows a specific pattern of behavior. Tom Sawyer is an archetype of a mischievous boy whose desire for adventure gets him in trouble. When Tom sees the natural stairway, "the ambition to be a discoverer seized him." What do you think Tom will do next? Will his actions have positive or negative results?

Becky responded to his call, and they made a smoke-mark for future guidance, and started upon their quest. They wound this way and that, far down into the secret depths of the cave, made another mark, and branched off in search of novelties to tell the upper world about. In one place they found a spacious cavern, from whose ceiling depended a multitude of shining stalactites[2] of the length and circumference of a man's leg; they walked all about it, wondering and admiring, and presently left it by one of the numerous passages that opened into it. . . . Under the roof vast knots of bats had packed themselves together, thousands in a bunch; the lights disturbed the creatures and they came flocking down by hundreds, squeaking and darting furiously at the candles. Tom knew their ways and the danger of this sort of conduct. He seized Becky's hand and hurried her into the first corridor that offered; and none too soon, for a bat struck Becky's light out with its wing while she was passing out of the cavern. The bats chased the children a good distance; but the fugitives plunged into every new passage that offered, and at last got rid of the perilous things. Tom found a subterranean lake, shortly, which stretched its dim length away until its shape was lost in the shadows. He wanted to explore its borders, but concluded that it would be best to sit down and rest awhile, first. Now, for the first time, the deep stillness of the place laid a clammy hand upon the spirits of the children. Becky said:

"Why, I didn't notice, but it seems ever so long since I heard any of the others."

"Come to think, Becky, we are away down below them—and I don't know how far away north, or south, or east, or whichever it is. We couldn't hear them here."

[2]**stalactites** icicle-shaped deposits hanging from the roof of a cave

ANALOGY An analogy is a comparison that shows the similarities between two things. An analogy can help readers visualize characters, events, or objects in a story. In this paragraph, the author compares stalactites to a man's leg. What do you learn about the stalactites from this analogy?

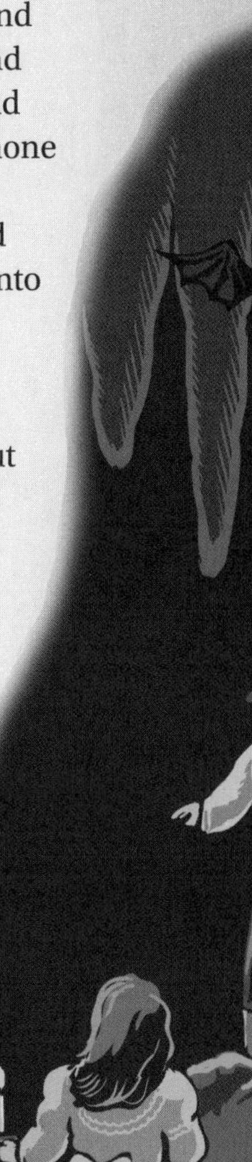

5 Becky grew apprehensive.

"I wonder how long we've been down here, Tom? We better start back."

"Yes, I reckon we better. P'raps we better."

"Can you find the way, Tom? It's all a mixed-up crookedness to me."

"I reckon I could find it—but then the bats. If they put our candles out it will be an awful fix. Let's try some other way, so as not to go through there."

10 "Well. But I hope we won't get lost. It would be so awful!" and the girl shuddered at the thought of the dreadful possibilities.

They started through a corridor, and traversed it in silence a long way, glancing at each new opening, to see if there was anything familiar about the look of it; but they were all strange. Every time Tom made an examination, Becky would watch his face for an encouraging sign, and he would say cheerily:

"Oh, it's all right. This ain't the one, but we'll come to it right away!"

But he felt less and less hopeful with each failure, and presently began to turn off into diverging avenues at sheer random, in desperate hope of finding the one that was wanted. He still said it was "all right," but there was such a leaden dread at his heart that the words had lost their ring and sounded just as if he had said, "All is lost!" Becky clung to his side in an anguish of fear, and tried hard to keep back the tears, but they would come. At last she said:

"Oh, Tom, never mind the bats, let's go back that way! We seem to get worse and worse off all the time."

15 "Listen!" said he.

Profound silence; silence so deep that even their breathings were conspicuous in the hush. Tom shouted. The call went echoing down the empty aisles and died out in the distance in a faint sound that resembled a ripple of mocking laughter.

DIALOGUE AND PLOT

In many stories, dialogue (conversation between characters) serves to move the plot (what happens in a story) forward. Tom says to Becky, "If [the bats] put our candles out it will be an awful fix. Let's try some other way, so as not to go through there," and Becky agrees. What happens as a result of this dialogue? How does it move the plot forward?

"Oh, don't do it again, Tom, it is too horrid," said Becky.

"It is horrid, but I better, Becky; they might hear us, you know," and he shouted again.

The "might" was even a chillier horror than the ghostly laughter, it so confessed a perishing hope. The children stood still and listened; but there was no result. Tom turned upon the back track at once, and hurried his steps. It was but a little while before a certain indecision in his manner revealed another fearful fact to Becky—he could not find his way back!

20 "Oh, Tom, you didn't make any marks!"

"Becky, I was such a fool! Such a fool! I never thought we might want to come back! No—I can't find the way. It's all mixed up."

"Tom, Tom, we're lost! we're lost! We never can get out of this awful place! Oh, why DID we ever leave the others!"

She sank to the ground and burst into such a frenzy of crying that Tom was appalled with the idea that she might die, or lose her reason. . . . Tom begged her to pluck up hope again, and she said she could not. He fell to blaming and abusing himself for getting her into this miserable situation; this had a better effect. She said she would try to hope again, she would get up and follow wherever he might lead if only he would not talk like that any more. . . .

So they moved on again—aimlessly—simply at random—all they could do was to move, keep moving. For a little while, hope made a show of reviving—not with any reason to back it, but only because it is its nature to revive when the spring has not been taken out of it by age and familiarity with failure.

25 By-and-by Tom took Becky's candle and blew it out. This economy meant so much! Words were not needed. Becky understood, and her hope died again. She knew that Tom had a whole candle and three or four pieces in his pockets—yet he must economize.

By-and-by, fatigue began to assert its claims; the children tried to pay attention, for it was dreadful to think of sitting down when time was grown to be so precious, moving, in some direction, in any direction, was at least progress and might bear fruit; but to sit down was to invite death and shorten its pursuit.

SUSPENSE Suspense is a state of uncertainty. An author uses suspense to maintain the reader's interest and keep the reader wondering about what will happen. What are Tom and Becky uncertain about in the story?

INFERENCE An inference is a guess based on evidence in a text. Becky agrees to try to have hope if Tom will stop blaming himself for their situation. What can you infer about Becky's feelings for Tom?

CHARACTERIZATION A writer reveals a character's personality through several elements of characterization—direct statements, action, dialogue, thoughts and emotions, and interactions with other characters. What is revealed about Tom's personality when he says, "Cheer up, Becky, and let's go on trying"? Which elements of characterization are being used?

POINT OF VIEW Point of view is the perspective from which a story is told. The three most common points of view are: third-person omniscient (the narrator knows everything about all characters), third-person limited (the narrator knows the thoughts and feelings of one character), and first person (the narrator is a character in the story and uses the personal pronoun "I"). While Tom and Becky are trapped in the cave, we learn that "The village of St. Petersburg still mourned." How does this information reveal the narrator's point of view?

At last Becky's frail limbs refused to carry her farther. She sat down. Tom rested with her, and they talked of home, and the friends there, and the comfortable beds and, above all, the light! Becky cried, and Tom tried to think of some way of comforting her, but all his encouragements were grown thread-bare with use, and sounded like sarcasms. Fatigue bore so heavily upon Becky that she drowsed off to sleep. Tom was grateful. He sat looking into her drawn face and saw it grow smooth and natural under the influence of pleasant dreams; and by-and-by a smile dawned and rested there. The peaceful face reflected somewhat of peace and healing into his own spirit, and his thoughts wandered away to bygone times and dreamy memories. While he was deep in his musings, Becky woke up with a breezy little laugh—but it was stricken dead upon her lips, and a groan followed it.

"Oh, how COULD I sleep! I wish I never, never had waked! No! No, I don't, Tom! Don't look so! I won't say it again."

"I'm glad you've slept, Becky; you'll feel rested, now, and we'll find the way out."

30 "We can try, Tom; but I've seen such a beautiful country in my dream. I reckon we are going there."

"Maybe not, maybe not. Cheer up, Becky, and let's go on trying."

. . . Tuesday afternoon came, and waned to the twilight. The village of St. Petersburg still mourned. The lost children had not been found. . . . Mrs. Thatcher was very ill, and a great part of the time delirious. . . . Aunt Polly had drooped into a settled melancholy, and her gray hair had grown almost white. The village went to its rest on Tuesday night, sad and forlorn.

Away in the middle of the night a wild peal burst from the village bells, and in a moment the streets were swarming with frantic half-clad people, who shouted, "Turn out! turn out! they're found! they're found!" . . .

The village was illuminated; nobody went to bed again; it was the greatest night the little town had ever seen. During the first half-hour a procession of villagers filed through Judge Thatcher's house, seized the saved ones and kissed them, squeezed Mrs. Thatcher's hand, tried to speak but couldn't—and drifted out raining tears all over the place. . . .

35 Tom lay upon a sofa with an eager auditory about him and told the history of the wonderful adventure, putting in many striking additions to adorn it withal; and closed with a description of how he left Becky and went on an exploring expedition; how he followed two avenues as far as his kite-line would reach; how he followed a third to the fullest stretch of the kite-line, and was about to turn back when he glimpsed a far-off speck that looked like daylight; dropped the line and groped toward it, pushed his head and shoulders through a small hole, and saw the broad Mississippi rolling by!

. . . He told how he went back for Becky[;] . . . how he pushed his way out at the hole and then helped her out; how they sat there and cried for gladness; how some men came along in a skiff and Tom hailed them and told them their situation and their famished condition; how the men didn't believe the wild tale at first, "because," said they, "you are five miles down the river below the valley the cave is in"—then took them aboard, rowed to a house, gave them supper, made them rest till two or three hours after dark and then brought them home.

IRONY Verbal irony occurs when a character's or narrator's words do not match what is really meant. Situational irony occurs when the outcome of an event is the opposite of what is expected. When the narrator says that Tom "told the history of the wonderful adventure," which type of irony is occurring? Why?

THEME A story's theme is the general idea about life that it reveals. One of this story's themes is that it is much easier to get into trouble than out of it. How does the story reveal this general idea about life? What are some other themes in the story?

Comprehension Check

Look back in *The Adventures of Tom Sawyer* to see how Tom thinks and behaves during the story. Think about how the author presents Tom through the narrator's eyes. Use the graphic organizer to develop a character sketch of Tom Sawyer.

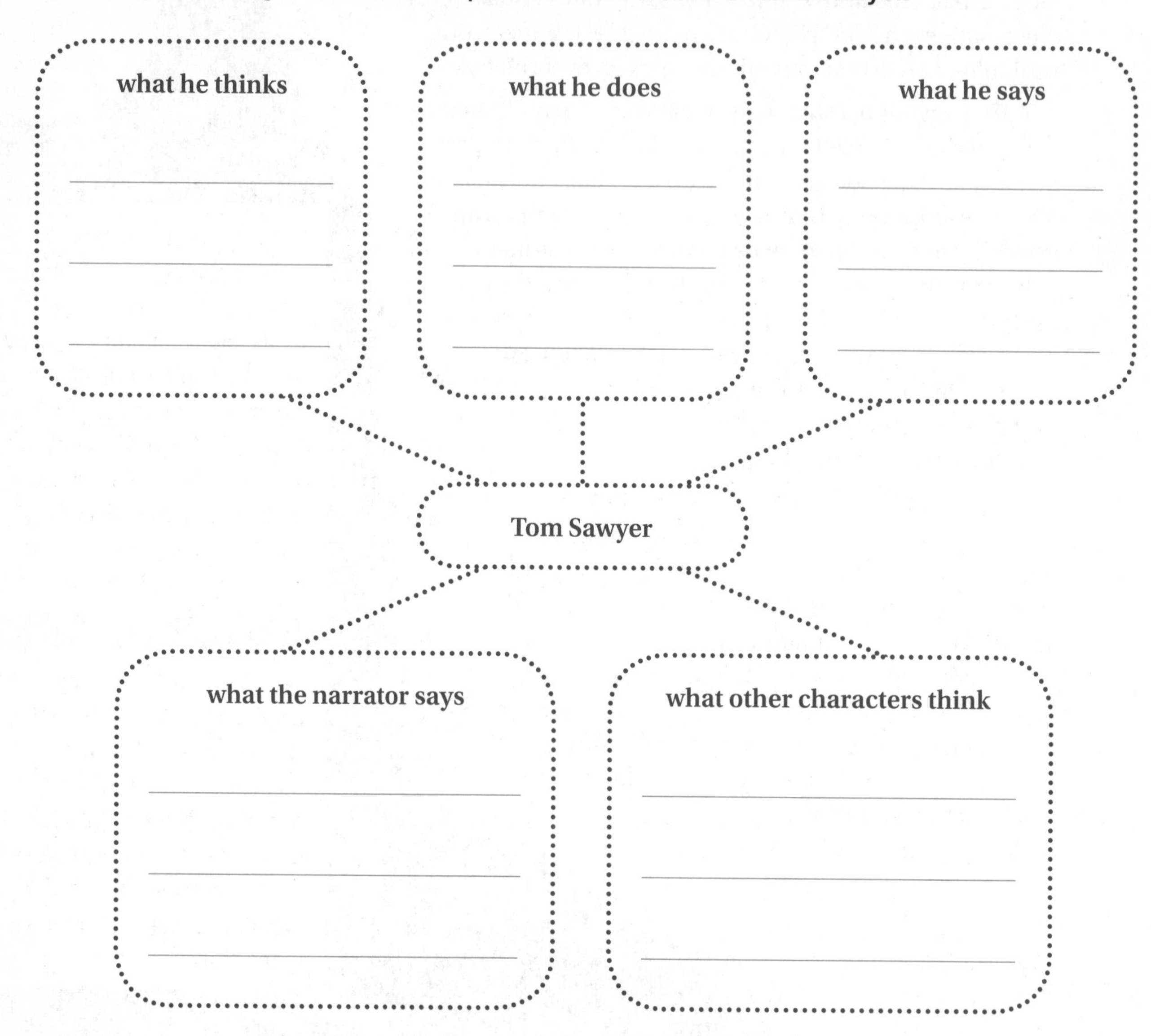

Vocabulary

Use the word map below to help you define and use one of the highlighted vocabulary words from the Share and Learn reading or another word your teacher assigns you.

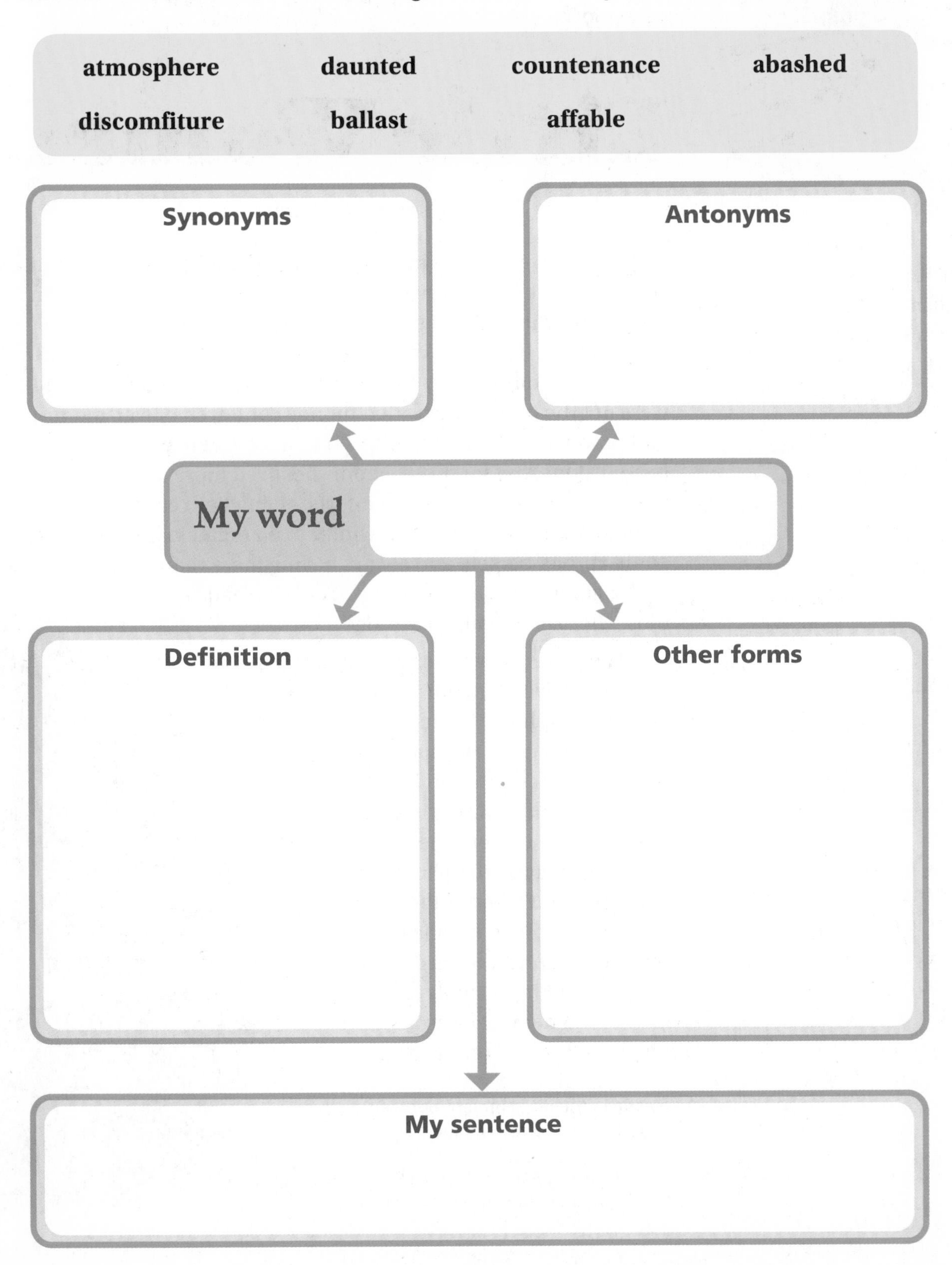

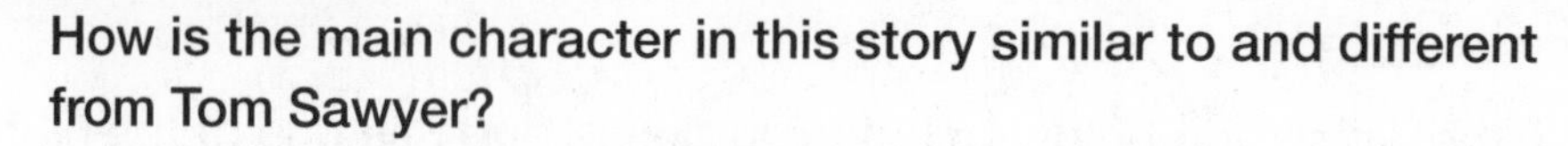

Share and Learn

Consider ▶ How is the main character in this story similar to and different from Tom Sawyer?

What various features of being young do these two characters illustrate?

from

Little Women

by Louisa May Alcott

THEME Look at the description of Jo in paragraph 1. Underline phrases that show that this story is about her pursuit of a dream.

ARCHETYPE Which phrase in paragraph 1 best describes a type of character you might see in other stories?

____

____

____

ANALOGY Circle the name of the fairy tale character in paragraph 2 that Jo is compared to. Explain how the author is saying the two characters are similar.

____

____

____

1 Though very happy in the social atmosphere about her, and very busy with the daily work that earned her bread and made it sweeter for the effort, Jo still found time for literary labors. The purpose which now took possession of her was a natural one to a poor and ambitious girl, but the means she took to gain her end were not the best. She saw that money conferred power, money and power, therefore, she resolved to have, not to be used for herself alone, but for those whom she loved more than life. The dream of filling home with comforts, giving Beth everything she wanted, from strawberries in winter to an organ in her bedroom, going abroad herself, and always having more than enough, so that she might indulge in the luxury of charity, had been for years Jo's most cherished castle in the air.[1]

The prize-story experience had seemed to open a way which might, after long traveling and much uphill work, lead to this delightful chateau en Espagne.[2] But the novel disaster quenched her courage for a time, for public opinion is a giant which has frightened stouter-hearted Jacks on bigger beanstalks than hers. But the "up again and take another" spirit was as strong in Jo as in Jack, so she scrambled up on the shady side this time and got more booty, but nearly left behind her what was far more precious than the moneybags.

[1]**castle in the air** a metaphor meaning that this was Jo's greatest dream

[2]**delightful chateau en Espagne** another reference to Jo's dream of having a comfortable home

She took to writing sensation stories,[3] for in those dark ages, even all-perfect America read rubbish.[4] She told no one, but concocted a "thrilling tale", and boldly carried it herself to Mr. Dashwood, editor of the *Weekly Volcano*. She had never read *Sartor Resartus*, but she had a womanly instinct that clothes possess an influence more powerful over many than the worth of character or the magic of manners. So she dressed herself in her best, and trying to persuade herself that she was neither excited nor nervous, bravely climbed two pairs of dark and dirty stairs to find herself in a disorderly room, a cloud of cigar smoke, and the presence of three gentlemen, sitting with their heels rather higher than their hats, which articles of dress none of them took the trouble to remove on her appearance. Somewhat daunted by this reception, Jo hesitated on the threshold, murmuring in much embarrassment.

"Excuse me, I was looking for the *Weekly Volcano* office. I wished to see Mr. Dashwood."

5 Down went the highest pair of heels, up rose the smokiest gentleman, and carefully cherishing his cigar between his fingers, he advanced with a nod and a countenance expressive of nothing but sleep. Feeling that she must get through the matter somehow, Jo produced her manuscript and, blushing redder and redder with each sentence, blundered out fragments of the little speech carefully prepared for the occasion.

"A friend of mine desired me to offer—a story—just as an experiment—would like your opinion—be glad to write more if this suits."

While she blushed and blundered, Mr. Dashwood had taken the manuscript, and was turning over the leaves with a pair of rather dirty fingers, and casting critical glances up and down the neat pages.

"Well, you can leave it, if you like. We've more of this sort of thing on hand than we know what to do with at present, but I'll run my eye over it, and give you an answer next week."

[3]**sensation stories** stories that may involve characters whose actions are not admirable

[4]**rubbish** refers to literature that is poorly written or has no moral value

ALLUSION Circle the name of the magazine in paragraph 3 that Jo might have read for fashion tips.

SETTING Based on the details in paragraph 3, what words would you use to describe the newspaper office?

____

____

____

CHARACTER Circle the words and phrases in paragraph 5 that the author uses to describe Mr. Dashwood.

INFERENCE What can you infer about Jo's feelings in paragraphs 5 through 7?

____

____

____

HUMOR Underline the description of the humor directed against Jo in paragraph 9.

POINT OF VIEW What does paragraph 9 tell you about the point of view of the narrator?

____

____

____

Now, Jo did *not* like to leave it, for Mr. Dashwood didn't suit her at all, but, under the circumstances, there was nothing for her to do but bow and walk away, looking particularly tall and dignified, as she was apt to do when nettled or abashed. Just then she was both, for it was perfectly evident from the knowing glances exchanged among the gentlemen that her little fiction of "my friend" was considered a good joke, and a laugh, produced by some inaudible remark of the editor, as he closed the door, completed her discomfiture. Half resolving never to return, she went home, and worked off her irritation by stitching pinafores[5] vigorously, and in an hour or two was cool enough to laugh over the scene and long for next week.

[5]**pinafores** garments worn over dresses or skirts, popular among girls in this time period

10 When she went again, Mr. Dashwood was alone, whereat she rejoiced. Mr. Dashwood was much wider awake than before, which was agreeable, and Mr. Dashwood was not too deeply absorbed in a cigar to remember his manners, so the second interview was much more comfortable than the first.

"We'll take this, if you don't object to a few alterations. It's too long, but omitting the passages I've marked will make it just the right length," he said, in a businesslike tone.

Jo hardly knew her own MS[6] again, so crumpled and underscored were its pages and paragraphs, but feeling as a tender parent might on being asked to cut off her baby's legs in order that it might fit into a new cradle, she looked at the marked passages and was surprised to find that all the moral reflections—which she had carefully put in as ballast for much romance—had been stricken out.

"But, Sir, I thought every story should have some sort of a moral, so I took care to have a few of my sinners repent."

Mr. Dashwood's editorial gravity relaxed into a smile, for Jo had forgotten her "friend", and spoken as only an author could.

15 "People want to be amused, not preached at, you know. Morals don't sell nowadays." Which was not quite a correct statement, by the way.

"You think it would do with these alterations, then?"

"Yes, it's a new plot, and pretty well worked up—language good, and so on," was Mr. Dashwood's affable reply.

"What do you—that is, what compensation—" began Jo, not exactly knowing how to express herself.

"Oh, yes, well, we give from twenty-five to thirty for things of this sort. Pay when it comes out," returned Mr. Dashwood, as if that point had escaped him.

[6]**MS** an abbreviation of the word *manuscript*

COMPARE AND CONTRAST FICTION
Compare and contrast how Tom and Jo each handle stressful situations in the two stories. How are they alike and different?

____

____

____

CONTEXT CLUES What context clues in paragraph 12 can help you determine the meaning of ballast?

____

____

____

CHARACTERIZATION
What do Mr. Dashwood's actions in paragraph 14 tell you about his personality?

____

____

____

SUMMARY How would you summarize the second interaction between Jo and Mr. Dashwood?

____

____

____

20 "Very well, you can have it," said Jo, handing back the story with a satisfied air, for after the dollar-a-column work, even twenty-five seemed good pay.

"Shall I tell my friend you will take another if she has one better than this?" asked Jo, unconscious of her little slip of the tongue, and emboldened by her success.

"Well, we'll look at it. Can't promise to take it. Tell her to make it short and spicy, and never mind the moral. What name would your friend like to put on it?" in a careless tone.

"None at all, if you please, she doesn't wish her name to appear and has no nom de plume,"[7] said Jo, blushing in spite of herself.

"Just as she likes, of course. The tale will be out next week. Will you call for the money, or shall I send it?" asked Mr. Dashwood.

25 "I'll call. Good morning, Sir."

As she departed, Mr. Dashwood put up his feet, with the graceful remark, "Poor and proud, as usual, but she'll do."

[7]**nom de plume** a French term meaning "pen name"; a name the author chooses to be called instead of using his or her given name

Anchor Standard Discussion Questions

Discuss the following questions with your peer group. Then record your answers in the space provided.

1. Jo goes through a lot of trouble to get her story published, yet she decides not to take credit for it. What does this decision reveal about Jo's values? Support your answer with evidence from the text.

2. The narrator describes Jo's second interview as "much more comfortable" than the first. Does Jo grow to like Mr. Dashwood? What is Jo's opinion of him by the end of the passage? Support your answers with evidence from the text.

Comprehension Check

1. How would you describe Jo based on what she does in the story? What character traits does she reveal through her actions?

2. Summarize Jo's dreams and her plan to make those dreams come true.

3. One of the themes of *The Adventures of Tom Sawyer* is about taking responsibility. How does this theme appear in *Little Women*?

Read On Your Own

Read another story, "Striking Out," independently. Apply what you learned in this lesson and check your understanding.

Lesson 2

Writing Responses to Literature

Many times during your school years, you will be asked to write a response to something you've read. For example, a teacher might ask you to evaluate the characters or plot of a story. Where do you start? What should you include? Today, you are going to read a response to a story that focuses on the importance of setting. Then you will write your own response to the same story, focusing this time on its theme. Both responses will be organized in much the same way.

ESSENTIAL QUESTION

How can writing be used effectively to analyze literature?

What's a Response to Literature?

A response to literature is a written analysis of any aspect of a story, play, poem, book, or some other written material. For example, a response might evaluate how one or more characters in a story interact, or it might examine a book as an example of a certain genre. A response to literature might explore an author's style of writing or explain the political theories in an essay. Sometimes, you will have to respond to a particular question or writing prompt about the text. Other times, you will be able to decide which aspect of the text you will write about.

A **response to literature** can be organized as outlined in the graphic organizer below. An effective response will usually include five or more paragraphs.

Introduction
Include a thesis, or main idea statement, that gives an interpretation of some aspect of the literature. Identify the title, author, and genre, and briefly summarize the text. Introduce reasons, or points, that explain your interpretation of the text.

↓

Reason #1 and Supporting Details
State your first point and support it with details from the text and/or other related evidence.

↓

Reason #2 and Supporting Details
State your second point and support it with details from the text and/or other related evidence.

↓

Reason #3 and Supporting Details
State your third point and support it with details from the text and/or other related evidence.

↓

Conclusion
Restate your thesis and summarize your main points. Leave the reader with some thoughts to consider.

Analyze a Mentor Text: Reading

You will respond to the story below. Read it carefully before reviewing the mentor text on the following pages.

Navajo Lessons

The van had been jolting over the rocky dirt road for more than an hour. "My teeth will fall out if we drive another mile," Celine thought bitterly.

She couldn't believe her grandmother lived so far away from everything. Even more unbelievable was the fact that her parents were making her and Josh spend their summer on the Navajo reservation in northern Arizona. Celine had planned a great summer—early-morning runs with Dora to get in tip-top shape for track; sunbathing at the pool with her friends every day; spending evenings dancing, laughing, and having fun at the Teen Center.

Then Mom received a letter from Aunt Billie. Cousin Sonia was getting ready to have her *Kinaaldá*, the Navajo girl's coming-of-age ceremony. Everyone was so excited, as there would be a big family party to celebrate. With that, she and Celine's dad decided to send Celine and Josh to their grandmother's house—not only for the *Kinaaldá*, but for the *entire* summer. Celine's mom caught the surprised expression on Celine's face that said, "for the *whole* summer?" Celine wondered why they couldn't all go home after the party.

"Grandmother misses you two," Mom had said. "It would be good for both of you to spend quality time with her."

A few days later, the van pulled up to her grandmother's hogan. Celine had been there before and was dreading seeing it again. The dirt floor, the lack of electricity and running water—all that and a few pieces of furniture would be her home for the next few months. Celine couldn't believe she had to spend the summer here, but this was her fate.

"*Yá'át'ééh*," Grandmother, *Shimásání*, greeted them. She only knew a few words of English, and even then it was difficult to understand her. The plan was that Celine and Josh would learn Navajo by necessity. If they wanted to communicate with anyone but each other, they'd have to speak Grandmother's language.

Celine survived the first few days by pointing and also by listening to her favorite music all day and night. It was almost as if she was living in denial.

Josh, on the other hand, was enjoying himself thoroughly; he was inquisitive about and interested in everything. He'd point at something, and Grandmother would say the word in Navajo. Josh would recite the word, and Grandmother would laugh and say it again, correcting his intonation. Then Josh would repeat it over and over again like a broken record until Celine thought she would scream.

Josh had even managed to find other human life near Grandmother's hogan. Granted, it was a mile away—Navajos didn't like to crowd one another. Even so, Josh didn't mind the lonesome hike down to the Begay hogan. There were two boys his age there, and the three of them would spend all day jabbering away in Navajo and chasing each other up and down the arroyos.

Celine had picked up only one Navajo word, *Shíká'anilyeed*—which means "help." It was ironic because it was how Celine felt and also all she heard all day long. "*Shíká'anilyeed*," Grandmother would say as she pointed to the pot on the stove that needed stirring. "*Shíká'anilyeed*," she said to Celine, intending for her to take the sheep out to graze.

Yet staying at Grandmother's wasn't all work. There were some special moments. Grandmother had a way of saying "Celine" that brimmed with affection. And every night, after Josh and Celine were snug in their sleeping bags, Grandmother would begin a long tale.

"What's she saying?" Celine would whisper to Josh. It all sounded like gibberish to her, but she could sense that whatever Grandmother was saying was important.

"Shh, this one's a story about Great-grandfather. He was a Code Talker in World War II. Code Talkers helped win the war against Japan because the Japanese couldn't decipher the Navajo language."

By the time Grandmother had finished her story, Josh would be fast asleep, while Celine would be lost in the dark, wondering about Great-grandfather's adventures.

Celine stuck to her training routine each morning when she went for a run. Even if she couldn't train with Dora, she would be in shape and conditioned for track when school started. One morning as she was returning to the hogan, Josh met up with her. He looked devastated: he was holding back tears.

"*Shimásání* is ill," he sobbed. "What are we going to do?"

Celine sprinted back to the Hogan, where she found Grandmother lying on her side. Celine heard Grandmother's shallow breathing and bravely fought her own feeling of panic. "We've got to get help!" shouted Celine. "You stay here with her. I'm going to run over to the Begays. They have a pickup truck, right?"

Josh nodded with his head resting against Grandmother's arm.

"She'll be all right, Josh. I'll be back soon." Celine quickly looked around to get her bearings. Which way was the Begay hogan? Could she run fast enough? Sweat streamed down her face and hair. How would she communicate? Could *she* ask for help?

Soon, though, the Begay hogan came into view, and the truck was parked nearby.

"Hello, hello?" she shouted. And then the words came to her. "*Shíká'anilyeed! Shimásání. Shíká'anilyeed!*" "Help! Grandmother. Help!" The grandfather was home. He grabbed the keys and they both rushed to the truck. They drove back to Grandmother's hogan in silence. When they arrived, they lifted her gently onto a blanket and into the back of the truck. Celine and Josh rode next to her, shading her from the blistering sun.

A few hours later, they were in the hospital in Tuba City, surrounded by family members. "You did the right thing," they told Celine. "Because of you, she got here in time. You run fast, like the Diné," they told her in English.

"Thank you, but please say it again," Celine prompted. "This time, in Navajo."

Analyze a Mentor Text: Response

This is an effective response to the story you just read. Read the response and then complete the activities in the boxes as a class.

The Importance of Setting

The setting controls everything in the story "Navajo Lessons." In this example of realistic fiction, Celine and her brother are sent to live on a reservation with their Navajo grandmother for the summer. Missing her friends back home, Celine resists learning Navajo, the only language her grandmother speaks. Celine resents being there—until one morning, when she suddenly has to get help for her ailing grandmother. In this story, the setting directly affects the characters, the plot, and the climax.

The setting affects how the main character, Celine, interacts with her grandmother. Celine does not understand or speak Navajo, which is her grandmother's only language. Celine reacts to the situation by withdrawing. For example, she spends her first days and nights at the reservation listening to music. At home, her behavior would have been very different. The setting affects the grandmother, too. Living by herself in the desert, she has had no need to learn English. Only Celine's brother, Josh, is not affected by the setting. A happy kid, he quickly adapts to living with Grandmother, finds friend, and starts learning how to speak and understand Navajo.

The setting also directly affects the plot. In fact, the story is based on how Celine responds to the setting—the Navajo reservation. If she were spending time with an aunt in the city or another relative in the suburbs, the plot would have been entirely different. Celine would have missed her friends, but she probably would not have felt so isolated. Plus, she most likely would have been able to communicate with those around her.

INTRODUCTION The introduction includes a thesis statement that gives the writer's interpretation of the text. Circle the thesis statement.

SUPPORTING DETAILS Paragraph 2 explains how the setting affects the three main characters in the story. Underline the evidence the writer uses to support the main point in this paragraph.

SUPPORTING DETAILS The writer does *not* use details from the story to support the main point presented in paragraph 3. What kind of evidence does the writer provide instead?

SUPPPORTING DETAILS Which details from the story support the main point discussed in paragraph 4?

CONCLUSION The conclusion summarizes the main points discussed in the response. How is the thesis restated here?

Even the story climax relies on the setting. In this isolated area, little help is available, and there are no working land phones or cell phones. In another, less remote setting, Celine and Josh probably would have called for an ambulance. Other people might have been nearby and available to help, too. Even if Celine had to go find help, she most likely would have been able to explain the problem in English instead of struggling with her limited Navajo. The setting contributes to the tension of the climax.

In conclusion, the setting of "Navajo Lessons" controls the entire story, from the characters to the plot to the climax. In another setting, the story would have unfolded differently. The setting establishes how the main characters interact and how the problem in the story is believable and solved. The setting supplies a key role for Celine, and she has a change of heart at the end of the story.

Think About It ► In your opinion, which point presented in this response is the most convincing?

Which point most strongly supports the importance of the setting in this story?

Vocabulary Study: Reference Materials

As you read, you will often encounter unfamiliar words. **Reference sources**, such as those described in the chart, can help you to find out the meaning of a word or term and the correct spelling. These resources will help you to understand the words you encounter in your reading and to use them correctly in your writing.

Dictionary	Lists words with their definitions, pronunciations, spellings, and parts of speech
Glossary	Lists words and meanings related to a certain topic or subject area, usually at the back of an informational text
Thesaurus	Lists words and their synonyms and antonyms

"Navajo Lessons" uses the word *arroyo*, which comes from the Spanish language. A thesaurus might tell you that this word is a noun that means "gulf, gorge, or break." A dictionary entry such as the one below will provide the definition as well as the pronunciation and part of speech.

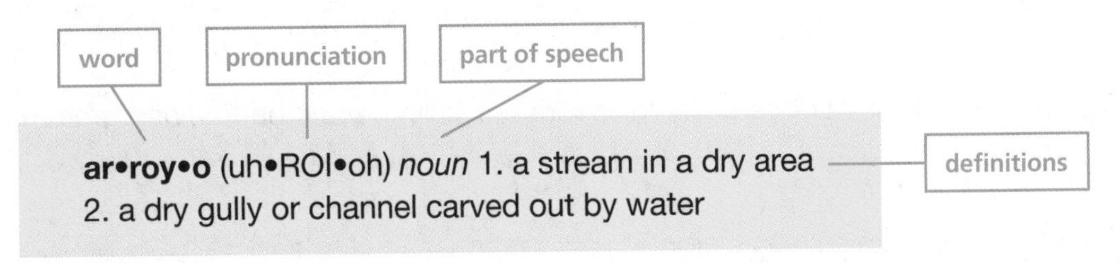

Work with your classmates to find out the meanings and parts of speech of these words from the story. Use print or digital reference materials to help you.

1. gibberish ______________________

2. devastated ______________________

3. intonation ______________________

Writing Process

Now that you have read and analyzed a response to literature, you are going to create your own response by following the steps of the writing process.

1. Get Ready: Brainstorm Begin by brainstorming possible ideas for a thesis and choosing the best one. Brainstorm main points that explain your thesis, and choose the strongest ones. Reread the story to gather supporting details or evidence.

2. Organize Use a graphic organizer to organize reasons and the details that support your thesis.

3. Draft Create the first draft of your response to literature.

4. Peer Review Work with a partner to evaluate and improve your draft.

5. Revise Use suggestions from your peer review to revise your response.

6. Edit Check your work carefully for errors in spelling, punctuation, and grammar.

7. Publish Create a final version of your response to literature.

Writing Assignment

In this lesson, you will write your own response to literature. As you write, remember the elements of the mentor text that were most effective. Read the following assignment.

> The theme of a story is its central message or lesson. Stories may have more than one theme. Identify the main theme of "Navajo Lessons." Support your choice with details from the story. Consider what the characters say and do, as well as how the characters change over the course of the story.

1. Get Ready: Brainstorm a Thesis

When you brainstorm, you think of as many ideas as you can and then record them. Don't edit yourself during this step—just let your ideas flow.

Below is the graphic organizer that the writer of the mentor text used to brainstorm a thesis about the importance of setting in "Navajo Lessons." After writing possible thesis statements in the box on the left, the writer reviewed them and chose the best one. The box on the right shows the thesis statement that the writer actually used.

List possible thesis statements for your response:

1. The setting is simply a backdrop for this story.
2. The setting is the most critical part of the story.
3. The setting affects the plot but not the characters.
4. The setting affects the characters but not the plot.

Which thesis statement will be the focus of your response?

The setting is the most critical part of the story.

Try It! Use a Brainstorming Graphic Organizer

Think about themes you could write about for your own response to literature. What, in your opinion, is the main theme of "Navajo Lessons"? Write possible thesis statements that identify the theme and explain why it is important. Then, choose one thesis statement to be the focus of your response.

List possible thesis statements for your response:

1. ______________________
2. ______________________
3. ______________________
4. ______________________

Which thesis statement will be the focus of your response?

____

____

____

Brainstorm Ideas

Next, you need to generate possible details and evidence that will support your chosen thesis. This is the time to record these details without worrying about their sequence or even about whether you will use them all. Here is how the writer of the mentor text used a graphic organizer to choose details from the passage that support her thesis.

SUPPORTING DETAILS The writer chooses details that are related to the setting of the story. The details in the left column support reasons in the right column. Circle the details that support her first reason.

SUPPORTING DETAILS The climax is the most exciting part of the story. Which details show the impact of the setting on the climax? Underline those details.

Possible Details or Evidence
The reservation is unfamiliar.
Celine is unhappy there.
She and her grandmother have no common language.
Celine withdraws from everyone.
Celine's brother makes friends in the new environment and learns Navajo.
Grandmother tries to connect with Celine.
Celine helps Grandmother but is still unhappy.
There is no car or phone to get help for Grandmother.
Celine runs to neighbors for help.
She uses the few words of Navajo she has learned to ask for help.

Strongest Reasons
setting affects characters
setting affects plot
setting affects climax

Try It!

Use a Brainstorming Graphic Organizer

Now use the graphic organizer below to brainstorm support for your response. Think about how the details relate to one another. Based on the details you have selected, choose the three strongest reasons that support your thesis. Each of these will become the main point of a paragraph.

Possible Details or Evidence	Strongest Reasons

2. Organize

You are almost ready to begin a draft of your response to literature. A more detailed graphic organizer can help you further plan the ideas for your response to the story. You can then refer to the graphic organizer as you work. After deciding on the main ideas and supporting evidence to include in her response, the writer of the mentor text completed this graphic organizer.

INTRODUCTION In the introduction, you:

- state your thesis and identify the title of the selection
- briefly summarize the selection
- introduce the reasons that support your thesis

SUPPORTING PARAGRAPHS In body paragraphs, you:

- give main reasons that explain your thesis
- support the points with relevant details and evidence from the selection

CONCLUSION In the final paragraph, you:

- restate your thesis
- summarize your main points
- add something for your reader to consider

Introduction

- Thesis: The setting controls the story in "Navajo Lessons."
- Celine and her brother stay with Grandmother.
- The setting affects characters, plot, and climax.

Reason #1 and Supporting Details

- Focus on how setting affects the characters.
- Celine withdraws. She listens to music night and day.
- Grandmother has no reason to learn English.

Reason #2 and Supporting Details

- Focus on how the setting affects the plot.
- Celine would react differently if living with an aunt in a city, her grandfather in the suburbs, or a cousin on a farm.
- She would make friends more easily if everyone spoke English.

Reason #3 and Supporting Details

- Focus on how the setting affects the climax: Celine runs for help.
- In a different setting, they would have phones to call for help.
- There would probably be more adults who speak English.

Conclusion

- Restate the thesis: the setting controls the story.
- Summarize the three reasons given above.
- The setting allows for Celine's change of heart.

Try It! Organize Your Response to Literature

Now use the graphic organizer below to organize the ideas and details you want to use in your draft.

Introduction

Reason #1 and Supporting Details

Reason #2 and Supporting Details

Reason #3 and Supporting Details

Conclusion

3. Draft

Now it's time to write the first draft of your response to literature. Remember, your goal is to get your ideas down on paper in an organized way. You can worry about spelling, punctuation, grammar, and other issues later, when you revise your writing.

Writer's Craft: Formal Style

Style is not just what the writer says but how the writer says it. A **formal style** of writing is carefully composed and usually avoids contractions, slang, and other casual language. An **informal style** of writing is more conversational and has the quality of everyday speech. Your writing style should be appropriate to your task, purpose, and audience.

	Sample Task	Purpose and Audience	Example of Language
Formal Style	Informative essay	• To convey information about a topic • Teacher	observe
Informal Style	E-mail	• To say hi • Friend	take a look

Notice how the writer of the mentor text uses a formal style of writing.

FORMAL STYLE
Words such as *establish* and *interact* are precise and formal. What would be a more informal way of saying "how the main characters interact"?

____

____

____

In conclusion, the setting of "Navajo Lessons" controls the entire story, from the characters to the plot to the climax. In another setting, the story would have unfolded differently. The setting establishes how the main characters interact and how the problem in the story is believable and solved. The setting supplies a key role for Celine, and she has a change of heart at the end of the story.

Try It! Write Your First Draft

Using a computer or a separate sheet of paper, create the draft of your response to the literature. Use this checklist to help you as you write.

- ✓ In your introduction, state the thesis. Provide the title of the literature selection and briefly summarize the story.
- ✓ In each of the next three paragraphs, give a reason that explains the thesis. Provide evidence from the text to support each of your main points.
- ✓ In your conclusion, restate your thesis. Stress how your three main reasons explain the thesis. Give the reader something to think about.
- ✓ Use a formal style.

Tips for Writing Your First Draft

- **Think about the best order for your three reasons. Writers usually place the strongest reason first.**
- **As you draft, write each supporting paragraph on an index card. This makes it easier to move paragraphs around to determine the best order for supporting details.**

4. Peer Review

Here is an early draft of the mentor text. Read it with your partner and answer the questions in the boxes. Later, you will find out how the writer's partner evaluated this draft.

INTRODUCTION The writer does not start with a thesis statement but begins by summarizing the story. What other basic information is missing?

In this story, Celine and her brother are sent to live in the desert with their grandmother for the summer. Missing the kids back home, Celine resists learning Navajo. One morning, she suddenly has to get help for her ill grandmother. In this story, the setting directly affects the characters, the plot, and the climax.

SUPPORTING DETAILS The second paragraph does a good job of explaining how the setting affects Celine. What other information should be included here?

The setting affects how the main character, Celine, interacts with her grandmother. Celine is unable to speak Navajo but now lives with someone who speaks only this language. She withdraws. For example, she spends her first days and nights listening to music. At home, her behavior would have been very different.

SUPPORTING DETAILS The writer says the plot would have been different in a different setting. What else should this paragraph include?

The setting also directly affects the plot. In fact, the story is based on how Celine responds to this setting. If she were spending time with an aunt in the city or a grandfather in the suburbs, the plot would have been entirely different.

Even the story climax relies on the setting. In this isolated area, little help is available, and there are no working land phones or cell phones. In another, less remote setting, Celine and Josh probably would have called for an ambulance. Other people might have been nearby and available to help, too.

CONCLUSION The writer repeats the thesis and mentions three main reasons that support it. What other details could be added?

In conclusion, the setting of "Navajo Lessons" controls the entire story, from the characters to the plot to the climax. In another setting, the story would have unfolded differently.

An Example Peer Review Form

This peer review form shows how a partner evaluated the draft of the mentor text shown on the previous page.

The introduction states the thesis and the title of the story. **The writer summarizes the story with enough details to help readers understand the response.**	You did a good job of *summarizing the story.* You could improve your response to literature by *stating the thesis at the beginning of the introduction. You should also give the title of the story.*
The next three paragraphs each develop reasons to support the thesis. **The writer uses evidence from the text to support each reason.**	You did a good job of *choosing three reasons that explain why setting is very important in this story.* You could improve your response by *adding more details about how the setting affects the other characters and how the story would have been different in a different setting.*
The writer uses a formal style that is appropriate for the task, purpose, and audience.	You did a good job of *using formal language in the first paragraph.* You could improve your response by *replacing the word "kids" in the second sentence with a more formal word.*
The conclusion stresses how the three reasons support the thesis. **It gives the reader something to think about.**	You did a good job of *restating your thesis.* You could improve your response by *adding more details about each of the three reasons. You should also leave the reader thinking about the story.*

Try It! Peer Review with a Partner

Now you will work with a partner to review each other's drafts. Use the peer review form below. If you need help, look back at the peer review form on the previous page.

The introduction states the thesis and the title of the story. The writer summarizes the story with enough details to help readers understand the response.	You did a good job of You could improve your response by
The next three paragraphs each develop reasons to support the thesis. The writer uses evidence from the text to support each reason.	You did a good job of You could improve your response by
The writer uses a formal style that is appropriate for the task, purpose, and audience.	You did a good job of You could improve your response by
The conclusion stresses how the three reasons support the thesis. It gives the reader something to think about.	You did a good job of You could improve your response by

Try It! Record Key Peer Review Comments

Now it's time for you and your partner to share your comments with each other. Listen to your partner's feedback, and write his or her key comments in the left column below. Then write some ideas for improving your draft in the right column.

My review says that my introduction	I will
My review says that my first main point	I will
My review says that my second main point	I will
My review says that my third main point	I will
My review says that my use of formal style	I will
My review says that my conclusion	I will

Use the space below to identify other ways you can improve your draft.

5. Revise

In this step of the writing process, you will find ways to strengthen your draft. The peer review form that your partner completed can help. Be sure to use your own ideas about how to improve each part of your response to literature. This checklist includes some things to think about as you prepare to revise.

Revision Checklist

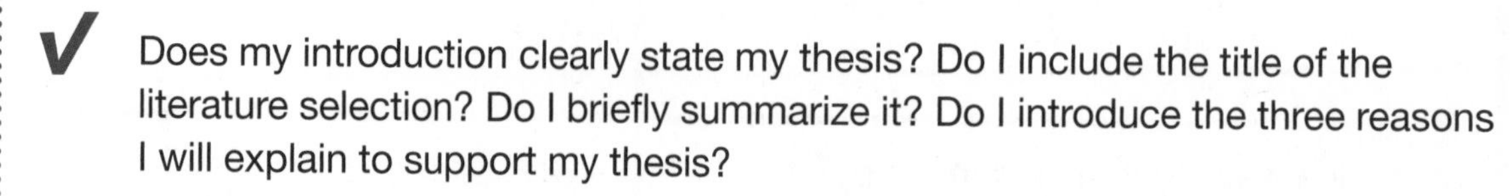

✓ Does my introduction clearly state my thesis? Do I include the title of the literature selection? Do I briefly summarize it? Do I introduce the three reasons I will explain to support my thesis?

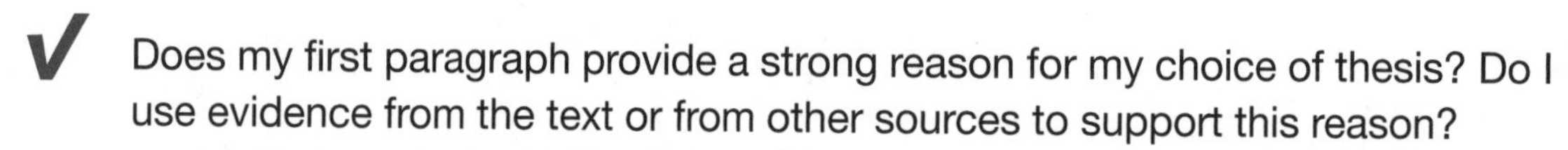

✓ Does my first paragraph provide a strong reason for my choice of thesis? Do I use evidence from the text or from other sources to support this reason?

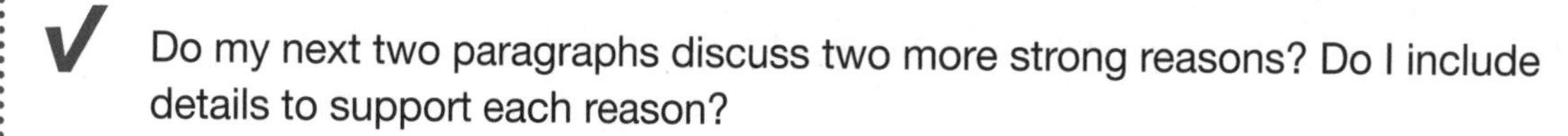

✓ Do my next two paragraphs discuss two more strong reasons? Do I include details to support each reason?

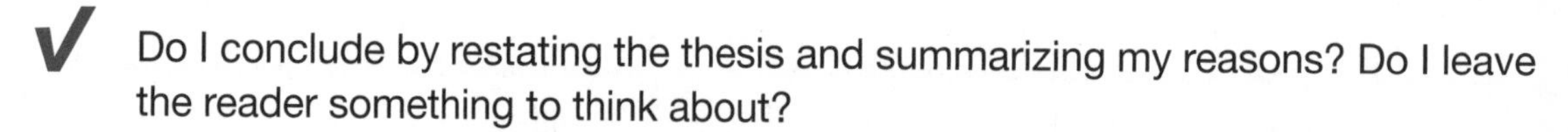

✓ Do I conclude by restating the thesis and summarizing my reasons? Do I leave the reader something to think about?

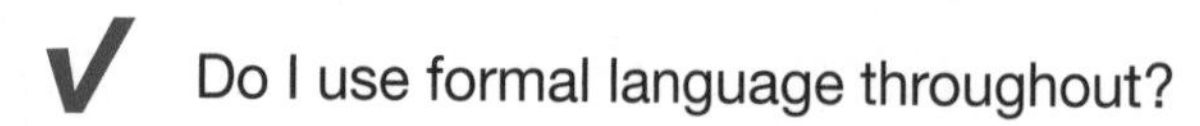

✓ Do I use formal language throughout?

Writer's Craft: Varying Sentence Structure

Writing that uses the same structure can be dull. To spice up your writing, you can add introductory words or phrases or reverse the order of the subjects and verbs. You might use a question instead of a statement. This sentence from the mentor text is an example of varied structure.

> Missing her friends back home, Celine resists learning Navajo, the only language her grandmother speaks.

VARYING SENTENCE STRUCTURE The writer could have written this: "Celine misses her friends back home. She resists learning Navajo. That is the only language her grandmother speaks." Instead, the writer combined these three sentences into one. Why is writing in short, choppy sentences not always the best choice?

____

____

Try It! Revise Your Response to Literature

Varying your sentence structure will make your writing more interesting—for you as well as your readers. Notice how the writer of the first example revised it to vary the sentence structure. Circle the revisions the writer has made. Next to each revision, explain why the writer made that change.

Original Text:

Karen reached the top of the mountain after a long trek. She found the notebook just where she had left it. She stuffed it into her backpack and smiled. She had not lost the song she had been writing for weeks. That night, she would sleep well.

Revised Text:

When Karen reached the top of the mountain after a long trek, she found the notebook just where she had left it. As she stuffed it into her backpack, she smiled. The song she had been writing for weeks was not lost. That night, she would sleep well.

Writing Assignment

Now it's time to revise the draft of your response to literature. Continue working on a computer or a separate sheet of paper. Review the assignment, repeated below, and the revision checklist to make sure you have included everything you need.

The theme of a story is its central message or lesson. Stories may have more than one theme. Identify the main theme of "Navajo Lessons." Support your choice with details from the story. Consider what the characters say and do, as well as how the characters change over the course of the story.

6. Edit

After revising your response to literature, you will edit it, reading carefully to find any mistakes. Here's a checklist of some things to look for.

Editing Checklist

- ✔ Did you indent each paragraph?
- ✔ Are all of your sentences complete, with a subject and a verb? Did you divide any run-on sentences?
- ✔ Does each sentence end with the correct punctuation?
- ✔ Have you used commas, colons, and semicolons correctly?
- ✔ Are all of the words spelled correctly?

You can use these editing marks to mark any errors you find.

{ } Insert parentheses	—/m Insert em dash	◯ Close up space
# Add space	⊐ Indent	^ Insert
		⁄ Delete

This paragraph from a draft of the mentor text response shows how to use editing marks.

⊐ The setting also directly affects the plot ^(—/m) in fact, the story is based on how Celine responds to this specific setting. If she were spending time with an aunt in the city or a grand ◯ father in the suburbs, the plot would have been entirely different. Celine would have missed her friends, but she probably would not ^(#) have felt so isolated. Plus, she would have been able to talk with those around her.

Language Focus: Spelling Hints

Even good writers sometimes have trouble spelling words correctly. Spelling errors can cause your readers to question the ideas in your writing. To avoid spelling errors, make a list of the words that you have difficulty spelling.

1. **Words that end in *-e*:**

Drop the final *e* when the suffix begins with a vowel:
separate + -ing = separating

Keep the final *e* when the suffix begins with a consonant:
engage + -ment = engagement

2. **Words using *ie* or *ei*:**

Use *ie* generally: *piece*   After *c*, use *ei*: *receive*   Use *ei* in words with /ā/: *freight*

3. **Endings to words that end in *-y*:**

When a double consonant precedes the final *y*, change the *y* to *i* and add the ending:
hurry + -ed = hurried

When a consonant precedes the final *y*, keep the final *y* when adding the ending:
pry + -ing = prying

If a vowel precedes the final *y*, keep the final *y* and add the ending:
enjoy + -ed = enjoyed   *play + -ing = playing*

4. **Adding *-s* or *-es* to form plurals:**

Add *-s* to most words, including words that end in *-f*, *-ff*, *-ffe*, and *-o* (when preceded by a vowel). ***Exception:*** In words ending in *-fe* or *-ef*, change to *-ves*, as in *thieves* and *wives*.

Add *-es* to words that end in *-s*, *-ss*, *-sh*, *-x*, *-z*, *-ch*, and *-o* (when preceded by a consonant), as in *caucuses*, *classes*, *splashes*, *foxes*, *quizzes*, *munches*, *tomatoes*.

Circle the misspelled words in the following paragraph from a draft of the mentor text.

The setting establishs how the main characters interact and how the problem in the story is believeable and solved. The setting supplys a key role for Celine, and she has a change of heart at the end of the story.

Try It! Language and Editing Practice

Find a spelling error in each sentence. Write the word correctly on the line next to each sentence.

1. ____________ I tryed to help my aunt in her garden whenever I could.

2. ____________ There was a huge crop of tomatos that summer.

3. ____________ One morning, flashs of lightning signaled that a fierce storm was on its way.

4. ____________ The nieghbors helped us pick the ripe plants before the storm arrived.

5. ____________ Mrs. Lewin bravly grabbed the last plant just as it started to thunder.

Now use editing marks to fix errors in punctuation, capitalization, and spelling.

The two brothers watched the large hawk circleing above Granite park. Just past the oak tree, a hungry family of foxs was on the prowl and small mice were scrambling to find a hiding place. The weather, dryer than it had been for dekades, meant little to eat for both animals and people. The brothers wondered when the rains would come and bring some relief?

Try It! Edit Your Response to Literature

Now edit your response to literature. Use this checklist and the editing marks you have learned to correct any errors you find.

- [ ] Did you indent each paragraph?
- [ ] Are all of your sentences complete, with a subject and a verb? Did you separate any run-on sentences?
- [ ] Does each sentence end with the correct punctuation?
- [ ] Have you used commas, colons, and semicolons correctly?
- [ ] Are all of the words spelled correctly?

Editing Tips

- Read your response aloud. Do your sentences all start with the subject? See if you can think of other ways to begin some of them.
- Read your paper backwards. This technique can help you catch spelling errors that your eyes might skip over otherwise.
- If possible, put your response aside for a few hours or overnight. When you read it again, your eyes—and brain—will be fresh and more likely to find errors.

7. Publish

Using a computer or a separate sheet of paper, create a neat final draft of your response to literature. Correct all errors that you identified while editing. Be sure to give your response an interesting title.

The final step is to publish your work, perhaps using one of these ideas:

- Combine the class's responses into a book, along with a copy of the literature selection. Place the book in the school library or media center.
- Display the class's responses to the story on a bulletin board, arranged around a copy of the selection.
- Meet in small groups to read your responses aloud and compare your thesis statements. Use evidence from your own response to support your thesis in a class debate.
- Use the evidence from your response to create a poster. Include images and words.

Technology Suggestions

- **Upload your response to literature onto a class or school blog.**
- **Start a blog that discusses the literature that you read in your class. Offer your opinions about the theme, setting, characters, plot, and so on.**

Lesson 3

Reading Literary Nonfiction

Look at this photograph of the Brooklyn Bridge in New York City.

What circumstances do you think led to the construction of this bridge?

ESSENTIAL QUESTION

How are true stories important in understanding significant events of the past?

Listen and Learn

Consider ▶ Why is the variety of cultures in the United States such an important part of the nation's character?

How can this cultural diversity remind us of the importance of freedom?

An Unbreakable Code

FIGURATIVE VS. LITERAL LANGUAGE In literal language, the words mean the same as their dictionary definitions. Figurative language involves the use of words and phrases to mean something other than their dictionary definitions. Look at paragraph 1. Is the phrase "the target of a surprise attack" literal or figurative language? What about "Americans heard the call of duty"? Explain the difference.

CONTEXT CLUES Context clues are words and phrases around a difficult word that can help a reader determine its meaning. Look at the word *fluent* in paragraph 2. What do you think it means? Which context clues helped you determine the meaning? Now do the same with *decipher.*

1 On December 7, 1941, the U.S. Naval Base at Pearl Harbor, Hawaii, was the target of a surprise attack by the Japanese. When President Franklin Roosevelt and the U.S. Congress entered World War II the next day, many Americans heard the call of duty. More than 3 million people enlisted in the military in 1942. One of them was young Chester Nez, an eighteen-year-old Navajo. He and twenty-eight other Navajo would become known as the "original 29," an elite, top-secret group of Navajo marines that would play a crucial role in helping the United States defeat Japan.

Fighting in the Pacific Ocean was a challenge for U.S. troops, in part because the battlefield included thousands of square miles of ocean. Military aircraft, ships, and ground operations needed to communicate efficiently across these vast distances. Troops transmitted messages to each other using wireless radios. However, the Japanese could tap in to this radio communication. Many Japanese soldiers were fluent in English and could translate these messages. The U.S. military developed a variety of code systems, but either the Japanese could break them, or the codes were so complicated that the U.S. military needed hours to decipher them. American troops needed a simple, unbreakable code.

When a civilian named Philip Johnston learned about the U.S. military's need for an unbreakable code, he had an idea.

The son of a missionary, Johnston had grown up on a Navajo reservation and was one of a small group of non-Navajo who knew their language. He also understood how difficult the language was to learn.

Navajo is purely an oral language with no alphabet. Meanings of Navajo words are carried by their spoken syllables, with slight variations in tone or pronunciation that can completely change the meaning of a word. Navajo was a challenge even to speakers of other Native American languages.

5 Johnston thought Navajo would be perfect as a secret U.S. military code, but it would not be easy to convince military officials to agree. The U.S. military had already tried to make use of Native American languages as codes during wartime. Choctaw soldiers tried to send secret messages during World War I, and the Chippewa and other groups had been recruited as messengers at the start of World War II. Students from other countries, including those of U.S. enemies, were already studying Native American languages. Using his deep knowledge of Navajo combined with the availability of Navajo recruits, Johnston was able to convince top military officials to develop a new system. In April 1942, Johnston recruited twenty-nine men from the Navajo reservation in Arizona. These young men were eager to enlist to fight for their country. They did not know that they were about to become the first Navajo Code Talkers.

The new recruits were sent to San Diego to begin the Marine Corps basic training course. Some had never traveled outside the Navajo reservation, ridden on a bus, or seen a large city. Many—including Chester Nez—barely met the weight requirement to be a marine, and at least one new soldier turned out to be only fifteen years old. However, the challenges of herding sheep and hauling buckets of water across vast distances in the Arizona desert had prepared them all for the physical demands of boot camp. They were able to practice military drills for hours and march long distances with heavy packs on their backs. The twenty-nine Navajo members of Platoon 382 successfully completed the seven-week marine basic training course and were ready for their next assignment—to create an unbreakable code.

CONNOTATION AND DENOTATION Many words can have similar literal meanings, or denotations. However, their connotations—the emotions or attitudes they express—can be different. In paragraph 5, the author describes the young men as *eager* to enlist. How would a reader's impression be different if the author used the word *willing* instead?

MAIN IDEA AND SUPPORTING DETAILS The main idea is what a text is mostly about. Supporting details help to convey, or show, the main idea. What is the main idea of paragraph 6? Which details support this main idea?

CONCLUSION A conclusion is a decision you make about all or part of the passage based on information from the text, inferences you make as you read, and your prior knowledge. Look at paragraph 7. What conclusion can you draw about the code? Which details support your conclusion?

WORD CHOICE AND TONE Authors choose words that will best convey the information as well as their attitude, or tone, toward the subject. Look at the words used in paragraph 9 to describe the situation on Guadalcanal. Which words help to illustrate the situation to the reader? What is the tone of the paragraph?

INFERENCE An inference is an idea that a reader reaches by putting the information in a text together with what he or she already knows. Look at paragraph 11. What inference can you make about Chester Nez? Which details led you to this inference?

The code they wrote consisted of about two hundred symbols, and it cut communication time from thirty minutes to about twenty seconds. It made clever use of the Navajo language on two levels. First, the group assigned a Navajo word to each letter of the alphabet, from A to Z. For example, the Navajo word for *ant*—*wol•la•CHEE*—stood for the letter *A*. The code became even more complicated when the Code Talkers added other Navajo words to stand for the same letters. The letter *A* could be *wol•la•CHEE* (ant), *be•la•SA•NA* (apple), or *tse•NILL* (ax). Next, they assigned Navajo words to frequently used military terms. A fighter plane was *dah•he•TIH•hi,* the Navajo word for *hummingbird*. Submarines were *BESH•lo* (iron fish) and battleships were *lo•TSO* (whales).

Due to the top-secret nature of the program, no written lists of the code were permitted, and Code Talkers had to both memorize every piece of the code and practice sending error-free messages. The code included such delicate shades of meaning that the slightest error could result in military disaster.

By July 1942, around the time the first Code Talkers were ready for battle, the Japanese were building an airstrip on an island in the South Pacific called Guadalcanal. It was crucial for the United States to place military bases on Pacific islands so the United States could attack Japan directly. U.S. Marines attacked and seized the airfield in August, beginning a series of intense battles on Guadalcanal that were devastating for both sides.

10 Over the next few months, both sides fought to land reinforcements in the area. Finally, in November, the U.S. Navy began to surpass the Japanese in the number of troops stationed on the islands. In early November, Chester Nez and the rest of the first group of Navajo Code Talkers were on their way to Guadalcanal.

On the journey over the Pacific Ocean, Nez reminded himself that the Navajo had always been warriors and protectors of their homeland. Still, at this moment he wondered whether he had made the right decision to leave high school to join the military. But as a warrior, he knew he had to protect his homeland.

On his first night in a foxhole on Guadalcanal, heavy raindrops fell and chilled Nez and his team to the bone. Artillery fire tore through the night, lighting up the sky and shaking the earth surrounding the men in the hole. Nez silently recited a traditional Navajo prayer:

In beauty I walk.
With beauty before me I walk.
With beauty behind me I walk.
With beauty around me I walk.
With beauty above me I walk.

Nez survived this first night in Guadalcanal, as well as every other night he spent in the South Pacific. During combat on the Japanese island of Iwo Jima in February 1945, one of the most decisive battles of the war, Code Talkers successfully transmitted over eight hundred messages in the first two hours of battle. After almost a month of fighting, the United States captured the island. Many members of the U.S. military believe that this victory—and the eventual victory over Japan—would not have been possible without the Navajo Code Talkers.

15 Returning from the war, the Code Talkers were heroes—heroes that nobody could know about. The Navajo code project was so secret that it remained classified for over twenty years. When the U.S. government finally declassified the project in 1968, the Navajo Code Talkers were still not officially honored. In July 2001, each of the "original 29" was awarded the Congressional Medal of Honor. The families of those who had died accepted the award in honor of their loved ones. Later that year, every Navajo Code Talker was awarded a silver medal for his unique service to the country.

Chester Nez went on to publish a memoir of his experience as a Navajo Code Talker. As the last living member of the "original 29," he can be sure that he and his fellow soldiers won an exceptional place in history.

COMPARE AND CONTRAST
When you compare texts, you tell the ways they are alike. When you contrast texts, you tell how they are different. Look at the prayer and the paragraph above it. What feelings does the language in each convey? How are the two different? Why do you think the author placed these two parts of the story next to each other?

SUMMARY A summary tells the most important ideas of a text in a few sentences. Look at paragraph 15. Summarize the experiences of the Code Talkers after the war.

Comprehension Check

Look back at "An Unbreakable Code" to understand the story of the Navajo Code Talkers. Think about the sequence of events that led to this project and the events of its aftermath. Add events to the timeline below to clarify the sequence of events relating to the Code Talkers from 1941 to 2001.

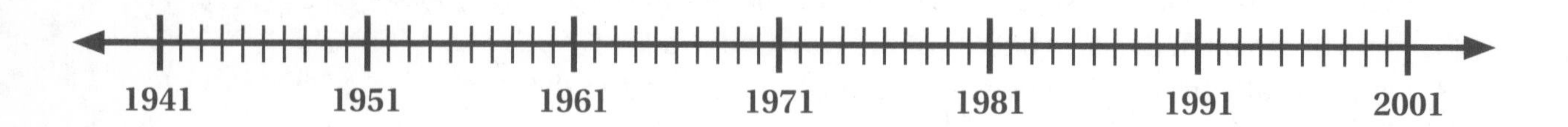

Circle two events that you think would be the most important for people to know about the Navajo Code Talkers and their experience. Then explain your choices.

Vocabulary

Use the word map below to help you define and use one of the highlighted vocabulary words from the Share and Learn reading or another word your teacher assigns you.

marvels	petition	commute
compressed	intervals	jurisdiction
innovation	ingenuity	

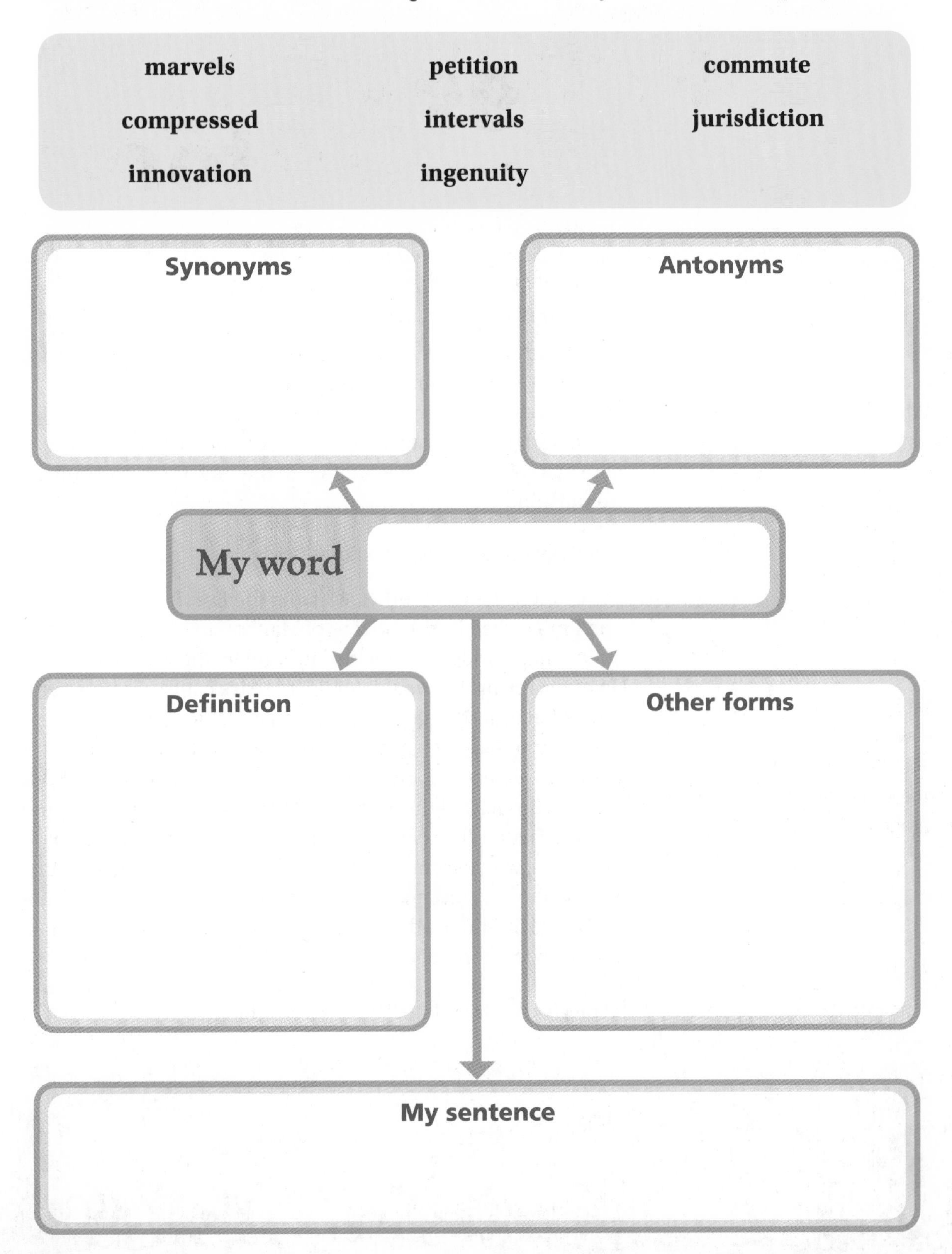

Share and Learn

Consider ▶ What structures in the United States help people to stay connected?

Why is it important that people in the United States feel connected?

Bridges with a History

1 *Against the city's gleaming spires,*
Above the ships that ply the stream,
A bridge of haunting beauty stands—
Fulfillment of an artist's dream.

ANALOGY To what does the poet compare the bridge? What about the two are similar?

____

____

____

These are the opening words of a poem by David Steinman, a bridge builder, about New York City's Brooklyn Bridge. The same words could also describe California's Golden Gate Bridge. These bridges, standing on opposite ends of the United States, were marvels of bridge technology at the time they were built and are still admired today.

The Beginnings of the Brooklyn Bridge

TEXT STRUCTURE How is paragraph 3 organized? Circle the words and phrases that help to identify the structure of this paragraph.

____

____

____

In 1802, the New York newspaper the *Evening Post* published a petition signed by the citizens of Manhattan and Long Island, stating that a bridge was needed to connect the two islands. However, the bridge would require massive cables to support it, and at that time, bridge design and architecture was not able to accommodate such heavy cables. Then, in 1867, the state legislature agreed to form a private company to construct a bridge between Brooklyn—the borough[1] at the south end of Long Island—and Manhattan. The city's growing population had been using ferryboats, which were usually crowded and very dangerous in bad weather, to commute across the East River. Legend holds that the Brooklyn Bridge's designer, John Roebling, was on a ferryboat during an ice storm when he created its design.

[1]**borough** one of five districts of New York City

A Builder for the Bridge

The bridge builder John Roebling was asked to design and manage the project, but before construction began, tragedy struck. Roebling's foot got caught between two planks on a ferryboat slip. His foot was crushed, and he soon died from tetanus. Roebling's son, Washington, took over, but he also suffered misfortune. He developed a crippling disease related to his work on the bridge.

5 To carry the weight of the massive cables, the bridge's towers had to be built on the floor of the river. To allow workers to excavate the sediment, hollow boxes were sunk into the river. The boxes were filled with compressed air to prevent water from leaking in. But when workers surfaced after digging underwater, their bodies had a hard time readjusting to the lower pressure. Nitrogen bubbles would build up in their blood and their tissues, resulting in what came to be called decompression sickness. Symptoms of this disease ranged from joint pain to paralysis to even death. Along with many workers on the Brooklyn Bridge, Washington Roebling developed this condition. However, he was determined to manage the job from his home. His wife, Emily, studied mathematics and engineering and worked with her husband to direct the project while he recuperated.

Something to Celebrate

When construction of the Brooklyn Bridge was complete, an opening celebration was held on May 24, 1883. Emily Roebling was the first to ride across the bridge. Pedestrians paid one cent to walk along the raised promenade, and eighteen thousand vehicles crossed for a five-cent toll each.

The American poet Walt Whitman described the Brooklyn Bridge as "the best, most effective medicine my soul has yet partaken." At the time of its creation, the Brooklyn Bridge was the world's longest suspension bridge, a bridge that is suspended from cables at each end and at intervals in between. It was also unique in that the wires in its cables—each of which was long enough to stretch from New York to London—were made from steel rather than iron. Roebling believed that steel would be an essential building material in the future.

CONNOTATION AND DENOTATION Three words in paragraph 4 suggest that the building started out as a disaster: *tragedy, crushed,* and *misfortune.* How would the interpretation be different if the writer had used these words instead: *accident, injured,* and *problem*?

____

____

____

CONTEXT CLUES Reread paragraph 6, and use context clues to determine the meaning of *promenade.* Explain how you determined the meaning.

____

____

____

FIGURATIVE AND LITERAL LANGUAGE Circle the sentence in paragraph 7 that uses figurative language.

No doubt, people of the day were worried about the safety of such a long bridge. They must have felt somewhat relieved when the circus owner P. T. Barnum paraded twenty-one elephants across the bridge to show off its strength.

Planning the Golden Gate Bridge

Around this time on the other side of the country, residents of San Francisco were using a ferry system to travel across the Golden Gate Strait, where the San Francisco Bay connects to the Pacific Ocean. Many people in this area wished for a bridge across the strait, but most engineers said it couldn't be done. For years, people thought that the project was impossible. However, as ferry traffic increased between San Francisco and Marin County across the strait, the possibility of a bridge was given more consideration.

ALLUSION What allusion does the writer use to illustrate the difficult task of building the bridge across the Golden Gate Strait?

10 Finally, in January 1923, representatives of the counties surrounding the strait met to discuss ways to move the bridge project forward. The meeting resulted in the formation of the Association of Bridging the Gate, a group of county representatives who took on the task of seeing the project through. Later that same year, legislation was passed that allowed counties to organize as one district, borrow funds, issue bonds, construct the bridge, and collect bridge tolls once construction was complete. Building the bridge would be a Herculean task, but it looked like it might finally become a reality.

Delays to the Project

SUMMARY Summarize the section called "Delays to the Project."

The U.S. War Department held jurisdiction over any construction that might affect shipping routes or military operations. The counties in the bridge district needed to be granted a permit from the War Department in order to begin any bridge construction. The process took up most of the year, but the permit was granted in December 1924.

However, ferry companies were strongly opposed to the project, claiming that the ferry ride was an important time for residents to spend relaxing together between work and home. These companies had enough money to carry out a long campaign against the project, and they successfully shifted opinion against the bridge for several years.

Over the next few years, ferry trips grew more and more crowded. The rides became more a source of frustration than relaxation for ferry riders. Opposition to the bridge project began to fade. Finally, in December 1928, the Golden Gate Bridge and Highway District was formed to put the bridge project back in motion.

Choosing a Builder

Joseph Strauss, a respected builder of more than four hundred bridges, had already submitted sketches of plans for a bridge across Golden Gate Strait back in 1921. Strauss was a major voice during the process of getting the project approved, insisting that it could be done more quickly and less expensively than many experts predicted. Strauss's proposal was chosen over those submitted by the country's top engineering firms. Because the project was so complex, many predicted that Strauss would never complete it. However, he fulfilled his longtime dream of bridging the Golden Gate—and the bridge was built faster and at a lower cost than expected.

15 Strauss worked quickly, but he was concerned about worker safety. He established strict rules for his builders. This project was the first that required workers to wear hard hats and glare-free goggles. Also, workers were given cream to protect their skin from the wind. They ate special diets to prevent dizziness. The most important innovation was a safety net stretching under the entire bridge. This device saved nineteen workers' lives and is now a standard part of construction regulations in the United States.

INFERENCE What inference can you make about Joseph Strauss? Underline the details that led you to your inference.

____

____

____

MAIN IDEA AND SUPPORTING DETAILS Write the main idea of paragraph 15 in your own words. Then underline the details in the paragraph that support the main idea.

____

____

____

COMPARE AND CONTRAST What similarities and differences do you notice about the stories of building the Brooklyn Bridge and the Golden Gate Bridge? In what way is this text structure useful for the reader?

____

____

____

WORD CHOICE AND TONE Circle the words in paragraph 16 about the Bridge Fiesta that you think the author chose to convey the significance of the opening of the bridge. What is the tone of the paragraph?

____

____

____

CONCLUSION Based on paragraph 18, what conclusion can you draw about the bridges? Underline the details that led you to your conclusion.

____

____

____

A Special Event

On May 27, 1937, the opening of the Golden Gate Bridge was celebrated with the Bridge Fiesta. An impressive crowd of two hundred thousand pedestrians crossed the bridge on the ten-foot-wide sidewalks on either side of the magnificent structure. The following day, President Franklin D. Roosevelt pushed a telegraph button from the White House, and a parade of official cars opened the bridge to automobile traffic. Strauss had been right—the project was completed ahead of schedule and below its budgeted costs.

The Bridges Today

At the time of its completion in 1937, the Golden Gate Bridge was the longest suspension bridge in the world, spanning 4,200 feet. Its length is over twice that of the Brooklyn Bridge. Since then, longer suspension bridges have been built around the world, including another one in New York. But these two bridges remain as symbols of engineering expertise and innovative ways of building connections.

Each year, millions of people drive over both of these marvels of human ingenuity, and few notice the structures themselves. Others, however, have taken the time to capture them in photographs and poems, which helps us all focus on their usefulness and beauty.

The Golden Gate Bridge, painted a deep orange, is one of the most photographed bridges in the world.

Anchor Standard Discussion Questions

Discuss the following questions with your peer group. Then record your answers in the space provided.

1. "Bridges with a History" traces the successes and obstacles faced by Strauss and the Roebling family. What is one theme that emerges from their stories? Support your answer with details from the selection.

2. What inference can you make about how the "original 29" might have felt when the military asked them to devise a code using the Navajo language? Use details from "An Unbreakable Code" to support your answer.

Comprehension Check

1. Why is the use of both literal and figurative language effective in literary nonfiction? Give examples of both in "Bridges with a History."

2. What innovations have made building bridges safer and stronger?

3. What are the main ideas of "An Unbreakable Code" and of "Bridges with a History"? Compare and contrast these main ideas.

Read On Your Own

Read another literary nonfiction text, "Brave Bessie Coleman," independently. Apply what you learned in this lesson and check your understanding.

Lesson 4

Writing Personal Narratives

Look at the people around you. How are you alike? How are you different? Do you enjoy the same sports, play the same computer games, or listen to the same music? You share more similarities than differences with the people around you, yet there is no one else in the world quite like you! What have you learned from the people and events in your life? How have your experiences, both positive and negative, influenced you? Readers sometimes learn and change as a result of reading about other people's experiences. One way to share your experiences is to write a personal narrative.

ESSENTIAL QUESTION

How could writing a personal narrative teach you about your own life?

What's a Personal Narrative?

Do you have a story to tell about an experience, an event, or a person that influenced your life? Think about how people and experiences have helped to shape you into the person you are today.

In a **personal narrative**, you share your experience with others. You describe something you've learned or an incident that changed you. The sequence of the events tells *your* story based on your real experiences, not ones you imagine. Read the ways to make your personal narrative effective.

Introduction

Begin with a hook that grabs the reader's attention and sets the scene. It might be a brief description of what you learned or what led to the important learning experience. Use the first-person point of view.

Body Paragraphs

Write about your experience in a logical order: beginning, middle, and ending. Use transitions, such as *first*, *next*, and *then*, to indicate sequence and the shift in time. Each paragraph should include descriptive details—thoughts, feelings, and dialogue—that help the reader see the experience from your perspective. Use those details and language to *show*, rather than tell, the reader.

Conclusion

Reflect on the experience or event and tell what you learned or how you changed.

Let's look at a personal narrative.

Analyze a Mentor Text

This is an example of an effective personal narrative. Read it and then complete the activities in the boxes as a class.

A Different Kind of Summer Vacation

The noise became louder and louder, like a supersonic aircraft approaching a runway. I thought I was dreaming. Propelled into the air like a rocket, I shot straight up in bed. With a loud boom, the doorknob hit the wall as my bedroom door flew open. "You aren't going to sit around the house all summer long doing nothing," my mother said loudly over the roar of the vacuum cleaner. "I have signed you up to caddy at the golf course," she continued. "You are going to be busy earning money this summer and spending your time productively. You start caddying tomorrow, bright and early," she added. I fell back onto my pillows and groaned.

After my mother's words sank in, I realized that this wasn't just a bad dream. It was a frightening nightmare! Why is it called summer vacation, I wondered, if it really isn't a vacation at all? Carrying someone's golf bag around a golf course was not a vacation. My back and feet ached just thinking about caddying. Sleeping, skateboarding, swimming, and hanging out with friends were what I had had in mind!

The next morning, I nervously reported to the caddy shack. The small, green-shuttered, white clapboard building was situated on the perimeter of the golf course. Approximately thirty-five other people crowded the main room. I recognized a few boys and girls from my school standing in the corner of the room. I quickly joined them. Curiously, we watched experienced caddies hoist heavy golf bags onto their shoulders and follow men and women across the emerald-colored grass.

INTRODUCTION To grab the reader's attention, writers often open with an amusing or engaging anecdote. Underline the sentences that hook the reader.

DIALOGUE Writers provide information in the words the characters say to each other. Draw a star next to the dialogue.

DESCRIPTIVE DETAILS The writer includes details that reveal his innermost thoughts and feelings. Circle the words and phrases that show how the writer feels about having to go to work.

TRANSITIONS Transitions are used to indicate the sequence of events or ideas. Circle a phrase that contains a transition.

POINT OF VIEW Personal narratives are written from the first-person point of view. Underline the words that show point of view.

SENSORY LANGUAGE Writers often use descriptive details that appeal to the reader's senses to engage the reader in the narrative. Draw a box around a descriptive detail that appeals to the reader's sense of sight.

CONCLUSION One effective way of concluding a narrative is to include a reflection. A reflection is the writer's analysis of how narrative events have affected him or her. Circle the sentences of reflection in the conclusion.

While the last few experienced caddies were heading out onto the course, the caddy master rounded up the fifteen remaining novices and rattled off the schedule for the day. "After completing the morning training session," he said, "you will go out on your first loop, or round, which will take most of the afternoon." He explained that, as a rule, beginners were only permitted to carry singles, or one bag at a time, until they gained some experience and proved they were capable of handling the work. However, later on we could earn twice the single rate for carrying doubles.

Finally the caddy master herded our group outside into the bright sunlight. The rolling green fairways were lined by hundreds of majestic oak and walnut trees beneath the cloudless blue sky. My mind was busy calculating how much money I could earn this summer. Suddenly, I realized that I might be able to earn enough money to pay for my ninth-grade trip and have some money left over to buy a new snowboard. As I looked around, I exchanged smiles with the other members of my group. This wasn't going to be a nightmare after all. Maybe this wouldn't be too bad. Perhaps it really was a blessing in disguise.

Think About It ▶

How did the writer make you want to continue reading the personal narrative?

What changed about the writer as a result of hearing the caddy master's introduction to the job?

How is this personal narrative organized?

Vocabulary Study: Context Clues

You can often use **context clues**, or the words that surround an unfamiliar word, to determine a word's meaning. The clue may be a synonym or an antonym. Sometimes, it's best to make a guess at the word's meaning and then use a dictionary to verify it. Determine the meaning of each underlined word in the chart using the strategy suggested. The first one has been done for you.

Strategy	Word or Phrase	Meaning
Look at words that surround the unfamiliar word or phrase.	Beginners were only permitted to carry <u>singles</u>, or one bag at a time, until they gained some experience.	one bag at a time
Guess the meaning of an unfamiliar word. Reread or use a dictionary to verify your guess.	We watched experienced caddies <u>hoist</u> heavy golf bags onto their shoulders.	
Look for relationships between words, such as synonyms or antonyms.	While the last few experienced caddies were heading out onto the course, the caddy master rounded up the fifteen remaining <u>novices</u>.	

Look back at the personal narrative on pages 63–64. Find unfamiliar or multiple-meaning words or phrases. Use one of the context clues strategies above to determine the meaning of each. Write one word or phrase in each box below, and write or illustrate its meaning.

Word: **Meaning:**	**Word:** **Meaning:**
Word: **Meaning:**	**Word:** **Meaning:**

Writing Process

Now that you have read and analyzed a personal narrative, you are going to create your own by following these steps of the writing process.

1. Get Ready: Brainstorm List several ideas you might want to write about. Choose one and think about the sequence of events. What events led up to that point? What happened afterward? Come up with descriptive details that will help the reader imagine the experience.

2. Organize Use a graphic organizer to organize the sequence of events and plan your personal narrative.

3. Draft Create the first draft of your personal narrative.

4. Peer Review Work with a partner to evaluate and improve your draft.

5. Revise Use suggestions from your peer review to revise your personal narrative.

6. Edit Check your work carefully for errors in spelling, punctuation, and grammar.

7. Publish Create a final version of your personal narrative.

Writing Assignment

In this lesson, you will write your own personal narrative. As you write, remember the elements of the mentor text that were most effective. Read the following assignment.

> People come in and out of our lives, but there are some people we never forget. Write a personal narrative about your best childhood friend. Discuss how you met, what kinds of things you did together, what challenges you faced, and what you learned from each other. Use descriptive details to show, not tell, your reader.

1. Get Ready: Brainstorm a Topic

The first step in writing a personal narrative is to choose your topic. Begin by listing several people, experiences, or events that you might want to write about. Think about what you learned or how you changed.

Here's how the author of the mentor text brainstormed topics.

Possible Topic	Significance of Event/Experience
1. Learning a Foreign Language	I learned French so I could talk with my new next-door neighbor. Being able to do so allowed me to learn about French culture. Now I want to study in France.
2. My First Summer Job	I was hoping to enjoy my summer vacation, but my mother made me work as a caddy. I realized that a summer job could be rewarding after all.
3. Making the Swim Team	I almost didn't try out for the swim team because I was afraid that I wouldn't make it. I did try out and made the team! I learned that to get what you want, you have to put in the effort, take risks, and manage your fears.

Try It! Use a Brainstorming Graphic Organizer

Now use the graphic organizer below to help brainstorm a possible focus for your narrative about your best childhood friend.

Topic: My Best Childhood Friend	Significance of Event/Experience
1. Possible focus:	
2. Possible focus:	
3. Possible focus:	

Brainstorm Ideas for Your Topic

Now that you've chosen a topic, use a graphic organizer to help capture your memories about the sequence of events and add details you might want to include in your personal narrative. Here is how the author of the mentor text used the graphic organizer.

DETAILS At this point, do not worry about presenting details in order. Just jot down anything you think is important along with your thoughts about each detail.

TOPIC The focus of your narrative must be broad enough so that you have plenty to write about but narrow enough to tackle in a few paragraphs.

CONCLUSION Identifying the significance of the event or experience is a way of reflecting on it. This will be helpful when you write your conclusion.

Detail: I planned to spend my vacation hanging out with friends, swimming, and skateboarding.

Feeling: Disappointed; I had planned a lot to do.

Detail: I worked as a caddy at a golf course. My mom signed me up.

Feeling: I thought my summer vacation was ruined.

Topic: My First Summer Job

Significance of Event/Experience: I was hoping to enjoy my summer vacation, but my mother made me work as a caddy. I realized that a summer job could be rewarding after all.

Detail: We got training in how to be a caddy. We were told how much we would be paid.

Feeling: We should be allowed to carry more so we can get paid more.

Detail: I started my job the next day. Some of the kids I knew from school were also working at the golf course.

Feeling: It was nice being outdoors on a green lawn, surrounded by trees and under a blue sky.

Detail: I figured out how much money I could make.

Feeling: I could pay for a school trip and buy stuff.

Try It! Use a Graphic Organizer for Brainstorming

Now use the graphic organizer below to brainstorm details and feelings for your personal narrative.

Detail:

Feeling:

Detail:

Feeling:

Topic: My Best Childhood Friend

Focus:

Detail:

Feeling:

Detail:

Feeling:

Detail:

Feeling:

2. Organize

You are almost ready to begin a draft of your personal narrative. You can use a graphic organizer to help arrange and develop the details that you gathered during brainstorming. You can then refer to the graphic organizer as you work through the different parts of your draft. The writer of the mentor text completed this graphic organizer.

INTRODUCTION

- Begin with an attention-grabbing hook.
- Set the scene.
- Tell how your experience began.

BODY PARAGRAPHS

- Describe the order of events.
- Build to the point where you realize the change.
- Use transitions.

DESCRIPTIVE DETAILS Be sure to add details that:

- show, not tell, the experience.
- appeal to the senses.

CONCLUSION Reflect on what you learned or how you changed as a result of the experience or event.

Introduction Where it all began: This isn't how I planned to spend my vacation.	**Possible hooks** Mom was vacuuming and woke me; she said I had a summer job. My summer is ruined.
Beginning Mom told me she had gotten me a job for the summer. I was going to work at the golf course as a caddy.	**Details:** It sounds like a lot of work. It makes me ache just thinking about it; nightmare!!
Middle I started the next day. We were trained about what to do. Some of my friends were also working as caddies that summer.	**Details:** Some kids from my class were also going to work there; the golf course is nice—sunny, trees, green lawn.
End We're going to be paid! I could earn some good money this summer.	**Details:** The more we can do, the more we'll be paid; I could use the money for school trip and snowboard.
Conclusion This isn't so bad after all. It might even turn out to be a good thing.	**Details:** Not bad at all!

Try It!

Organize your Personal Narrative

Now use the graphic organizer below to organize the sequence of events and descriptive details you want to use in the different paragraphs of your draft.

Introduction	**Possible hooks**
Beginning	**Details:**
Middle	**Details:**
End	**Details:**
Conclusion	**Details:**

3. Draft

Now it is time to write the first draft of your personal narrative. Remember, your draft does not have to be perfect! This is the time to use your notes, get your ideas down in an organized way, and experiment with different ways to use narrative techniques, such as dialogue, description, and reflection, effectively. You will have time to revise your writing later. Start by drafting your personal narrative on a computer or on a separate sheet of paper. Describe your best childhood friend and what you learned from each other. Use descriptive details and dialogue so that the reader will come to know your childhood friend, too.

Writer's Craft: Using Transitions

In a personal narrative, you can use transition words, phrases, and clauses to

- shift from one time frame or setting to another
- show the relationships among experiences and events
- make connections between thoughts and ideas
- move smoothly from one idea to the next

Transition words	before, next, after, while, during, however
Transition phrases	at the same time, in addition, as long as, another thing, as a rule

The author of the mentor text uses transition words and phrases in the fourth paragraph.

TRANSITIONS Read this section of the mentor text. Circle the transition word that contrasts the pay rate for singles and doubles. Then underline all remaining transitions.

While the last few experienced caddies were heading out onto the course, the caddy master rounded up the fifteen remaining novices and rattled off the schedule for the day. "After completing the morning training session," he said, "you will go out on your first loop, or round, which will take most of the afternoon." He explained that, as a rule, beginners were only permitted to carry singles, or one bag at a time, until they gained some experience and proved they were capable of handling the work. However, later on we could earn twice the single rate for carrying doubles.

Try It! Write Your First Draft

On a computer or a separate sheet of paper, create the draft of your response to the writing prompt. Remember to use words, phrases, and clauses that show clear relationships among ideas in your piece. Use this drafting checklist to help you as you write.

- ✓ A good introduction grabs the reader's attention. Begin with an exaggeration, an exclamation, or an amusing anecdote. Set the scene, and tell what your narrative will be about.
- ✓ Use the first-person point of view.
- ✓ Organize the event sequence so that it unfolds logically and naturally.
- ✓ Use descriptive details that appeal to the senses.
- ✓ Use dialogue and reflection to develop events and/or characters.
- ✓ Use a variety of transitions.
- ✓ Provide a conclusion that follows from and reflects on the experiences or events. State what you learned or how you changed.

Tips for Writing Your First Draft

- Start writing to get your ideas down. You may not use all that you write, but "freewriting" can help you think of more or different ways to convey your ideas.
- Focus on the event sequence. Do you want to tell events in the order in which they happened? Do you want to include a flashback to a related earlier event?
- Try to show, not tell, the reader. Think of your story as a movie. What do you picture in your mind? What sounds do you recall? What music was playing? Details like these appeal to many of the senses. Use those details to help the reader experience what you are describing.

4. Peer Review

After you finish your draft, you can work with a partner to review each other's drafts. Here is an early draft of the mentor text. Read it with your partner. Together, answer the questions in the boxes. Then we'll see how the writer's classmate evaluated the draft.

INTRODUCTION In the draft, the writer does not grab the reader's attention in the introduction. How might the writer make the hook more powerful?

BODY PARAGRAPHS The third paragraph would be more effective with additional descriptive details. Where could the writer add them? What transitions could the writer add to the fourth paragraph to make the sequence of events clearer?

CONCLUSION The conclusion could be stronger. What details and thoughts could the writer add to emphasize a change in attitude?

My Summer Vacation!

I thought I was dreaming. I shot straight up in bed. With a loud boom the doorknob hit the wall as my bedroom door flew open. "You aren't going to sit around the house all summer long with nothing to do," my mother said loudly over the noise of the vacuum cleaner. "I have signed you up to caddy at the golf course," she continued. "You start caddying tomorrow, bright and early," she added. I fell back onto my pillows and groaned. This was not how I planned to spend my summer vacation!

After my mother's words sank in, I realized that this wasn't a dream. It was a nightmare! Why is it called summer vacation, if it really isn't a vacation after all? Carrying someone's golf bag around a golf course was not a vacation. It was not what I had in mind at all.

The next morning, I reported to the caddy master. The building was set on the edge of the golf course. Approximately thirty-five other people crowded the room. I recognized a few kids and joined them. Curiously, we watched experienced caddies hoist golf bags onto their shoulders and follow men and women across the grass.

The last few experienced caddies were heading out onto the course. The caddy master rounded up the novices and explained the schedule for the day. "Complete the morning training session," he said. "You will be sent out on your first loop, or round." He explained that beginners were only permitted to carry singles until they gained some experience. Later on we would earn twice the single rate for carrying doubles.

Finally the caddy master herded our group outside into the sunlight. The fairways were lined by hundreds of trees, beneath the sky. My mind was busy calculating how much money I could earn. Maybe this wasn't so bad after all.

An Example Peer Review Form

This peer review form gives an example of how a classmate evaluated the draft of the mentor text shown on the last page.

Criteria	Feedback
The writer grabs the reader's interest in the introduction.	You did a good job of using dialogue. You could improve your personal narrative by making the beginning clearer.
The writer organizes the event sequence so that it unfolds logically and naturally. **The writer uses descriptive details that appeal to the senses.**	You did a good job of organizing the event sequence. You could improve your personal narrative by adding descriptive details to the third paragraph.
The writer uses transitions to make the writing flow smoothly and to connect ideas.	You did a good job of using some transitions. You could improve your personal narrative by adding more transitions in the fourth paragraph.
The writer uses dialogue and reflection to develop experiences, events, and/or characters. **The writer states what he or she learned or how he or she changed.**	You did a good job of telling what you were thinking as the events occur. You could improve your personal narrative by adding more details about how your life changed.

Try It! Peer Review with a Partner

Now you are going to work with a partner to review each other's personal narrative drafts. You will use the peer review form below. If you need help, look back at the mentor text writer's peer review form for suggestions.

The writer grabs the reader's interest in the introduction.	You did a good job of You could improve your personal narrative by
The writer organizes the event sequence so that it unfolds logically and naturally. **The writer uses descriptive details that appeal to the senses.**	You did a good job of You could improve your personal narrative by
The writer uses transitions to make the writing flow smoothly and to connect ideas.	You did a good job of You could improve your personal narrative by
The writer uses dialogue and reflection to develop experiences, events, and/or characters. **The writer states what he or she learned or how he or she changed.**	You did a good job of You could improve your personal narrative by

Try It!

Record Key Peer Review Comments

Now it's time for you and your partner to share your comments with each other. Listen to your partner's feedback, and in the left column, write down the key comments that you hear. Then write some ideas for improving your draft in the right column.

My review says that my introduction	I will
My review says that my event sequence and details	I will
My review says that my transitions	I will
My review says that my dialogue	I will
My review says that my conclusion	I will

Write anything else you notice about your draft that you think you can improve.

5. Revise

In this step of the writing process, you work on parts of your draft that need improvement. Use the peer peview form that your classmate completed to help you. You also use your own ideas about how to improve each part of your personal narrative. This checklist includes some things to think about as you get ready to revise.

Revision Checklist

- ✔ Does my introduction grab the reader's interest? Do I set the scene?
- ✔ Does the event sequence flow in a logical and natural manner?
- ✔ Do I use relevant descriptive details and sensory language?
- ✔ Do I use transitions to connect my ideas?
- ✔ Do I reflect on what I learned or how I changed as a result of the experience?

PRECISE LANGUAGE
One way to use precise language is to include descriptive action words that create strong images. Compare the sentence "I exchanged smiles with the other members of my group" to this one: "I smiled at the people in the group, and they smiled back." Both describe what happened. Which is more effective and precise? Why?

Writer's Craft: Using Precise Language

Precise language brings life to the images a writer creates. Specific words are stronger than general ones, and many words evoke feelings. The mentor text describes the trees as *majestic*. How would the meaning be less precise if the writer used the word *big* instead? What other details in the text are described precisely?

Finally the caddy master herded our group outside into the bright sunlight. The rolling green fairways were lined by hundreds of majestic oak and walnut trees beneath the cloudless blue sky. My mind was busy calculating how much money I could earn this summer. Suddenly, I realized that I might be able to earn enough money to pay for my ninth-grade trip and have some money left over to buy a new snowboard. As I looked around, I exchanged smiles with the other members of my group. This wasn't going to be a nightmare after all. Maybe this wouldn't be too bad. Perhaps it really was a blessing in disguise.

Try It! Revise Your Personal Narrative

Replacing general language with precise language is an important part of revising a personal narrative. Your revision should not be limited to changing adjectives. Choosing appropriate nouns and verbs can also make your writing more effective. For the following paragraph, replace each underlined word or phrase with more precise language. Rewrite the paragraph on the lines provided.

A <u>man</u> <u>took a picture</u> of the <u>girl</u> <u>standing</u> by a <u>tree</u>. <u>The color of her dress</u> matched her eyes. Her mother saw her <u>smile</u>. The child <u>looked just like</u> her <u>other</u> daughter at <u>that age</u>. <u>So much</u> had <u>changed</u> over the years.

____

____

____

____

____

Writing Assignment

Now it's time to revise the draft of your personal narrative. Continue working on a computer or on a separate sheet of paper. Review the assignment, repeated below, and the checklist. Doing so will help you make sure that you have included everything you need.

> People come in and out of our lives, but there are some people we never forget. Write a personal narrative about your best childhood friend. Discuss how you met, what kinds of things you did together, what challenges you faced, and what you learned from each other. Use descriptive details to show, not tell, your reader.

After revising your personal narrative, you will edit it. When you edit, you read very carefully to find any mistakes in your writing. Here's a checklist of some things to look for as you edit.

Editing Checklist

- ✓ Did you indent each paragraph?
- ✓ Did you use complete sentences?
- ✓ Did you check for sentence fragments and run-on sentences?
- ✓ Did you use correct punctuation?
- ✓ Did you spell each word correctly?

You can use these editing marks to correct any errors you find.

Indent	Close up space	# Add space
Add hyphen	Delete	^ Insert

This paragraph from an early draft of the mentor text shows how to use editing marks.

The next morning, I nervously reported to the caddy master. The small green shuttered, white clap board building was situated on the perimeter of the golfcourse. Approximatly thirty five other people crowded the mane room. I recognized a few boys and a girl from my school standing in the corner of the room. I quickly joined them. Curiusly, we watched experienced caddies hoist large golf bags onto their shoulders and follow men and women across the emerald-colored grass.

Language Focus: Using Verbals

A **verbal** is a word formed from a verb that is used as a noun, adjective, or adverb. **Gerunds**, **participles**, and **infinitives** are types of verbals.

A gerund acts as a noun and ends in *-ing*.

Running is good exercise. (gerund)

Running five miles a day is good for your heart. (gerund phrase)

A participle acts as an adjective.

A present participle ends in *-ing*.

The crying child ran home.

A past participle usually ends in *-ed* or *-en*.

The broken dish was on the floor.

The frightened cat hid under the couch.

An infinitive acts as a noun, an adjective, or an adverb. It is usually a verb preceded by the word *to*.

I love to read on rainy days.

We cleaned the house to prepare for the holidays.

To be late would upset my mother. (infinitive phrase)

Read this paragraph from the mentor text to find examples of verbals.

After my mother's words sank in, I realized that this wasn't just a bad dream. It was a frightening nightmare! Why is it called summer vacation, I wondered, if it really isn't a vacation at all? Carrying someone's golf bag around a golf course was not a vacation. My back and feet ached just thinking about caddying. Sleeping, skateboarding, swimming, and hanging out with friends were what I had had in mind!

VERBALS There are three types of verbals: gerunds, participles, and infinitives. A verbal can be used alone or as part of a verbal phrase. Underline the verbals and verbal phrases in this section of the mentor text.

Try It! Language and Editing Practice

Underline the verbal or verbal phrase in each sentence. Then identify the type of verbal on the line provided: *gerund (gerund phrase)*, *participle (present or past participial phrase)*, or *infinitive (infinitive phrase)*.

1. Cam likes to go fast on his skateboard when he zooms around at the skate park. ____________________
2. The reckless driver was ticketed for speeding. ____________________
3. The high school senior earning the highest score on the test will earn a full scholarship. ____________________
4. To improve your draft, you should use precise language and revise. ____________________
5. The stolen watch was not an expensive one. ____________________

Now use editing marks to correct the errors in this paragraph.

Snowboarding during winterbreak was all I could think about for weeks, before school let out. My family had a driving trip planned to Colorado. I had never in my life time seen real mountians. Illinois is pretty flat! I became addicted to snowbording last winter when I went to a small ski area not far from home. The joy that I felt as I flew down the runs got me hooked on skiing. After the first day I looked forward to weekends with my friends just hanging out on the slopes. I can't wait to snowboard in Colorado.

Try It! Edit Your Personal Narrative

Now edit your personal narrative. Use this checklist and the editing marks you have learned to correct any errors you find.

- [ ] Did you indent each paragraph?
- [ ] Did you use complete sentences?
- [ ] Did you check for sentence fragments and run-on sentences?
- [ ] Did you use correct punctuation?
- [ ] Did you spell each word correctly?
- [ ] Did you use verbals correctly?
- [ ] Did you use transitions effectively?

Editing Tips

- Read your writing aloud. Add any missing words, and correct any awkward sentence constructions. Ask yourself, "Did that sentence sound right?"
- Reread your writing several times. Each time, focus on something different. For example, focus on punctuation and spelling in one reading and effective use of strong verbs in another reading.
- Delete unnecessary words and phrases that clutter your narrative. Are there too many words when one strong, precise word would work better?

7. Publish

On a computer or a separate sheet of paper, create a neat final draft of your personal narrative. Correct all errors that you identified while editing your draft. Give your personal narrative an interesting title.

The final step is to publish your personal narrative. Here are some different ways you might choose to share your work.

- Form a writing club. Meet to read and discuss each person's personal narrative.
- Create a brochure to publicize your personal narrative and to capture readers' attention.
- Submit your personal narrative for publication in your school newspaper.
- Read your personal narrative to a classmate. Discuss what you learned or how you changed as a result of the event or experience.
- Create a classroom magazine that includes your personal narrative. Make enough copies to distribute to each student in the class.

Technology Suggestions

- **Upload your personal narrative onto your class Web site or blog.**
- **Save your personal narrative as a PDF document that can be easily sent by e-mail to family and friends.**

Lesson 5

Reading Historical Texts

Look at this photo of one of the national parks in the United States.

Who explored these areas, and which processes have led to their preservation?

ESSENTIAL QUESTION

How do historical texts help us better understand our world today?

Listen and Learn

Consider ▶ Why is it important to ensure that certain areas of natural beauty are preserved?

How does an area of the country become legally preserved and protected?

A Place to PROTECT

1 Native Americans called the place Yellow Rock River, probably because of the color of the sandstone bluffs that line a portion of the banks of the Yellowstone River. When explorers told stories about the area, they said it was a place where the earth rumbled and shook under their feet. Smoke billowed upward from the cracks between the rocks, and enormous jets of hot water shot from the ground. Pools of boiling mud interrupted the landscape, and the river had cut a vast canyon with steep walls.

Many people refused to believe what the explorers said. It all seemed too fantastic to be real.

PRIMARY AND SECONDARY SOURCES A primary source is a document, speech, image, or other piece of evidence created by someone who was present when an event occured. A secondary source is something created or written about an event that the writer did not experience. Often the writer of a secondary source uses primary sources as evidence to support what is written. Look at paragraph 3. Why did Langford travel to the area? Is his illustrated article a primary source or a secondary source?

1870: The Langford Expedition

To scrutinize[1] the claims, Nathaniel Langford organized an expedition in 1870. When Langford returned from the Yellowstone area, he wrote a magazine article about what he had seen. The article was illustrated with drawings that were based on Langford's verbal descriptions to the artist.

Langford hoped that the United States Congress would vote to set the Yellowstone lands aside as a park for everyone to enjoy. But there was a problem. Many people doubted that the Yellowstone area was anything like Langford's description of it. Nonetheless, the idea of a national park, which everyone could appreciate and enjoy, was born.

[1]**scrutinize** to inspect or examine

1871: The Hayden Expedition

5 Dr. F. V. Hayden decided to persuade Congress to make Yellowstone a park by leading another expedition there to find and bring back indisputable evidence. A geologist, Hayden was often called upon by the United States government to do land surveys. One of his jobs was to survey the territories that the United States had annexed.[2] He had already seen Yellowstone, so he knew that its wonders were real. However, he needed evidence.

As William Henry Jackson wrote in his autobiography, *Time Exposure*:

> *That was where I came in. No photographs had as yet been published, and Dr. Hayden was determined that the first ones should be good. A series of fine pictures would not only supplement his final report but also tell the story to thousands who might never read it.*

Hayden recruited Jackson for the expedition. Jackson had already made a name for himself with his photographs of the American West, and this was not his first trip to Yellowstone. He knew what to look for, and he had a good idea of the kind of photographs that would prove the area was something special that should be preserved.

Hayden's expedition spent the summer of 1871 exploring the Yellowstone area. They returned with photographs that revealed a place even more amazing than the stories had made it seem.

[2]**annexed** taken possession of

DOMAIN-SPECIFIC VOCABULARY Many subjects or fields of study use vocabulary that has a specific meaning within that subject. In paragraph 5, the word *surveys* is specific to the fields of geography and geology. What do you think it means within these fields?

COMPARE AND CONTRAST TEXTS When comparing texts, you look for similarities and differences between two or more texts. The basis for comparison can include many things: genre, point of view, facts and opinions, and approaches to the topic. Paragraph 6 includes an excerpt from an autobiography—a text written by a person about his or her own life. In what ways is the text of the autobiography different from the historical text in paragraph 5? In what ways is it the same?

GLOSSARY A glossary is a list of specialized words that appear in the text, along with their definitions. It is usually found at the end of the text. Which word on this page would likely appear in the glossary of a social studies book?

FACT, OPINION, REASONED JUDGMENT A fact is something that can be observed or proven. An opinion is a personal view that someone believes about a certain issue. A reasoned judgment is similar to an opinion in that it can change from person to person. However, it is based on facts, logic, or reason. Look at paragraph 9. Was the idea that Yellowstone was "worthless" a fact, an opinion, or a reasoned judgment?

1872: Success!

Meanwhile, back in Washington, Langford had run into some people who had an aversion[3] to the idea of making Yellowstone a national park. Some people in Congress thought Yellowstone seemed "worthless" because the area didn't have any exploitable[4] resources. They didn't think Yellowstone was valuable.

10 When Langford explained the problem to him, the recently returned Dr. Hayden had an idea. Before the Yellowstone National Park bill came up for a vote, he placed a selection of Jackson's photographs on the desk of every member of the Senate and House of Representatives.

Jackson's photographs were persuasive. In 1871, people were not used to such images. A photograph was a remarkable thing, and the members of Congress had never seen photographs like these. Nor had they ever seen land like the place that the photographs showed.

[3]**aversion** feeling against

[4]**exploitable** able to be used to make money or for some other benefit

VISUAL INFORMATION An author may use a map or other graphic to further explain or enhance the words of a text. Look at this map of Yellowstone National Park. What do you notice about the entrances, and why do you think they were designed this way?

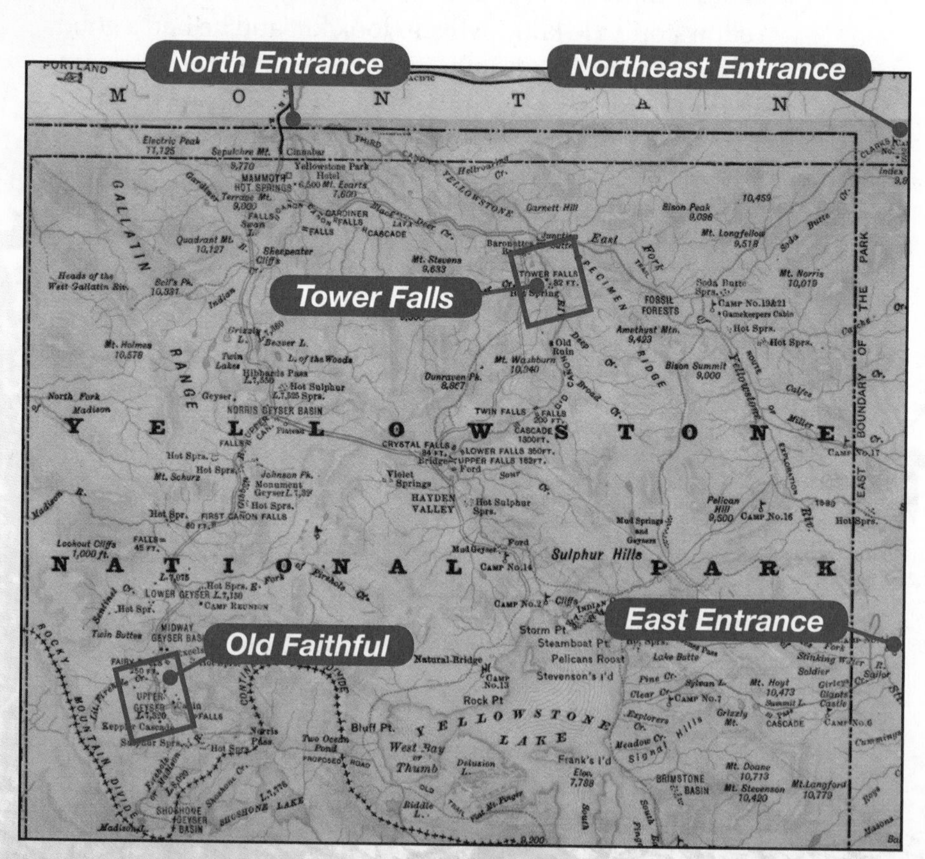

Fortunately, Hayden's idea worked. After viewing Jackson's photographs, Congress voted in favor of making Yellowstone the first national park in the United States. Today, more than 3 million people visit the park every year. It seems that none of these people would consider the park's geysers, hot springs, waterfalls, and wildlife "worthless."

TEXT STRUCTURE Many historical texts are organized in a cause-and-effect structure. An event is explained in terms of the causes that led to it. Look at paragraph 12. What does it suggest is the immediate cause of Congress voting to make Yellowstone a national park? What are some of the other causes that led to this event?

How to Become a National Park

A community or a local organization submits a proposal to the National Park Service.

↓

The National Park Service surveys the area for these criteria:

- It is an outstanding example of a certain resource.
- It exhibits a complete and undamaged example of the resource.
- It illustrates natural or cultural themes of the United States.
- It offers exceptional opportunities for recreation or for scientific study.

↓

The National Park Service submits its study to Congress.

↓

Congressional committees hold hearings.

↓

Congress votes on whether the area should become part of the National Park System.

STEPS IN A PROCESS Processes are designed so that steps are followed in a certain order. For land to gain status as part of the National Park System, a proposal must first be sent to the National Park Service. Which of these steps do you think is most important?

Comprehension Check

Look back in "A Place to Protect" to follow the series of events that led to the establishment of the first national park in the United States. Think about the actions different people took to make Yellowstone a national park. Use the graphic organizer to understand this sequence of events.

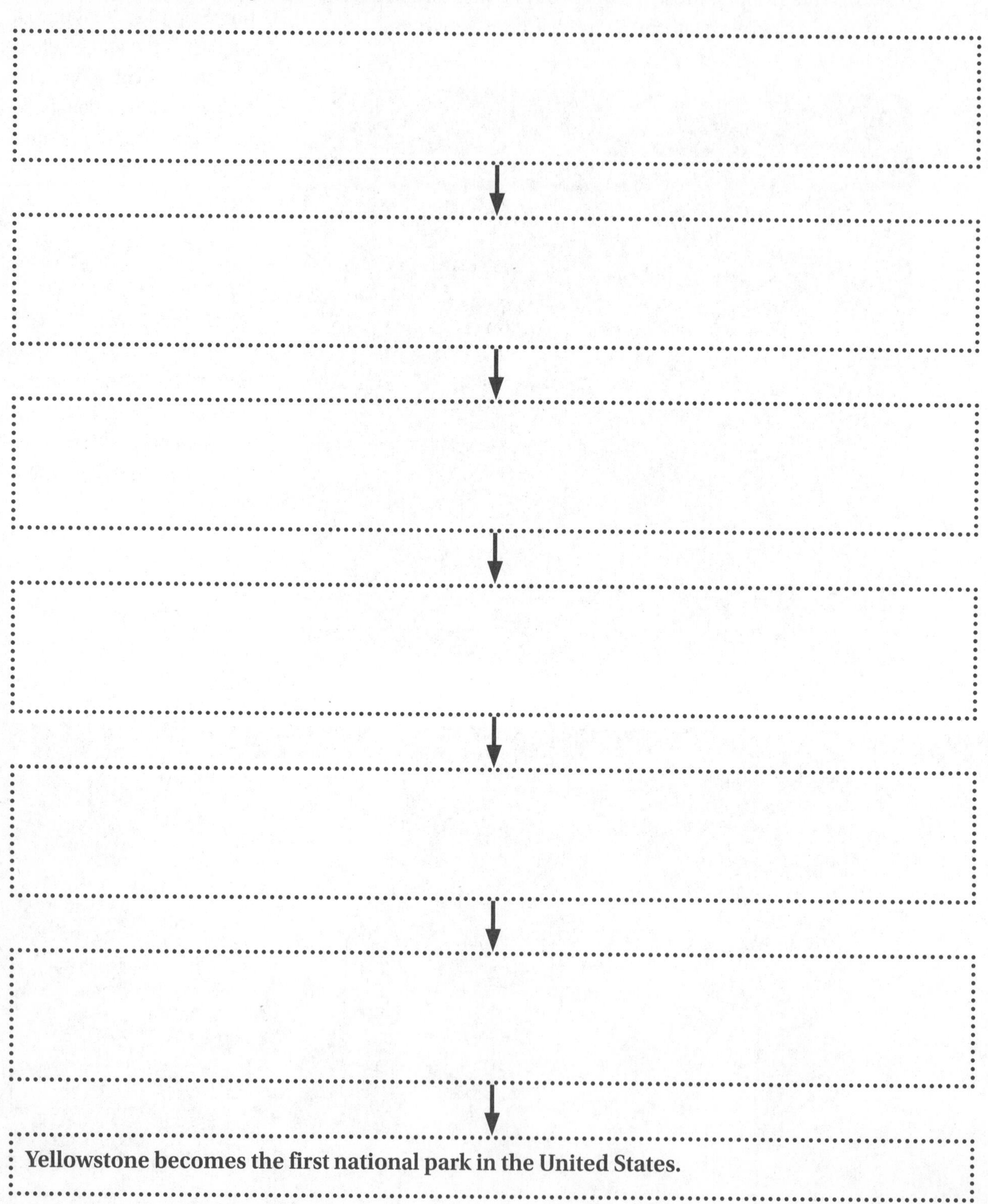

Yellowstone becomes the first national park in the United States.

Vocabulary

Use the word map below to help you define and use one of the highlighted vocabulary words from the Share and Learn reading or another word your teacher assigns you.

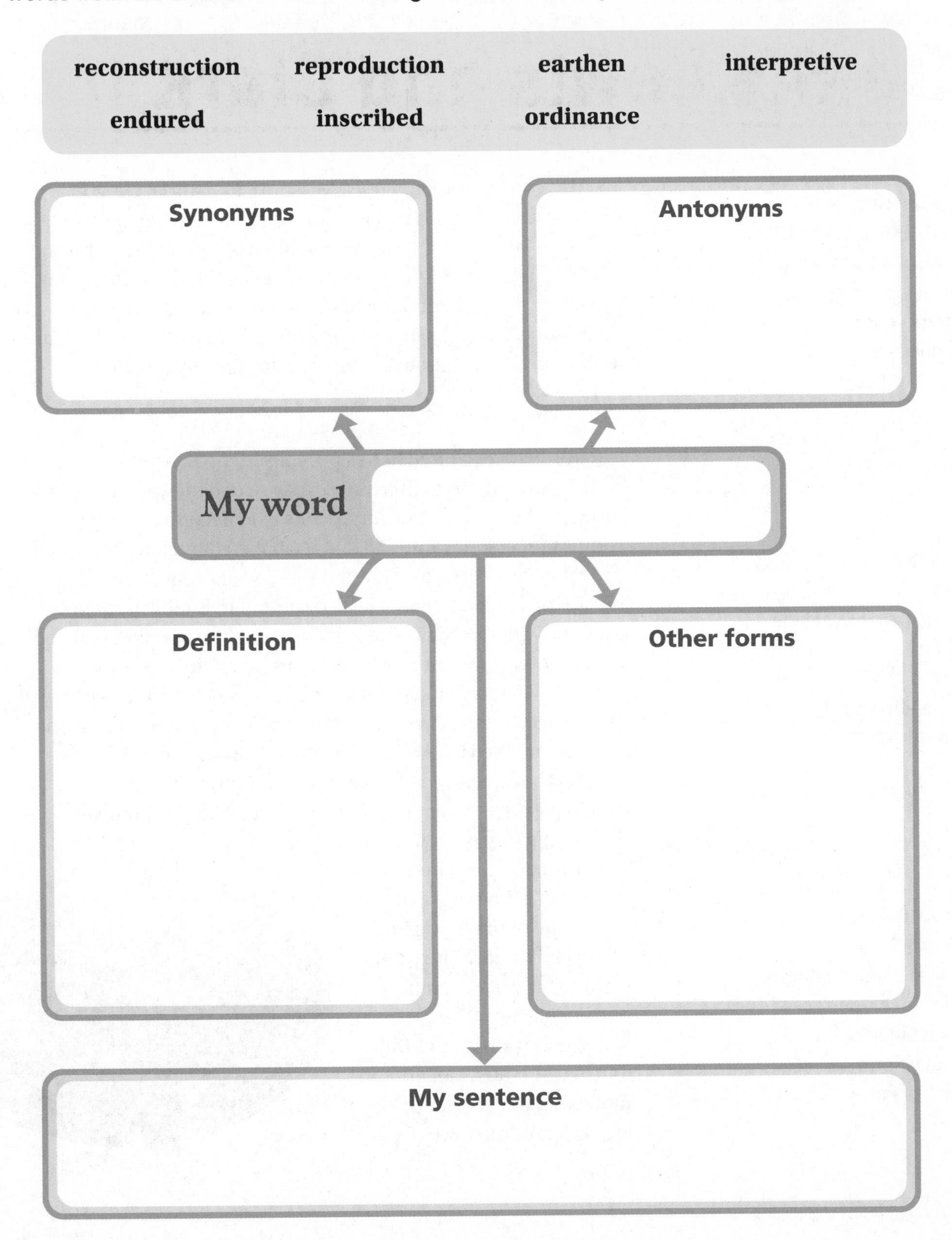

Share and Learn

Consider ▶ What do you think explorers of the American West expected to find?

What are the advantages and risks of exploring new territory?

On the Lewis and Clark Trail

FACT, OPINION, AND REASONED JUDGMENT
Circle one fact and underline one opinion in paragraph 1. Is the opinion a reasoned judgment? Why or why not?

____

____

TEXT STRUCTURE
Underline the words and phrase(s) that indicate the text structure. Is this article structured chronologically, by cause/effect, or by comparison/contrast?

____

____

COMPARE AND CONTRAST TEXTS
What kind of information is provided in this passage? How is it different from the information provided in "A Place to Protect"?

____

____

1 You can fly from St. Louis, Missouri, to Astoria, Oregon, in about five hours. Or you can follow in the footsteps of the explorers Meriwether Lewis and William Clark and travel some 3,700 miles up the Missouri River, across the Rocky Mountains, and down the Columbia River to the Pacific coast. For speed, take an airplane, but to have more fun, you might want to visit some spots along the Lewis and Clark National Historic Trail.

The Corps of Discovery

In 1803, the United States purchased the Louisiana Territory from France. Much of this huge expanse of land was wilderness, known only to the Native Americans who lived there. President Thomas Jefferson wanted to know what the land and its animals and plants were like, and if there was a water route that would lead to the Pacific Ocean. He also wanted to establish friendly relations with the Native Americans. Jefferson asked his trusted secretary, Meriwether Lewis, to lead an expedition. Lewis enlisted William Clark as his co-leader. Together, they assembled a group called the Corps of Discovery. Thirty-three volunteers, mostly from the U.S. Army, gave more than two years of their lives for the adventure of a lifetime. After months of planning, the Corps of Discovery set off from what is now Wood River, Illinois, on May 14, 1804. You can read the history of the expedition's remarkable adventure in the landscape of the Lewis and Clark Trail today. The trail, winding its way through parts of eleven states, lets you retrace portions of the journey by water, car, and on foot. Read more to learn about highlights of the trail.

Up the Mighty Missouri

The expedition proceeded up the Missouri River by boat, stopping to meet with Native Americans wherever they found them. Near Sioux City, Iowa (1), you can visit a monument to Sergeant Charles Floyd, the only member of the Corps to die during the expedition, probably of a burst appendix. His comrades buried him on a rounded hill, which Lewis and Clark named Floyd's Bluff. The expedition spent its first winter at Fort Mandan, which they built near a cluster of Mandan and Hidatsa villages in what is now central North Dakota. A reconstruction of the fort (2) is located about 12 miles south of the original site. Several miles north of that is the Knife River Indian Villages National Historic Site (3). Here you can see a film and exhibits about the Mandan and Hidatsa as well as a furnished reproduction of a Hidatsa earthen lodge. In June 1805, Lewis and Clark reached the Great Falls (4) of the Missouri River at what is now Great Falls, Montana. It took the expedition a month to carry six huge dugout canoes[1] and many supplies 18 miles around the falls. At the Lewis and Clark National Historic Trail Interpretive Center in Great Falls, exhibits cover the whole Lewis and Clark journey.

A hands-on exhibit called the Missouri River Mile-O-Meter lets you experience how difficult it was to haul the canoes upriver. At another exhibit, you can hear the four-language translation chain Lewis had to use to bargain for horses with the Shoshone (English to French to Hidatsa to Shoshone).

[1]**dugout canoes** canoes made from hollowed-out tree trunks

CONCLUSION What conclusion can you draw about the difficulty of the expedition? Circle the details and evidence that led you to that conclusion.

____

____

____

GLOSSARY Underline any words in this paragraph that would likely be found in a glossary.

VISUAL INFORMATION At what point on the trip home did Lewis and Clark separate? Where did their paths meet again?

____

____

The Trail of the Lewis and Clark Expedition

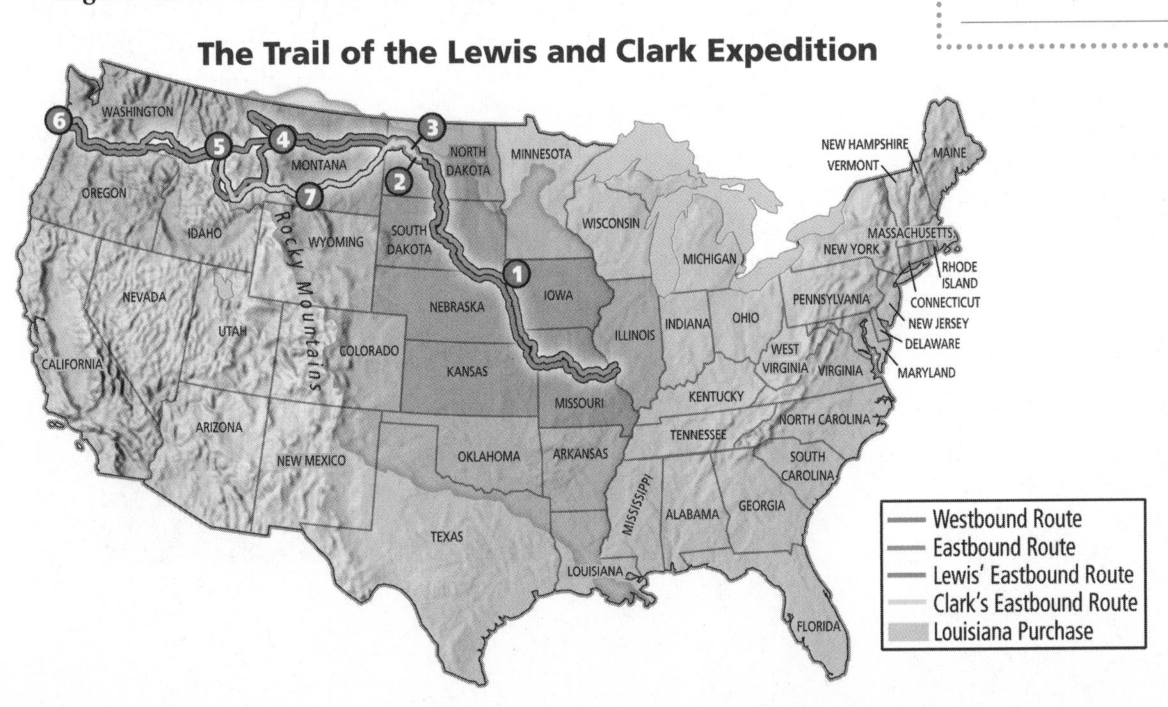

DOMAIN-SPECIFIC VOCABULARY What does the geology-related word *terrain* mean? How can you verify its meaning?

PRIMARY AND SECONDARY SOURCES Is the quotation from Sergeant John Ordway's writing a primary source or a secondary source? Explain how you know.

STEPS IN A PROCESS Which detail in this process shows that a territory could not become a state based on population alone?

Across the Mountains to the Sea

When the explorers reached the Rocky Mountains, the expedition followed the Lolo Trail (5) over the Bitterroot Range. They crossed some of the most rugged terrain in the mountains in freezing, wet weather and on starvation rations. Today, there are hiking trails that will give you a taste of the trip without the hardships endured by the expedition. Eventually, the team reached the great Columbia River, where the men built canoes and rode the river to the Pacific Ocean. Since winter was coming, the men constructed Fort Clatsop (6) near what is now Astoria, Oregon. Near the original site stands a reconstruction of the fort, where interpreters will answer your questions and let you test out Clark's bed or try on a buckskin jacket.

Going Home

5 On March 23, 1806, the expedition headed home. About 28 miles east of present-day Billings, Montana, Clark climbed a 200-foot sandstone rock, which he named Pompey's Pillar (7) in honor of the expedition's youngest member. On a path leading to the top, Clark inscribed his name and the date. Today, at Pompey's Pillar National Historic Landmark, you can see the inscription and take a guided walk that covers local history, animals, and plants. The expedition arrived in St. Louis on September 23, 1806. As Sergeant John Ordway wrote, ". . . the people of the town gathered on the bank and could hardly believe that it was us, for they had heard and had believed that we were all dead and were forgotten." And they have not been forgotten since. Just over two hundred years later, their history-making journey can still be read in the landscape of the American West.

How Northwest Territories Became States

The Northwest Ordinance of 1787

A township that reaches a population of 5,000 adult males becomes a territory.

A territory forms its own government.

A territory that reaches a population of 60,000 adult males and females can draft a constitution.

After approval from Congress, the territory becomes a state.

Anchor Standard Discussion Question

Discuss the following questions with your peer group. Then record your answers in the space provided.

1. Even though "On the Lewis and Clark Trail" is a historical text, it projects a unique tone. In the box, list words or phrases that contribute to the tone of the passage. On the lines below, explain how the connotation of these words reveals the author's attitude toward his or her subject.

Comprehension Check

1. How is the text mainly organized in "On the Lewis and Clark Trail"?

2. Summarize Lewis and Clark's journey, making sure to describe events in the order they took place.

3. Compare and contrast the articles "A Place to Protect" and "On the Lewis and Clark Trail." Are they primary or secondary sources? Explain how you know.

Read On Your Own

Read another historical text, "The Second War of Independence," independently. Apply what you learned in this lesson and check your understanding.

Lesson 6

Reading Drama

Look at this photo of the actors on stage.

How do their props and actions help tell the story?

ESSENTIAL QUESTION

How does presenting a story in a dramatic form influence the way it is told?

Consider ▶ Do you remember discovering something for the first time?

What would a production of this play look like?

A Grand Geyser

Cast of Characters

***Liu Xiang**, a young man from China*
***Dr. William Hayden**, a geologist*
***William Henry Jackson**, a photographer*
***James Stevenson**, assistant to Dr. William Hayden*

Scene 1

Setting: *The edge of a canyon, where an expedition team is exploring Yellowstone country.*

(Enter Liu Xiang and James Stevenson.)

Liu Xiang: *(climbing off his mule)* This canyon is breathtaking. I've never seen anything like it!

James Stevenson: *(chuckling)* Nor have I! Does this wondrous display of natural beauty erase your regret about joining our expedition?

Liu Xiang: Yes, sir, it does. Three weeks of trudging over this rugged terrain has not been easy. But seeing a sight like this makes the all the hard work worth it!

James Stevenson: I agree. When I signed on to manage the logistics of this trip for Dr. Hayden, I, too, had my misgivings. But having been Dr. Hayden's assistant, I know how committed he is to exploring the terrain of the American West.

Liu Xiang: No one believed the rumors about steam exploding from the earth or mud seething in boiling pools. I joined the trip so I could see these amazing wonders for myself. It seemed much more exciting than working on the transcontinental railroad, as many of my friends are doing in California.

James Stevenson: Well, Liu, that is important work as well. But even if there is nothing more to see here in Yellowstone country, the sight of this awe-inspiring canyon alone will have made the trip worthwhile.

(Exit.)

DRAMATIC IRONY Dramatic irony is a situation in which the audience knows something that the characters do not. How is dramatic irony shown in the final lines of scene 1? What effect does it create?

Scene 2

Setting: *A bit further down into the canyon.*

(Enter Dr. William Hayden and William Henry Jackson.)

Jackson: Well, Dr. Hayden, it certainly must have been excruciating work for you to get our government to support this expedition!

Hayden: Indeed, it was. As a geologist, I am enthralled by the extraordinary features of the land. As the next step, I must persuade Congress to make Yellowstone a national park.

Jackson: How do you think you'll be able to achieve that? Many of the leaders in Washington do not understand the value of preserving such a vast area of land that could be exploited in other ways.

10 **Hayden:** Oh, my good man. What better way to use this land than as a giant scientific laboratory? The natural phenomena in Yellowstone can teach us a great deal about geology. We've barely scratched the surface of this geologic gold mine, so to speak!

Jackson: Yes. A site like Yellowstone needs to be preserved and protected so that others can study and marvel at its unfathomable beauty.

Hayden: It does, my friend. And your photographs will be crucial for making our vision a reality. Shall we continue?

Jackson: By all means! My camera is ready and willing!

(Exit.)

DENOTATION AND CONNOTATION Many words are similar in their dictionary meanings, or denotations. However, the meaning that each word suggests or implies—its connotation—may be different. How would the meaning of Hayden's first lines be different if he had said "*Yes*, it was. As a geologist, I'm *interested in* the *unusual* features of the land"?

FIGURATIVE VS. LITERAL LANGUAGE Authors use literal language when they want the reader to understand their words exactly as written. When authors use figurative language, however, their words take on deeper meanings. Figurative language can make writing more interesting, but the reader will need to infer what the author is really trying to say. What examples of figurative language can you find in Hayden's lines? What does he mean?

DRAMATIC STRUCTURE Most plays are organized into one or more acts. Each act is made up of several scenes. Scenes often change when the setting or the characters on the stage change. Stage directions tell the actors where to enter and exit and as well as how to say their lines. In Stevenson's first line in scene 3, the stage direction is to interrupt Xiang. What other stage directions are in the opening lines of scene 3?

DIALOGUE The lines each actor is supposed to say in the drama make up the dialogue. Lines of dialogue appear after the character's name and sometimes after a stage direction. Xiang's first line in scene 3 is "You're welcome, sir. It's been an honor to accompany you . . ." What is Stevenson's first line of dialogue?

FIGURATIVE LANGUAGE VS. LITERAL LANGUAGE Which character uses literal language to describe what he sees, and which character uses figurative language? What is the effect of each?

Scene 3

Setting: *Later that day, farther into the basin of the canyon.*

(Enter Dr. William Hayden, William Henry Jackson, Liu Xiang, and James Stevenson.)

Jackson: Liu, I can't thank you enough for all of your assistance today. Photographs from these cameras might finally offer some tangible proof of the natural wonders of Yellowstone.

15 **Xiang:** You're welcome, sir. It's been an honor to accompany you—

Stevenson: *(interrupting Xiang)* Ssshhh! Listen! Can you hear a rumbling in the distance?

Hayden: *(furrowing his brow)* Jackson, prepare to use that camera of yours.

Jackson: *(coating his glass plate with photographic chemicals)* There may not be enough time!

(All four men remain silent and watchful as the ground continues to shake. Suddenly, in the distance, a great eruption begins. The men stare at a fixed point offstage.)

Hayden: Here we are, my friends, witnesses to one of Yellowstone's most fascinating features—
a geyser erupting!

20 **Stevenson:** That water must be reaching heights of almost 200 feet. It's astounding!

Xiang: It's like a witch's cauldron exploding out of the earth!

(The men continue to stare offstage.)

Scene 4

Setting: *Same place, two hours later.*

(The four men are sitting around a fire.)

Jackson: Well, it's fortuitous that the geyser erupted for over ten minutes. What great luck! We have numerous photographs showing the hot water eruptions as well as the steam that followed.

Stevenson: Like an underground teakettle! Liu, will you be accompanying us on our journey back to Washington?

Xiang: Unfortunately not, my friends. I would rather stay here to see what other awe-inspiring sights the American West has to reveal to me. If that geyser was just a glimpse of the impressive natural wonders this area has to offer, I can only imagine what awaits me!

25 **Hayden:** Yes, it was rather grand, wasn't it?

(Curtain.)

COMPARE AND CONTRAST
Written information can be presented in a variety of ways to help the reader gain understanding. "A Grand Geyser" presents information in dramatic form as well as with photographs and informative text. How is the text in the orange oval similar to and different from the dramatic text?

Yellowstone National Park

Dr. Hayden was successful in convincing Congress to name Yellowstone as the first national park in the United States. In fact, Yellowstone National Park became the first national park in the world.
The park includes more than three hundred geysers, some of which—such as the Grand Geyser—were named by Dr. Hayden. With more than 2 million acres, Yellowstone National Park is larger than the states of Rhode Island and Delaware combined.

Comprehension Check

Look back at the structure of "A Grand Geyser." Drama is organized into acts and scenes, but it typically also follows a narrative plot structure that includes exposition, rising action, climax, and falling action. Use the plot diagram below to depict the plot structure of the play.

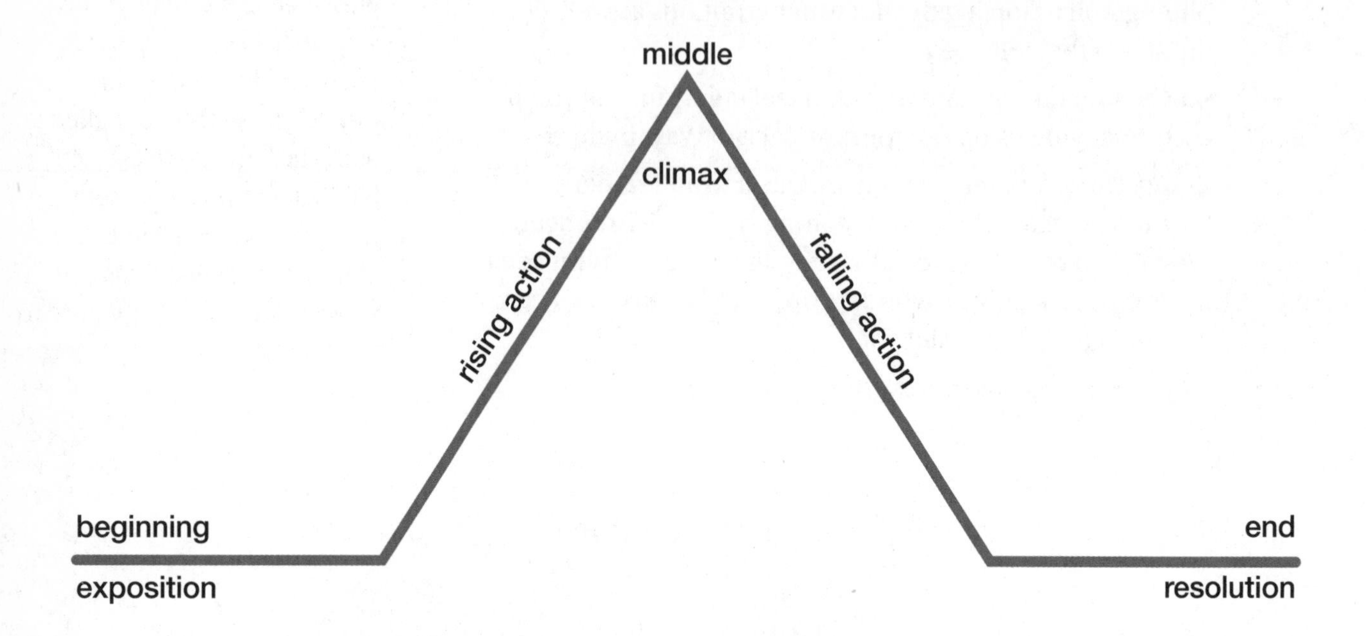

Vocabulary

Use the word map below to help you define and use one of the highlighted vocabulary words from the Share and Learn reading or another word your teacher assigns you.

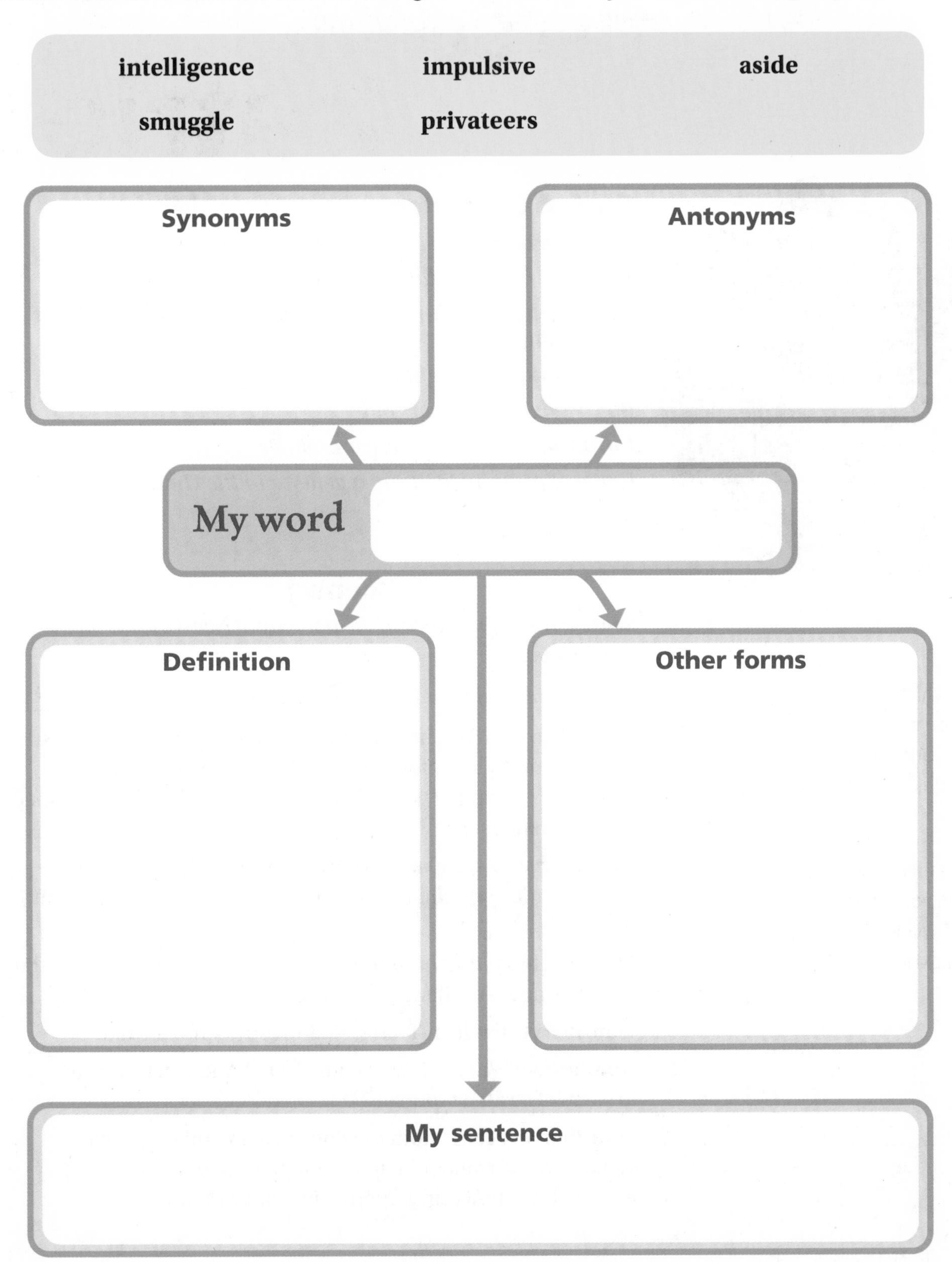

Consider ▶ How can setting and staging affect the story in a drama?

What can a writer do to propel the action in a drama?

The Surprise Patriot

Cast of Characters

Jean-Pierre*, fourteen-year-old boy living in New Orleans*

Papa*, Jean-Pierre's father, owner of a shipping warehouse*

Jean Lafitte*, French-born American patriot, commander of private ship*

Dominique*, Jean Lafitte's brother*

Boy*, eight or nine years old*

Corporal Jones*, an American soldier*

General Andrew Jackson*, a general in the United States Army*

Soldier

Scene 1

Setting: *A shipping dock in the port city of New Orleans on the Mississippi River.*

(Jean-Pierre and his father are stacking crates.)

Papa: Jean-Pierre, scurry over to the main square and request that Captain Moret inform us about when he will unload his cargo. Please explain to him that there is enormous storage space in the warehouse.

Jean-Pierre: Yes, Papa! *(runs toward stage left and almost collides with Dominique and Jean Lafitte as they enter)* Pardon me, sirs.

Jean Lafitte: *(places his hands on the boy's shoulders)* What's the rush, young man? Identify yourself.

Jean-Pierre: I'm Jean-Pierre, sir. I'm fourteen years old.

5 **Dominique:** Where did you come from? And where are you off to in such haste all by yourself?

Jean-Pierre: I come from the docks, sir. I'm off to the main square on an errand for Papa. *(pause, thinking)* And I go off by myself all the time, sir. Nobody's in charge of me, sir.

PLOT Which incident sets the action of this drama in motion? Underline the point at with this incident occurs.

PROPELLING ACTION How can you tell this incident will lead to what occurs next?

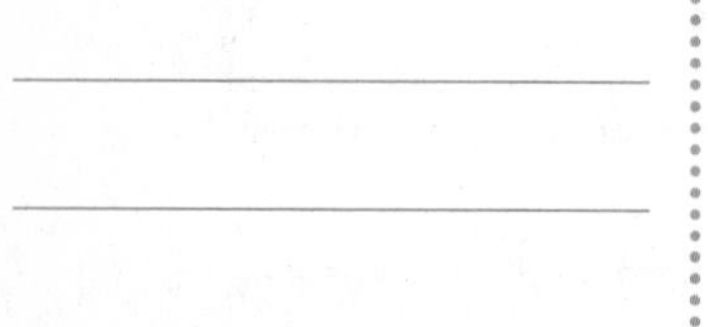

Dominique: Ah, the docks. I'm sure a boy your age loves the excitement of the docks, yes? But aren't you fearful of the enemy ships anchored down the river?

Jean-Pierre: Yes, sir, I do. And no, sir, I'm not.

Jean Lafitte: Ah, brave young lad, then you are a patriot?

10 **Jean-Pierre:** *(pauses, looks confused)* Umm, quite likely, sir.

Jean Lafitte: In any case, you must know about General Andrew Jackson, who has come to keep our great city free from the British. And perhaps you know where he resides?

Jean-Pierre: I know where the general keeps his headquarters, sir.

Jean Lafitte: Excellent. My brother and I have important business to discuss with the general, but he is . . . reluctant to meet with us. We must arrange for an "accidental" meeting. Do you see my point, young man?

Jean-Pierre: *(excitedly)* Yes, sir!

15 **Dominique:** Splendid! Run your papa's errand, then off you go to the general's headquarters to gather information.

Jean Lafitte: Yes, be our little bloodhound and sniff out clues about the general's habits. Where does he take his refreshment? At what time of day? You understand, yes?

Jean-Pierre: Indeed I do, sir.

Dominique: Excellent. Meet us here at the same hour tomorrow, and bring the intelligence we need. Your patriotic duty will be its own reward, young lad. Off you go!

(Jean-Pierre exits)

Dominique: My dear brother, surely you are not relying on an impulsive young boy to take part in our battle against the British?

20 **Jean Lafitte:** Dominique, if the British seize control of one of America's most important port cities, they will not stop! These states will not be treated as colonies!

(Exit Jean Lafitte and Dominique.)

FIGURATIVE LANGUAGE VS. LITERAL LANGUAGE Both Dominique and Jean Lafitte ask Jean-Pierre to do the same thing. Which one uses literal language and which one uses figurative language? In what way do they use them?

____

____

CHARACTERIZATION Describe the character of Jean-Pierre. How does his view of himself differ from that of Dominique and Jean Lafitte?

____

____

SETTING How does the setting contribute to the secrecy in the drama?

____

____

THEME What idea do Jean-Pierre and Jean Lafitte both seem to value? How might this idea contribute to a theme of the play? Circle the words and phrases that relate to this theme.

____

____

DRAMATIC IRONY Circle the stage direction that helps you to identify an example of dramatic irony.

SUMMARY Summarize the events of this scene.

____

____

____

MAIN IDEA What is the main idea of this scene, in relation to Jean-Pierre's character?

____

____

____

Scene 2

Setting: *Royal Street, New Orleans, outside of General Andrew Jackson's headquarters.*

(Boy pulls a wagon of crates along the street. Enter Jean-Pierre, running.)

Jean-Pierre: *(looking around, frantic)* Surely there must be an inn or a public house somewhere nearby where the general takes his refreshment.

Boy: *(overhearing)* Say, what's that you utter about the general?

Jean-Pierre: Oh, greetings. Maybe you can assist me.

Boy: *(suspiciously)* And how's that? *(aside to the audience)* The British have resorted to using young men to acquire information about the general! Well, we'll just see about that, won't we? *(to Jean-Pierre)* What do *you* want to know, sir?

25 **Jean-Pierre:** Have you seen the general anywhere near here? Do you know where he takes his tea?

Boy: *(proudly)* Sure, I see the general. Old Hickory himself. He's got a weak stomach. All he eats is boiled rice. *(pointing)* I happen to know he's at that inn every day precisely at noon. *(suddenly clamps his own hand over his mouth and turns to the audience)* Drat!

(Enter an American soldier.)

Boy: Corporal Jones, sir! This boy, he's been asking all kinds of questions about the general. Wants to know all about where and when he eats and the like.

Soldier: *(grabs Jean-Pierre by the arm)* Well, well, what have we here? You spies are getting younger and younger. I think it's time for us to start interrogating him.

(Jean-Pierre twists out of the soldier's grasp and exits at a run, with the soldier following.)

Scene 3

Setting: *Jean-Pierre's father's shipping warehouse. Papa, Jean Lafitte, and Dominique are engaged in a serious discussion in low voices.*

(Enter Jean-Pierre.)

Jean-Pierre: *(out of breath)* Papa, you'll never believe— *(halts in surprise upon seeing Jean Lafitte and Dominique)*

30 **Papa:** Jean-Pierre, remember your manners. We have the honor of the presence of Jean Lafitte, the most famous private commander in the city. He and his brother are helping us to defend New Orleans from the British.

Jean-Pierre: *(nervous and confused)* P-p-pleased to meet you, sir.

Jean Lafitte: *(chuckling)* Don't worry, my good lad. We're just discussing some shipping business with your papa.

Dominique: Indeed, sir. We have men and weapons to offer, and you can help us smuggle them into the country.

Jean Lafitte: But first, we must convince the general that we are privateers and not pirates. He doesn't seem to understand the difference.

35 **Jean-Pierre:** I have the information you need. I can lead you to the general, sir.

(Jean Lafitte and Dominique exit, following Jean-Pierre, while Papa stares in amazement.)

DENOTATION AND CONNOTATION In these lines, both characters talk about bringing men and weapons into the country. What is the connotation of each character's words?

____

____

____

DIALOGUE What does Papa's dialogue with Jean-Pierre reveal about Papa's feelings toward Jean Lafitte?

____

____

____

Lafitte's Blacksmith Shop

DRAMATIC STRUCTURE Why isn't scene 4 incorporated into scene 3? What is the effect of separating this incident?

COMPARE AND CONTRAST In what ways are the final scenes of "A Grand Geyser" and "The Surprise Patriot" similar? In what ways are the dramas different?

Scene 4

Setting: *Royal Street, outside the general's headquarters.*

(Jean Lafitte and Dominique stand in the street talking quietly while Jean-Pierre looks around nervously. A tall, slim man in the uniform of a general enters and begins to stride past them.)

Jean Lafitte: Excuse me, sir, General Jackson, may I have a word?

(General Jackson pauses and fixes Lafitte with a stony stare, which gradually softens to a smile. Jackson, Lafitte, and Dominique exit. Jean-Pierre stares after them, beaming and standing a bit taller and straighter than before.)

(Curtain.)

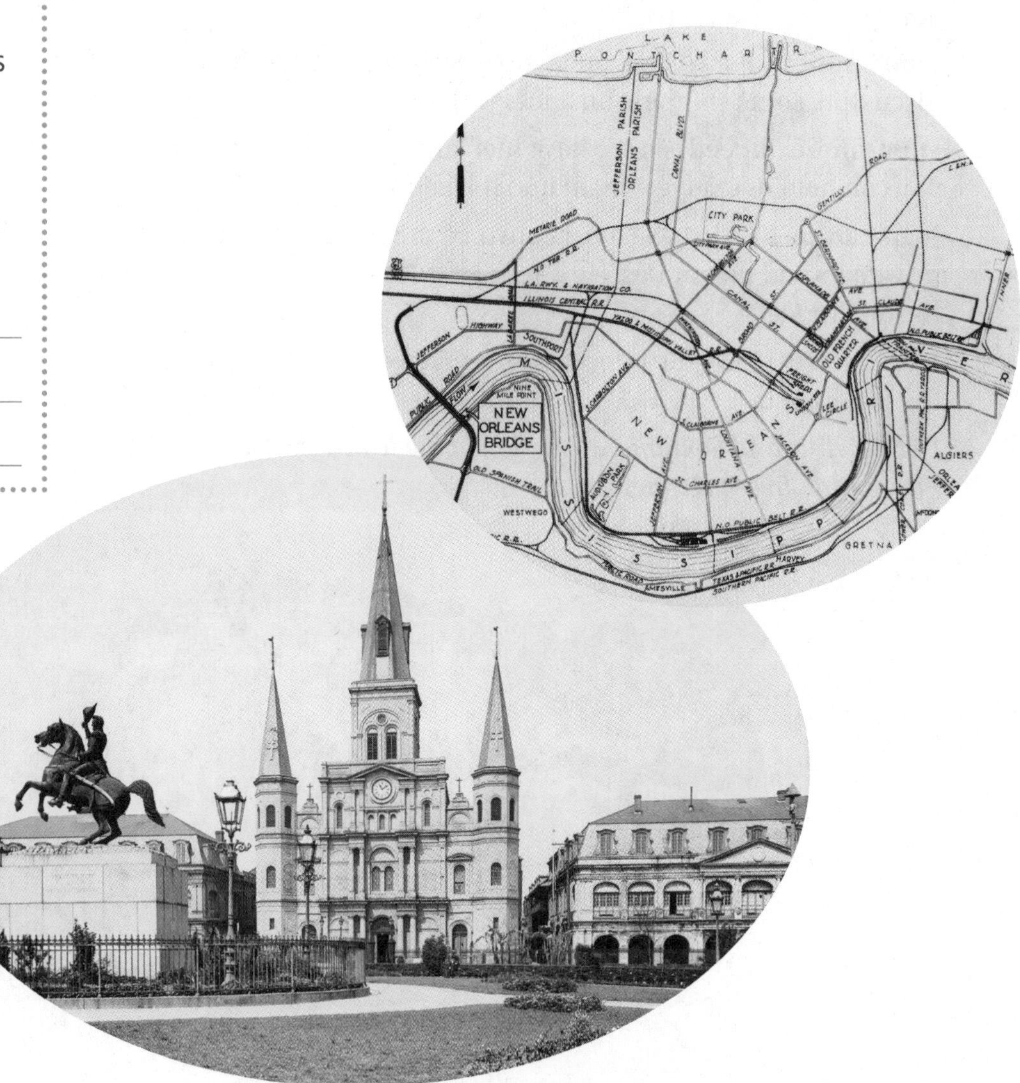

Andrew Jackson Monument
in front of St. Louis Cathedral

Anchor Standard Discussion Question

Discuss the following question with your peer group. Then record your answers in the space provided.

1. If you were chosen to direct a stage production of "The Surprise Patriot," what tone would the play have? How would you project this tone? Support your choice of tone with details from the text. Be sure to address dramatic irony in your answer.

Comprehension Check

1. Are any of the characters in "The Surprise Patriot" alike? Explain.

2. Identify a key line of dialogue in "The Surprise Patriot" that served to propel the action forward.

3. Evaluate the author's use of stage directions. How do the stage directions contribute to the meaning of the dialogue? Support your answer with details from the passage.

Read On Your Own

Read another drama, "Learning of Fly," independently. Apply what you learned in this lesson and check your understanding.

Lesson 7

Reading Poetry

Look at this image of the moon's reflection on the water.

Why might an image like this inspire poets?

ESSENTIAL QUESTION

How do the imagery, mood, and tone of a poem reflect human emotion?

Listen and Learn

Consider ▶ How do you think mythological figures can teach us about being human?

Can images from nature do the same?

Endymion

by Henry Wadsworth Longfellow

POETRY STRUCTURE
Poems are often divided into stanzas, or groups of lines. How many stanzas does the poem have? What is similar about the structure of all the stanzas in this poem? (Hint: Think about how long the lines are and which ones rhyme.)

IMAGERY Poets use imagery—language that appeals to the senses—to create a vivid experience for the reader. Look at stanza 1. To what does the poet compare the rays of the moon? What other visual imagery does the poet use in the first two stanzas?

Endymion is a figure in Greek mythology who was known for his desire for perpetual sleep. According to myth, Diana, a goddess associated with the moon, loved to gaze upon Endymion's beauty while he slept.

1 The rising moon has hid the stars;
Her level rays, like golden bars,
  Lie on the landscape green,
  With shadows brown between.

5 And silver white the river gleams,
As if Diana, in her dreams
  Had dropt her silver bow
  Upon the meadows low.

10 On such a tranquil night as this,
She woke Endymion with a kiss,
  When, sleeping in the grove,
  He dreamed not of her love.

Like Dian's kiss, unasked, unsought,
Love gives itself, but is not bought;
15 Nor voice, nor sound betrays
Its deep, impassioned gaze.

It comes,—the beautiful, the free,
The crown of all humanity,—
In silence and alone
20 To seek the elected one.

It lifts the boughs, whose shadows deep
Are Life's oblivion, the soul's sleep,
And kisses the closed eyes
Of him who slumbering lies.

25 O weary hearts! O slumbering eyes!
O drooping souls, whose destinies
Are fraught with fear and pain,
Ye shall be loved again!

No one is so accursed by fate,
30 No one so utterly desolate,
But some heart, though unknown,
Responds unto his own.

Responds,—as if with unseen wings,
An angel touched its quivering strings;
35 And whispers, in its song,
"Where hast thou stayed so long?"

SYMBOL A symbol is an object or action that represents something else that might be more complex. In "Endymion," Longfellow uses Diana's kiss as a symbol. Look at lines 9–16. What does Diana's kiss symbolize, and in what ways?

RHYME SCHEME Rhyme scheme, the pattern of rhymes in a poem, is written as a string of letters, with each letter representing an end sound. For example, the rhyme scheme of the stanzas in "Endymion" is *aabb* (*deep*, *sleep*; *eyes*, *lies*). Sometimes, the lines do not rhyme perfectly but are instead very close in sound. This is called half rhyme or slant rhyme. Which pairs of end words show examples of half rhyme?

MOOD Mood is the general atmosphere the poet creates for the reader. How does the poet create a mood of reassurance and hope in lines 29 through 32?

TONE The tone of a poem is the poet's attitude toward the subject of the poem. If the subject of "Endymion" is love, what tone does the poem convey about this subject? What words or other features help to show the tone?

Comprehension Check

Each stanza of "Endymion" describes a visual or symbolic scene that expresses the poet's ideas about love. Use the storyboard below to draw scenes that most vividly represent the meaning of each of the four stanzas. Don't worry about your drawing skill—use stick figures, clip art, or pictures from magazines for your storyboard. Then write a caption in your own words explaining what is happening in each scene. Finally, answer the question at the bottom of the page.

1.

2.

3.

4.

How would you summarize the poet's feelings or understanding of love?

Vocabulary

Use the word map below to help you define and use one of the highlighted vocabulary words from the Share and Learn reading or another word your teacher assigns you.

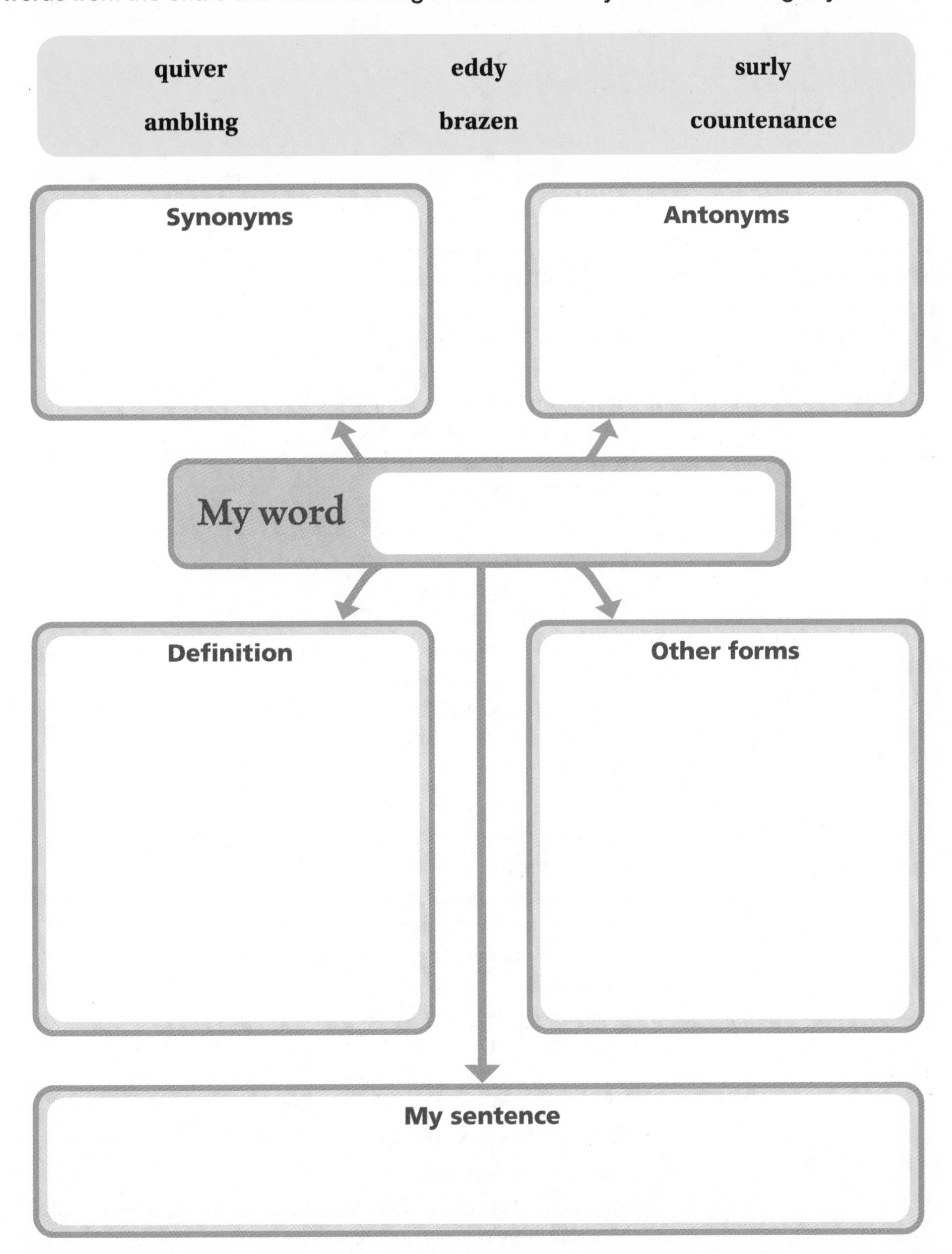

Share and Learn

Consider ▶ What makes the Lady of Shalott so fascinating to the speaker?

Why is the Lady of Shalott drawn to the knight?

from

The Lady of Shalott

by Alfred Lord Tennyson

INFERENCE What can you infer about the dwelling or home of the Lady of Shalott? Circle the details that led you to this inference.

____

____

____

MOOD What is the mood of the first three stanzas? Circle any words or phrases that indicate the mood.

____

____

____

1 On either side the river lie
Long fields of barley and of rye,
That clothe the wold[1] and meet the sky;
And thro' the field the road runs by
5 To many-tower'd Camelot;[2]
And up and down the people go,
Gazing where the lilies blow
Round an island there below,
The island of Shalott.

10 Willows whiten, aspens quiver,
Little breezes dusk and shiver
Through the wave that runs for ever
By the island in the river
Flowing down to Camelot.
15 Four grey walls, and four grey towers,
Overlook a space of flowers,
And the silent isle embowers[3]
The Lady of Shalott.

Only reapers, reaping early,
20 In among the bearded barley
Hear a song that echoes cheerly
From the river winding clearly;
Down to tower'd Camelot;
And by the moon the reaper weary,
25 Piling sheaves in uplands airy[4]
Listening, whispers, " 'Tis the fairy
Lady of Shalott."

[1]**clothe the wold** cover the hilly country

[2]**Camelot** the legendary kingdom of King Arthur

[3]**embowers** shelters or encloses

[4]**piling sheaves in uplands airy** stacking up the bundles of grain stalks harvested that day in the wide-open hills

There she weaves by night and day
A magic web with colours gay.
30 She has heard a whisper say,
A curse is on her if she stay
To look down to Camelot.
She knows not what the curse may be,
And so she weaveth steadily,
35 And little other care hath she,
The Lady of Shalott.

And moving through a mirror clear[5]
That hangs before her all the year,
Shadows of the world appear.
40 There she sees the highway near
Winding down to Camelot;
There the river eddy whirls,
And there the surly village churls,[6]
And the red cloaks of market girls
45 Pass onward from Shalott.

Sometimes a troop of damsels[7] glad,
An abbot[8] on an ambling pad,
Sometimes a curly shepherd lad,
Or long-hair'd page[9] in crimson clad
50 Goes by to tower'd Camelot;
And sometimes through the mirror blue
The knights come riding two and two.
She hath no loyal Knight and true,
The Lady of Shalott.

[5]**through a mirror clear** weavers placed mirrors across from their looms so they could see their work as they completed it

[6]**churls** people with no manners

[7]**damsels** young women

[8]**abbot** a religious official

[9]**page** messenger

SYMBOL In lines 28–36, the reader learns that there is a curse on the Lady of Shalott if she looks upon the royal city of Camelot. What might the web that she weaves symbolize?

____

____

____

IMAGERY What imagery is used in lines 28–36 to suggest Lady Shalott's mood? How is the imagery different in lines 37–45? What might the "shadows" symbolize in line 39?

____

____

____

THEME How do lines 46–54 reflect loneliness and solitude? Underline the line that best illustrates this theme.

____

____

____

RHYME SCHEME Label one stanza of the poem with the correct rhyme scheme by placing the appropriate letter at the end of each line.

FIGURATIVE VS. LITERAL LANGUAGE When the Lady of Shalott says, "I am half sick of shadows," how is her use of the word *shadows* both literal and figurative? What triggers this remark?

____

____

____

POETRY STRUCTURE Look at the fifth and ninth line of each stanza. How does the second stanza on this page depart from this structure? What might this structural change suggest?

____

____

____

55 But in her web she still delights
To weave the mirror's magic sights,
For often through the silent nights
A funeral, with plume[10] and lights
And music, went to Camelot;
60 Or when the Moon was overhead,
Came two young lovers lately wed.
"I am half sick of shadows," said
The Lady of Shalott.

A bowshot from her bower-eaves,
65 He rode between the barley sheaves,
The sun came dazzling thro' the leaves,
And flamed upon the brazen greaves[11]
Of bold Sir Lancelot.
A red-cross[12] knight forever kneel'd
70 To a lady in his shield,
That sparkled on the yellow field,
Beside remote Shalott.

[10]**plume** decorative feathers

[11]**greaves** armor

[12]**red-cross** highly decorated, accomplished

His broad clear brow in sunlight glow'd;
On burnish'd hooves his war-horse trode;
75 From underneath his helmet flow'd
His coal-black curls as on he rode,
As he rode down to Camelot.
From the bank and from the river
He flashed into the crystal mirror,
80 "Tirra lirra,"[13] by the river
Sang Sir Lancelot.

She left the web, she left the loom,
She made three paces through the room,
She saw the water-lily bloom,
85 She saw the helmet and the plume,
She look'd down to Camelot.
Out flew the web and floated wide;
The mirror crack'd from side to side;
"The curse is come upon me," cried
90 The Lady of Shalott.

And down the river's dim expanse
Like some bold seer in a trance,
Seeing all his own mischance—
With a glassy countenance
95 Did she look to Camelot.
And at the closing of the day
She loosed the chain, and down she lay;
The broad stream bore her far away,
The Lady of Shalott.

100 Lying, robed in snowy white
That loosely flew to left and right—
The leaves upon her falling light—
Thro' the noises of the night,
She floated down to Camelot:
105 And as the boat-head wound along
The willowy hills and fields among,
They heard her singing her last song,
The Lady of Shalott.

[13]**"Tirra lirra"** made-up tune

ARCHETYPE Which descriptions of Lancelot show him as an archetype of the "knight in shining armor"? Typically, what is this type of character supposed to do?

____

____

____

SYMBOL Circle the symbol that represents bad luck.

ALLUSION Camelot and the Knights of the Round Table are common allusions in popular culture. On the lines below, list at least two allusions to Camelot you've seen in books, movies, or on television.

____

____

____

POINT OF VIEW To whom does *they* refer in line 107? What is the point of view of this poem?

____

____

____

TONE What is the overall tone of the poem? Circle any words in the last three stanzas that reveal the poet's tone.

____

____

____

COMPARE AND CONTRAST POEMS How is the topic of love portrayed differently in "Endymion" and in "The Lady of Shalott"?

____

____

____

Heard a carol, mournful, holy,
110 Chanted loudly, chanted lowly,
Till her blood was frozen slowly,
And her eyes were darkened wholly,
Turn'd to tower'd Camelot.
For ere she reach'd upon the tide
115 The first house by the water-side,
Singing in her song she died,
The Lady of Shalott.

Who is this? And what is here?
And in the lighted palace near
120 Died the sound of royal cheer;
And they crossed themselves for fear,[14]
All the Knights at Camelot;
But Lancelot mused a little space
He said, "She has a lovely face;
125 God in his mercy lend her grace,
The Lady of Shalott."

[14]**they crossed themselves for fear** made the sign of the cross as a form of a prayer

Anchor Standard Discussion Question

Discuss the following question with your peer group. Then record your answer in the space provided.

1. Which lines of "The Lady of Shalott" contain the turning point of the poem? Explain how this point alters the remainder of the poem.

Comprehension Check

1. Describe the imagery in "The Lady of Shalott."

2. Think about what happens to the Lady of Shalott. What might she symbolize?

3. Compare the moods of "Endymion" and "The Lady of Shalott."

Read On Your Own

Read another poem independently. Apply what you learned in this lesson and check your understanding.

Lesson 8

Writing Fictional Narratives

Have you ever wondered what it might be like to have a high-risk job in which a typical workday consists of situations that most people will never face? Think of a real-life job that fits this description, and then create a character who has this job. Consider the challenges and obstacles that this character must face daily and how he or she overcomes them.

ESSENTIAL QUESTION

Which plot and narration techniques contribute to an engaging fictional narrative?

What's a Fictional Narrative?

Have you ever thought of what it would be like to have a dangerous but exhilarating and important job? What dangers would you have to face on a daily basis? How would you overcome them and succeed or even survive? You can use your imagination to write a fictional narrative about characters in a dangerous line of work.

A **fictional narrative** is a story about made-up characters and events. Like other narratives, a fictional narrative has a specific setting and one or more characters who face conflicts and solve them. The setting, characters, and/or events may be realistic or based on fantasy.

The story may be told from the first-person point of view by one of the characters (using the pronoun *I*). It can also be told from the third-person point of view by a narrator who is not part of the story (using pronouns like *he*, *she*, and *they*).

Introduction
Indicate the time and place of your story, and introduce the main character or characters. Establish who will be narrating, or telling, the story.

Plot/Problem/Conflict
Show your main character facing an important problem or conflict. Explain how your character tries to overcome this problem. Describe the actions the character takes and show how he or she interacts with others.

Climax
Make this part of the story the most suspenseful and exciting. Tell how your character finally succeeds in overcoming the problem.

Resolution
Show what happens after the climax. Bring the story to an end.

Let's look at a fictional narrative.

Analyze a Mentor Text

This is an example of an effective fictional narrative. Read it and then complete the activities in the boxes as a class.

It's Just My Job

A siren blast pierced the air, calling Marisa and the other smokejumpers to report to duty. For several days, ground crews had been fighting a slow-burning forest fire started accidentally by a careless camper. All this time, a steady wind had been pushing the fire toward the lake, where it would burn out. That's why Marisa was surprised that the smokejumpers were being called in for such a "deadly" fire.

Within fifteen minutes, she and the other jumpers were in a plane, circling above the fire. The winds were accelerating, carrying away burning embers and starting new fires in areas that the ground crews could not reach. Then Marisa understood why jumpers had been called in.

Wearing her parachute, Marisa floated weightlessly toward the forest with the other smokejumpers. Parachutes that carried tools floated down with them. Upon landing, Marisa immediately smelled the bitter smoke and heard the fire roaring like an oncoming train. The jumpers quickly got to work. However, after a few hours, Marisa made a frightening discovery. "The wind has changed! It's blowing toward the east!" she yelled to the team leader. The fire was heading toward the cabins and the park lodge!

INTRODUCTION The writer introduces Marisa as the main character and describes her as a smokejumper. This paragraph implies that smokejumpers fight difficult fires, unlike the ground crews. From which point of view will this story be told?

PLOT A sequence of events makes up the plot. In this narrative, it increases the tension. What events make the situation increasingly dangerous?

CLIMAX The climax of a story is the highest point of interest or excitement. It is often the major turning point in the action. What events and details show that this is the climax?

RESOLUTION In a story's plot, the resolution describes the solution to the conflict. Why is a resolution important in a narrative? Why does the writer not end the story immediately after the climax?

The smokejumpers began the backbreaking work of establishing a fire line. They worked for days just to clear a brush-free path that they hoped would stop the ferocious wall of flame. Just as they finished, the fire roared up to the fire line—but then stopped! And at that moment, it began to rain—a real downpour. Once the rain stopped and the flames were out, the jumpers still weren't finished. They got down on their hands and knees and carefully felt every acre of ground to make sure it was cool. There were no hot spots. Their hard work had paid off.

At last, the leader radioed for a helicopter to pick up the smokejumpers. They had been fighting the fire for five days with very little rest. As they waited for the helicopter, Marisa thought about how good it was going to feel to shower and fall into bed. Fighting fires was just her job, but it could be very tiring! As the smokejumpers were boarding the helicopter, the team leader smiled at the smoky jumpers and joked, "We've been fired, so let's all get out of here!"

Think About It ▶ How does the writer show you the dangers that smokejumpers face?

Does the narration style add to or take away from the suspense of the story?

Vocabulary Study: Figures of Speech

As you read, you are likely to encounter figures of speech, such as similes, idioms, and puns. A **simile** is a type of figurative language that compares two things or ideas using the word *like* or *as*. For example, *His unshaved face was like grassy stubble*. An **idiom** is a figurative expression with a commonly understood meaning that is different from its literal meaning. A **pun** is a word that has a double meaning and is often used for humorous effect. Often, clues in the surrounding sentence or paragraph can help you understand figures of speech.

Read the following sentence from the fictional narrative on pages 125–126, and look at the underlined simile. What two things are being compared?

> Upon landing, Marisa immediately smelled the bitter smoke and heard <u>the fire roaring like an oncoming train.</u>

The ______________________ is compared to a ______________________.

This simile helps the reader imagine ______________________.

Look at the paragraph below from the fictional narrative. The underlined phrase is an idiom, and the underlined word is a pun. How do clues from this paragraph help you understand the meaning of the idiom <u>fall into bed</u> and the two meanings of the pun *fired*?

> At last, the leader radioed for a helicopter to pick up the smokejumpers. They had been fighting the fire for five days with very little rest. As they waited for the helicopter, Marisa thought about how good it was going to feel to shower and <u>fall into bed</u>. Fighting fires was just her job, but it could be very tiring! As the smokejumpers were boarding the helicopter, the team leader smiled at the smoky jumpers and joked, "We've been <u>fired</u>, so let's all get out of here!"

Meaning of *fall into bed*: ______________________

Context Clues: ______________________

Meanings of *fired*: ______________________

Context Clues: ______________________

Writing Process

Now that you have read and analyzed a fictional narrative, you are going to create your own narrative by following the steps in the writing process.

1. Get Ready: Brainstorm List several topics that you might want to write about. Choose the one that interests you most. Brainstorm details about your topic, including possible conflicts. Choose a main character and a setting.

2. Organize Use a graphic organizer to organize the events and details you plan to include, and arrange them in the correct sequence.

3. Draft Create the first draft of your fictional narrative. Don't worry too much about making mistakes. Get your ideas down.

4. Peer Review Work with a partner to evaluate and improve your draft.

5. Revise Use suggestions from your peer review to revise your narrative.

6. Edit Check your work carefully for errors in spelling, punctuation, and grammar.

7. Publish Create a final version of your fictional narrative.

Writing Assignment

In this lesson, you will write your own fictional narrative. As you create the piece, remember the elements of the mentor text that were most effective. Read the following assignment.

> The narrative "It's Just My Job" is about a person who has a dangerous but important job. Write a fictional narrative about another character who has an interesting career. Demonstrate the obstacles the character faces on a typical workday or in a typical situation, and explain how he or she overcomes them.

1. Get Ready: Brainstorm

When you brainstorm, you think of as many ideas as you can. Start by making a chart like the one below and filling in the first column with the names of careers and jobs that interest you. Then fill in the middle column with reasons to choose that job or career for this writing assignment. Finally, complete the third column. After that, you should have the information you need to select the topic for your fictional narrative.

Here's how the author of the mentor fictional narrative began brainstorming ideas.

Possible Career/Job	Reason to Choose	What I Already Know
firefighter	An active day can be exciting and dangerous.	My uncle is a firefighter.
emergency medical technician (EMT)	Sometimes their actions can save lives.	I've seen EMTs at work.
smokejumper	There is always risk and tension in this job.	I read about a real smokejumper.

Try It!

Use a Brainstorming Graphic Organizer

Now use the chart below to help brainstorm ideas for your own fictional narrative.

Possible Career/Job	Reason to Choose	What I Already Know

Brainstorm Ideas for Your Topic

Now that you've chosen a topic, you need to map out your narrative and brainstorm ideas and details to include. After deciding to write about a smokejumper, the author of the mentor text used the first column of the graphic organizer below to record possible details and the second column to review them. Then the author decided which ones to include.

INTRODUCTION The introduction needs to include enough details about the main character to enable readers to understand the story. Give details about the setting, as well.

PLOT Choose an exciting event that will require the main character to take action. The climax will occur when the main character has to confront the conflict.

RESOLUTION Choose a way to wrap up the story so there is a resolution to the problem.

Introduction	How will this detail add to the story?
Training for smokejumpers	Good background, but might slow down the story
Background details about Marisa	Need to choose details carefully
Tools and equipment and how they are used	May be too much detail for a short narrative
Place and time of the story	I can include details to show this.
Plot	**Which problem is best?**
Someone lost in the forest?	I don't think smokejumpers find lost people—unless they are lost in a fire.
A fire out of control?	Sounds good!
Smokejumper in trouble?	Possible?
Climax	**How does the character solve the problem?**
The smokejumper faces a dangerous situation and must act quickly.	Creates a fire line. It stops the fire just in time.
Resolution	**How does the story come to an end?**
Stay there? Go home?	The main character reflects on a job well done.

Try It! Use a Graphic Organizer for Brainstorming

Now use the graphic organizer below to brainstorm details and events for your fictional narrative. You can always add more details and make other changes as you write your draft. You can also delete details or events that do not fit into your narrative after all.

Introduction	How will this detail add to the story?
Plot	**Which problem is best?**
Climax	**How does the character solve the problem?**
Resolution	**How does the story come to an end?**

2. Organize

You are almost ready to begin a draft of your own fictional narrative. A more detailed graphic organizer can help you further organize the ideas you have chosen to include and describe events in sequence. You can then refer to this graphic organizer as you work through the parts of your draft. After deciding on the main events and details to include in the mentor text, the writer completed this graphic organizer.

INTRODUCTION Set the scene by grabbing the readers' interest, introducing the main character, and including only enough details so readers will understand your story.

Introduction

- Main character: Marisa
- Experienced smokejumper working with a team
- Based in a wilderness camping area
- Called only for dangerous fires

PLOT Describe the challenge facing the main character. Use chronological order to tell how he or she works to solve the problem.

Plot/Problem/Conflict

- A forest fire is getting out of control; blown by wind; set by camper.
- Smokejumpers fly over it and parachute down near it.
- They seem to be putting the fire out at first.
- Wind picks up, blowing fire toward people and buildings.

CLIMAX Show how the main character solves the problem. Include details that convey the tension of the moment.

Climax

- Smokejumpers have to clear a fire line so the fire has no fuel.
- Very hard work; takes days
- Fire line stops fire; rainstorm helps puts out flames.
- Smokejumpers feel ground to see if it's cool: no hot spots.

RESOLUTION Describe what happens after the problem is solved.

Resolution

- Helicopter comes to pick up smokejumpers.
- They are tired and dirty.
- Marisa says it's just her job.

Try It! Organize your Fictional Narrative

Now use the graphic organizer below to organize the ideas and descriptive details you want to use in your draft.

Introduction

Plot/Problem/Conflict

Climax

Resolution

3. Draft

Now it is time to write the first draft of your fictional narrative. Remember, your draft does not have to be perfect! This is the time to use your notes and get your ideas down in an organized way. You will have time to revise your writing later.

Writer's Craft: Using Dialogue

Dialogue is a conversation between characters. It can provide important information and also bring readers into the story. The author of the mentor text uses dialogue to make the danger seem more real.

DIALOGUE
Dialogue should be written as a character would speak. How does this dialogue help show the urgency of this situation?

____

____

____

The jumpers quickly got to work. However, after a few hours, Marisa made a frightening discovery. "The wind has changed! It's blowing toward the east!" she yelled to the team leader. The fire was heading toward the cabins and the park lodge!

What the characters say and how they say it can reveal their personalities. Their words can also help propel the action. The author of the mentor text uses dialogue to let us know what the leader is like and to move the action forward.

DIALOGUE
Underline the dialogue in this paragraph. What does the dialogue reveal about the team leader's personality and about what will happen next?

____

____

____

At last, the leader radioed for a helicopter to pick up the smokejumpers. They had been fighting the fire for five days with very little rest. As they waited for the helicopter, Marisa thought about how good it was going to feel to shower and fall into bed. Fighting fires was just her job, but it could be very tiring! As the smokejumpers were boarding the helicopter, the team leader smiled at the smoky jumpers and joked, "We've been fired, so let's all get out of here!"

Try It! Write Your First Draft

On a computer or a separate sheet of paper, create a draft of your response to the writing prompt. Remember to include dialogue. This draft checklist can help as you write.

- ✓ Set the scene for your story, and grab your readers' attention. Briefly introduce your main character and the setting.
- ✓ Describe the problem that your main character faces.
- ✓ Explain how the character tries to solve this problem.
- ✓ Write how your character finally solves the problem.
- ✓ Explain what happens after the problem is solved.
- ✓ Include dialogue and realistic details and experiences.

Tips for Writing Your First Draft

- Write down key phrases about the chosen career before you begin writing. You might just hint at some of them in your narrative, but keeping them in mind will help you give readers a clear idea of the career you have chosen as a topic.
- Focus on the event sequence. You can add more descriptive words and details after you have determined a logical sequence.
- Focus on ideas, not details. You will revise and edit later, so you can make any necessary changes then. In drafting, it's the ideas that count.

4. Peer Review

Here is an early draft of the mentor text. Read it with your partner and answer the questions in the boxes. Later, you will find out how the writer's partner evaluated the draft.

INTRODUCTION The writer does not make it clear that Marisa is part of a team. The setting also is not clear. What other basic information should be added to this introduction?

PLOT The writer needs to add more details to the plot. What details could be added to the third paragraph? What could be added to the fourth paragraph?

RESOLUTION This ending needs more details to help the reader imagine the characters, setting, and mood. How would you improve the ending?

Smokejumpers

A siren blast called Marisa to report to duty. For several days, the wind had been blowing a fire toward the lake, where it would burn out. That's why Marisa was surprised that she was being called in for such a "deadly" fire.

Within fifteen minutes, she and the other jumpers were in a plane, circling above the fire. The winds were blowing harder, carrying away burning embers and starting new fires in areas that the ground crews could not reach. Then Marisa understood why jumpers had been called in.

Wearing her parachute, Marisa floated toward the forest with the other firefighters. Parachutes that carried tools floated down with them. Upon landing, the jumpers quickly got to work. However, after a few hours, Marisa yelled, "The wind has changed! It's blowing toward the east!" The fire was heading toward the cabins and the park lodge!

The firefighters built a fire line and worked for two days to put out the fire. When it was finally out, they were tired and dirty. Still, they had to get down on their hands and knees and feel every inch of ground to make sure it was cool.

At last, the leader radioed for a helicopter to pick up the smokejumpers. They had been fighting the fire for five days. Marisa and her team were dirty and tired.

A Sample Peer Review Form

This peer review form shows how a partner evaluated the draft of the mentor text shown on the previous page.

Criteria	Feedback
The introduction sets the scene for the story and grabs the interest of readers.	You did a good job of *grabbing my attention.*
The writer offers enough details to help readers understand the story.	You could improve your fictional narrative by *telling more about Marisa. Why is she being called for a fire? Is she a firefighter?*
The writer explains the problem that the characters face and how they try to solve it.	You did a good job of *telling why the fire is dangerous.*
The writer explains how the characters finally solve the problem.	You could improve your fictional narrative by *adding more details about how Marisa and her team are fighting the fire and how they finally put it out. What's a fire line?*
The story includes dialogue to make the characters come alive.	You did a good job of *using "then" in the second paragraph. You also used transitions to show the sequence.*
	You could improve your fictional narrative by *adding more dialogue. You used dialogue only one time.*
The resolution explains what happens after the problem is solved.	You did a good job of *explaining how they looked for hot spots after the fire was out.*
	You could improve your fictional narrative by *adding more details about what the smokejumpers do next or how they feel now that the fire is out.*

Try It! Peer Review with a Partner

Now you will work with a partner to review each other's fictional narrative drafts. Use the peer review form below. If you need help, look back at the peer review form on the previous page.

The introduction sets the scene for the story and grabs the interest of readers. **The writer offers enough details to help readers understand the story.**	You did a good job of You could improve your fictional narrative by
The writer explains the problem that the characters face and how they try to solve it. **The writer explains how characters finally solve the problem.**	You did a good job of You could improve your fictional narrative by
The story includes dialogue to make the characters come alive.	You did a good job of You could improve your fictional narrative by
The resolution explains what happens after the problem is solved.	You did a good job of You could improve your fictional narrative by

Try It! Record Key Peer Review Comments

Now it's time for you and your partner to share your comments with each other. Listen to your partner's feedback, and write his or her key comments in the left column. Then write some ideas for improving your draft in the right column.

My review says that my introduction	I will
My review says that my use of details	I will
My review says that my explanation of the problem	I will
My review says that how the characters finally solve the problem	I will
My review says that my use of dialogue	I will
My review says that my ending	I will

Use the space below to write anything additional you can think of to improve your draft.

5. Revise

In this step of the writing process, you work on parts of your draft that need improvement. Use the peer review form that your partner completed to help you. Be sure to use your own ideas about how to improve each part of your fictional narrative. This checklist includes some things to think about as you get ready to revise.

Revision Checklist

- ✓ Does my introduction grab the reader's interest? Do I introduce the characters and the setting briefly but clearly?
- ✓ Did I choose a problem or conflict for my character or characters to solve and portray it in a way the reader can understand?
- ✓ Do my characters finally manage to solve this problem in a believable way?
- ✓ Do I explain what happens after the problem is solved?
- ✓ Do I use dialogue to help my story come alive?

Writer's Craft: Using Sensory Language

Sensory language tells what something looks, sounds, feels, smells, and even tastes like. Using sensory language helps draw readers into a scene, making them feel as if they are actually there. Now look at this paragraph from the mentor text for examples of sensory language.

Wearing her parachute, Marisa floated weightlessly toward the forest with the other smokejumpers. Parachutes that carried tools floated down with them. Upon landing, Marisa immediately smelled the bitter smoke and heard the fire roaring like an oncoming train. The jumpers quickly got to work. However, after a few hours, Marisa made a frightening discovery. "The wind has changed! It's blowing toward the east!" she yelled to the team leader. The fire was heading toward the cabins and the park lodge!

SENSORY LANGUAGE Sensory language appeals to the senses of sight, hearing, touch, smell, and taste. Underline the sensory language in this paragraph. What is another way that sensory language could be used in this paragraph?

____

____

____

Try It! Revise Your Fictional Narrative

Using sensory language is an excellent way to strengthen a fictional narrative, but try not to limit yourself to the sense of sight. Consider what the characters might hear, feel, smell, or even taste. To practice using sensory language, rewrite the following paragraph, inserting at least two examples of sensory language.

> Jeff and the other police officers coming on the shift headed for the meeting room to get an update on what had taken place during the night. The room was crowded, but Jeff found a seat toward the back of the room. Some of the officers had brought coffee in with them.

____

____

____

____

____

Writing Assignment

Now it's time to revise the draft of your fictional narrative. Continue working on a computer or on a separate sheet of paper. Review the assignment, repeated below, and the checklist to make sure you have included everything you need.

> The narrative "It's Just My Job" is about a person who has a dangerous but important job. Write a fictional narrative about another character who has an interesting career. Demonstrate the obstacles the character faces on a typical workday or in a typical situation, and explain how he or she overcomes them.

6. Edit

After revising your fictional narrative, you will edit it, reading carefully to find any mistakes. Here's a checklist of some things to look for.

Editing Checklist

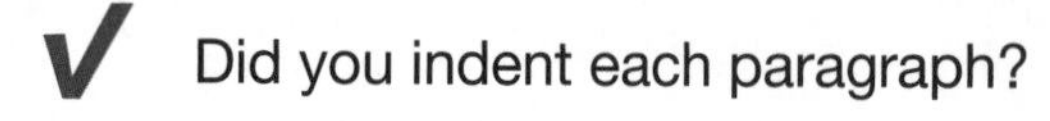

- ✔ Did you indent each paragraph?
- ✔ Are all of your sentences complete, with a subject and a verb? Did you separate any run-on sentences?
- ✔ Does each sentence end with the correct punctuation?
- ✔ Have you used commas, colons, and semicolons correctly?
- ✔ Are all of the words spelled correctly?

You can use these editing marks to mark any errors you find.

^ Insert comma	— Insert em dash	Close up space
# Add space	^ Insert	Reverse order

This paragraph from the draft of the mentor text shows how to use editing marks.

Waring her parachute, Marisa flaoted towardthe forest with the other firefighters. Parachutes that carried tools floated down with them. Upon landing the jumpers quick got to work. However, after a few ours, Marisa yelled, "The wind has changed! It's blowing toward the east!" The fire heading to ward the cabins and the park lodge!

Language Focus: Verb Voice

Verbs can be in either the **active voice** or the **passive voice**. In a sentence using the active voice, the subject is carrying out an action. In a sentence using the passive voice, the subject is being acted upon. Both uses can be effective in narrative fiction writing.

> Active: The rain put out the fire. (The subject is acting.)
> Passive: The fire was put out by the rain. (The subject is being acted upon.)
>
> Active: The smoke drifted over the countryside.
> Passive: The smoke was pushed to the east by the wind.

Most writers prefer using the active voice because it almost always makes a sentence clearer, shorter, and stronger. However, writers can use the passive voice when they do not want to name the actor or when the actor is not important.

For example, this sentence is in the passive voice to avoid embarrassing a player:

> A pass was dropped in the last seconds of the game, leading to a loss.

Passive voice is used in this sentence because the actor is not important:

> The packages were mailed out yesterday.

Look for examples of active and passive voice in this paragraph from the mentor text.

> Within fifteen minutes, she and the other jumpers were in a plane, circling above the fire. The winds were accelerating, carrying away burning embers and starting new fires in areas that the ground crews could not reach. Then Marisa understood why jumpers had been called in.

VERB VOICE The subject is carrying out an action in active voice. The subject is being acted upon in passive voice. Reread the third sentence of this paragraph. The two verbs are *understood* and *had been called.* Explain whether each of these verbs is active or passive. If a verb is in passive voice, explain why that is acceptable.

Try It! Language and Editing Practice

Mark each sentence *A* for *active voice* or *P* for *passive voice.* Then circle the subject in each passive sentence. Underline the verb in each active sentence.

1. ____ Drinking his cup of hot coffee, Sam faced the day with excitement.
2. ____ He had been drawn to life in the outdoors since childhood.
3. ____ After weeks of training, Sam was going to cut down his first tree.
4. ____ A logger could be seriously hurt or even killed by a falling tree.
5. ____ Sam felt confident, though, for he had learned how to drive wedges into trees to make them fall just the right way.

Now use editing marks to correct the errors in this paragraph.

Rosa looks at her new class of EMT students, and freezes. Although the students she has trained are capable she is terrified as usual. There was so much the students need to be learned. They will have to know how to move injured people without causing further harm. They will have to learn how to treat patience in distress. Any mistake can be fatel. Rosa looks around the room again. Inspired by the students eager faces, she begins the first leson.

Try It!

Edit Your Fictional Narrative

Now edit your response to the writing prompt. Use this checklist and the editing marks you have learned to correct any errors you find.

- [ ] Did you indent each paragraph?
- [ ] Are all of your sentences complete, with a subject and a verb? Did you separate any run-on sentences?
- [ ] Do most or all of your sentences use active voice?
- [ ] Does each sentence end with the correct punctuation?
- [ ] Have you used commas, colons, and semicolons correctly?
- [ ] Are all of the words spelled correctly?

Editing Tips

- **Read your narrative slowly several times. Each time you read, focus on something different, such as punctuation in one reading and spelling in another reading.**
- **Ask a classmate, friend, or family member to read your narrative aloud. Listen for any parts that sound awkward. You might need to rewrite that sentence or paragraph or just punctuate it differently.**

7. Publish

On a computer or a separate sheet of paper, create a neat final draft of your fictional narrative. Correct all errors that you identified while editing. Be sure to give your narrative an interesting title.

The final step is to publish your work, perhaps using one of these ideas:

- Combine the class's fictional narratives into a book. Copies might be placed in the school media center.
- Record your story for other students to enjoy.
- Read your fictional narrative aloud to a younger class.
- Arrange for one of the class's narratives to be read as part of the morning announcements one day a week.

Technology Suggestions

- **Upload your fictional narrative onto a class or school blog.**
- **Use your narrative as the starting point for a blog on a specific topic.**
- **Record a podcast in which you read your narrative aloud. Invite classmates to contribute to a recorded discussion about the narrative.**

Lesson 9

Reading Scientific and Technical Texts

Look at this Amazon rain-forest canopy.

Why is it important to protect this kind of land?

ESSENTIAL QUESTION

How do authors present complex information in ways that readers can understand?

Listen and Learn

Consider ▶ What are the causes of forest fires?

Can fire ever be beneficial to a forest?

LET IT BURN?

STEPS IN A PROCESS
Scientists follow a specific procedure called the scientific method. It starts with a question and a hypothesis, or educated guess, about the answer. Then scientists test the hypothesis and analyze the results. Why is it important for all scientists to follow this process? Look at paragraph 1. What question and hypothesis do you think scientists used in their investigation of forest fires?

PROBLEM AND SOLUTION
Many science articles are organized by a problem-solution structure. That is, the article states a problem or issue, then gives details about possible solutions for that problem. Look at paragraph 2. Can you identify the problem?

1 "Only you can prevent wildfires" is Smokey Bear's message. This highly recognizable character has been campaigning against forest fires since 1944. Preventing unexpected wildfires is important to preserving the wilderness and to saving lives. This might lead you to wonder why a growing number of scientists actually want to let some forest fires burn.

Odd as it may seem, forest fires can actually be beneficial. They act like forest vacuum cleaners and rid areas of flammable debris, such as dead limbs and underbrush. They temporarily reduce disease, weeds, and harmful insects. Forest fires also recycle nutrients into the soil to rejuvenate forests and encourage the growth of new vegetation. For these reasons, some people argue that certain forest fires should be allowed to burn. Sometimes they even start fires, called prescribed burns, on purpose.

In 2004, a prescribed burn in the Loxahatchee National Wildlife Refuge in Florida helped stop the spread of a wildfire that was started by lightning. The wildfire fizzled out when it reached the area where the prescribed burn had been done. The homes of many bird species were saved as a result.

Not everyone agrees that forest fires are good. Fires can spread as fast as 14.29 miles per hour (23 kph), so they can be very challenging for firefighters to control. Opponents of natural fires and prescribed burns are quick to point out that when forest fires run amok,[1] the results are tragic. They point out a parkland fire that ran wild after it started as a prescribed burn a few years ago in Los Alamos, New Mexico. That fire caused $1 billion of damage, including the loss or damage of 260 homes, 1,500 archaeological sites, and 44,000 acres of land (more than 178 million m^2).

[1]**run amok** get out of control

SCIENTIFIC SYMBOLS
Scientific and technical writing often include scientific symbols, such as measurements or chemical formulas. Look at the measurements in the parentheses in paragraph 4. What do these measurements stand for?

FACT VS. SPECULATION
A fact is something that can be observed or proven. Speculation is a conclusion based on incomplete evidence. Look at paragraph 4. What is one fact in paragraph 4? Is the idea that prescribed burns always cause tragic results a fact or speculation?

STEPS IN A PROCESS Most states require that a specific process be followed before conducting a prescribed burn. Look at this sample procedure. Which of the steps for conducting a prescribed burn is the best example of the "planning an investigation" step of the scientific method?

BEFORE CONDUCTING A PRESCRIBED BURN . . .

1. Become familiar with state fire laws.
2. Monitor any bans on burning.
3. Educate yourself about prescribed burns.
4. Clarify burn objectives.
5. Write a burn plan.
6. Construct fire guards.
7. Prepare a map.
8. Obtain personal protection equipment.
9. Identify hazards.
10. Anticipate the smoke's direction.
11. Assemble a crew.
12. Notify your neighbors.

DOMAIN-SPECIFIC VOCABULARY Scientific texts usually include words that mean specific things in certain fields. Look at paragraph 5. What do you think "mop-up operations" refers to?

5 The threat of danger exists not only for land and homes but also for the people who live near the fires and for the firefighters who risk their lives attempting to put out the flames. The danger does not end when the fire goes out and mop-up operations are completed. Air pollution, landslides, floods, erosion, and damage to the ozone layer can all result from wildfires.

Some experts claim that no matter how much care and preparation are involved, there is always an element of risk with prescribed burns. Not only is there the chance that a fire can get out of control, but plant and animal populations can also be negatively affected. Experts point to studies that show a decrease in the number of herb plants, as well as in the numbers of animals such as millipedes and certain ant and beetle species, that results from prescribed burns.

TEXT STRUCTURE Some scientific texts are organized by category, or by ideas that can be grouped together. If this article had been organized by category, what might the categories be?

People in favor of prescribed burns say that blazes set by fire experts rarely get out of control. They argue that not permitting fires to burn is actually more dangerous and can lead to a greater risk of catastrophic[2] fires. When fires occur after years of suppression,[3] flames spread rapidly and furiously through thick and overgrown trees and vegetation. Under those conditions, flames are not limited to the ground. The flames shoot up trees, causing what are called crown fires.

CONTROLLED BURN AHEAD

[2]**catastrophic** relating to a sudden event that causes great distress

[3]**suppression** the act of putting an end to something

From 1998 to 2010, between 0.88 and 3.14 million acres were burned each year. The most acres were burned in 2007, and the smallest number of acres were burned in 1998. The average number of acres burned over ten years was 2.47 million.

VISUAL INFORMATION
Information in a science article is often represented by a chart or graph. Look at the information in the graph and in the paragraph that precedes it. What details in the graph are not described in the text? Why might scientific information be presented visually instead of being expressed in words?

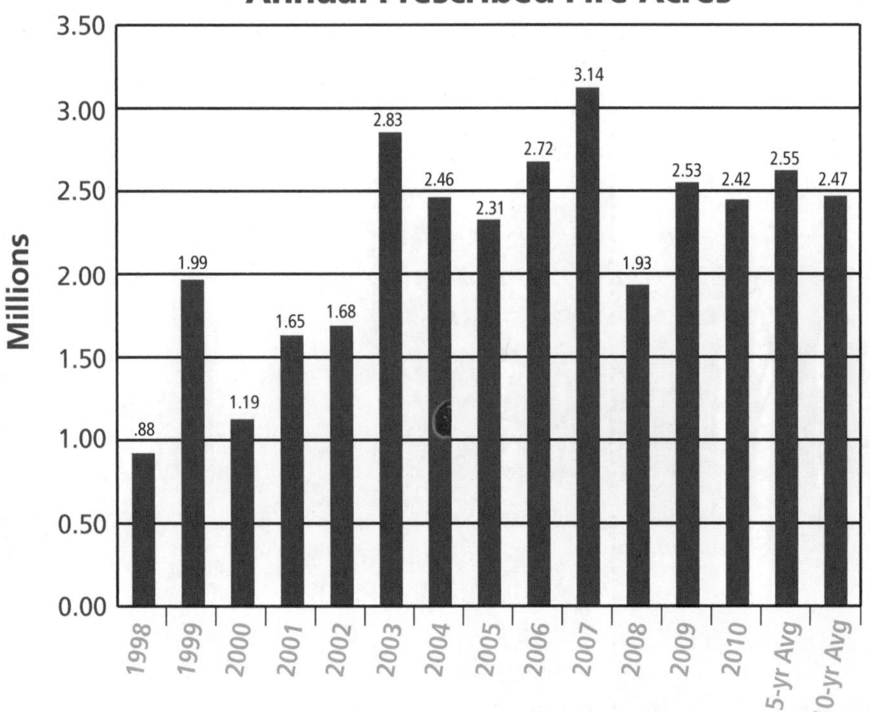

All fires come with a certain element of danger, and safety can never be completely guaranteed. However, prescribed burns may protect natural resources and wildlife from more serious destruction, increasing the chances that the forest will grow and thrive in years to come. Though the practice of setting controlled fires may be controversial, its intended outcome focuses on safety and long-term preservation.

Comprehension Check

Look back in "Let It Burn?" to identify the arguments for and against prescribed burns. Use the graphic organizer to record the arguments mentioned in the text. Then think about the pros and cons of this practice. State your opinion about it at the bottom of the page, citing evidence to support it.

Arguments FOR Prescribed Burns	Arguments AGAINST Prescribed Burns

I think prescribed burns are/are not a good practice. I think this because

Vocabulary

Use the word map below to help you define and use one of the highlighted vocabulary words from the Share and Learn reading or another word your teacher assigns you.

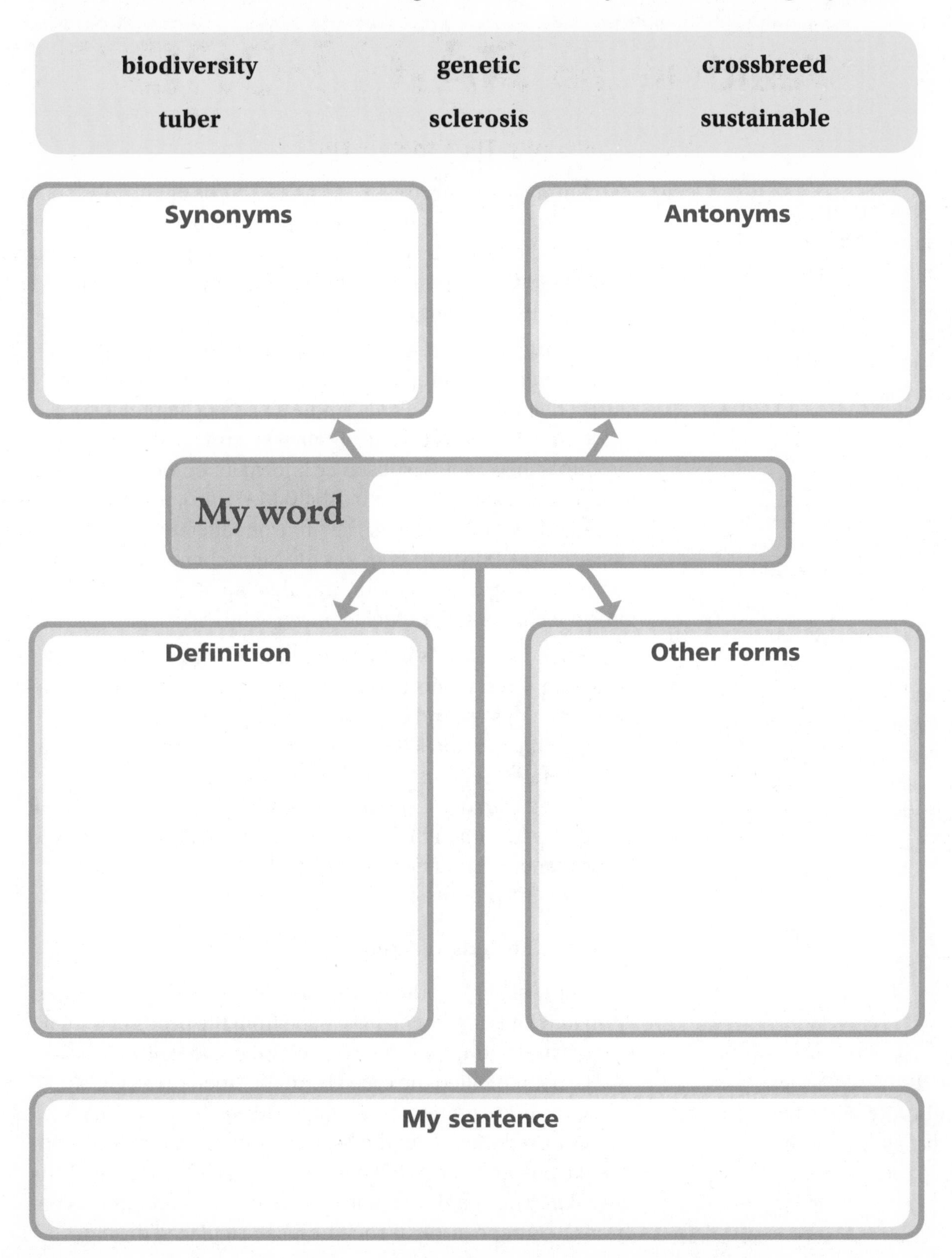

Share and Learn

Consider ▶ Why should the rain forests be protected?

To what kinds of "wealth" do you think the title of this article refers?

Wealth in the RAIN FORESTS

DRAW CONCLUSIONS What conclusion can you draw about the value of some plants in the rain forest? Underline the details and evidence you used to draw your conclusion.

COMPARE SCIENTIFIC TEXTS How is the information and data in this article presented differently from the information and data in "Let It Burn?" Which presentation is more effective?

DOMAIN-SPECIFIC VOCABULARY Circle the words that are specific to science in paragraph 3.

Biodiversity: The Variety of Life

1 From tall canopy trees to ferns and herbs on the forest floor, tropical rain forests contain more species of plants than any other place on the earth. A warm, moist climate helps create this great biodiversity. The numerous rain-forest plants and trees provide a variety of useful foods and materials.

Rain-forest plants produce chemical compounds that protect them from predators—insects and animals—or that attract helpful insects. For example, to attract helpful insects, a West African rain-forest shrub called katemfe (kah•TEM•fee) produces the sweetest substance known in the world. This plant compound, called thaumatin (thaw•MAH•tin), is 100,000 times sweeter than table sugar. In the Amazon rain forest, sap from copaiba (ko•PYE•bah) trees has the same chemical properties as diesel fuel. Experiments show that this sap might one day be processed and used for fuel to power vehicles.

Scientists use this natural storehouse of genetic material from rain-forest plants to crossbreed plants and create disease-resistant crops around the world. During the 1970s, a plant disease attacked and killed nearly the entire corn crop in the United States. Scientists searched for wild corn plants to crossbreed with domestic corn plants. They discovered a small stand of wild corn in the Mexican rain forest. Researchers used these plants to produce new breeds that are more disease-resistant and produce higher yields of corn.

Food for the Gods and People

Many of our favorite foods and flavorings originally came from rain forests. Chocolate is made from the beans of a small Central and South American tree called cacao (kuh•KAY•oh). Native people called the cacao bean the "food of the gods." Ancient stone carvings show that the Maya drank chocolate. The Aztecs mixed water with the beans and flavored the drink with vanilla, pimiento, and chili pepper. They called the bitter drink *chocolatl*. The Spanish explorer Hernán Cortés brought cocoa beans to Europe in 1528. The Europeans replaced the chili peppers with sugar, and chocolate became a popular hot drink. Europeans were probably not used to the spicy heat from the chili peppers, and preferred their drinks sweeter.

5 Another popular drink comes from the guarana (gwahr•uh•NAH) vine in the Brazilian Amazon. The brown guarana bean contains four to five times more caffeine than a coffee bean. International soft-drink manufacturers sell millions of bottles of guarana soda in Brazil and other parts of South America. People in these areas must like their caffeine as much as we do in the United States!

Cassava, or manioc, is a food eaten by many people in tropical countries. Tapioca (ta•pee•OH•kuh) comes from this starchy tuber, which is the thick underground stem of the plant. The cassava root, however, has a deadly secret. It contains a compound called linamarin (lyn•uh•MAR•in) that produces a poison. Cassava must be carefully soaked in water, baked, and dried before it is safe to eat.

FACT VS. SPECULATION
Circle one fact each about cacao and guarana on this page. Draw a line through one statement in each paragraph that is speculation rather than fact.

REASONED JUDGMENT
What reasoned judgment can you make about the use of plants from the rain forest?

___

___

___

The Healing Power of the Rain Forest

For thousands of years, native peoples of the rain forest have used plant material for their health needs. Native healers, called shamans, have a storehouse of knowledge about the medicinal qualities of native plants.

However, it wasn't until the 1970s that scientists began to study rain-forest plants seriously. The 1970s was an era of great concern for and interest in the environment. Scientists wanted to learn more about natural medicines derived from rain-forest plants. Researchers studied with shamans and collected plants for laboratory analysis. One discovery was the wild rosy periwinkle plant from Madagascar. Chemicals from this plant destroyed certain types of cancer tumors. Today, doctors treat Hodgkin's disease and leukemia with drugs made from this plant. Rosy periwinkle is now cultivated throughout the tropics for battling cancer.

TEXT STRUCTURE
Skim the article from the beginning. What text feature helps you understand how the article is organized?

Even natural poisons found in the rain forest can become useful medicine. Native hunters in South America dip their arrows in a poison made from the bark of the liana (lee-AH-nuh) vine. The poison, curare (kyoo•RAHR•ee), paralyzes prey, making it easier to catch. The substance is used by surgeons to paralyze muscles during operations. Researchers isolated another substance from this plant called d-turbocuarine (tur•boh•QWAH•reen), which is now used to treat multiple sclerosis, Parkinson's disease, and other muscular disorders.

SCIENTIFIC SYMBOLS
Circle the chemical symbols in paragraph 10. What does each symbol represent?

PROBLEM AND SOLUTION Underline the statement that describes how manufacturers tried to solve the problem of needing more rubber for tires. Why didn't their solution work?

Treasure from the Hevea Tree

10 In the mid-1800s, inventors discovered a way to make rubber from latex. Latex is a gum—the thick, milky-white sap found just beneath the bark of hevea (heev•EE•uh) trees in the Amazon. To protect itself from insects, the tree "weeps" sticky and poisonous latex when the bark is cut. The latex also contains natural rubber. Unfortunately, the rubber made from latex becomes brittle in cold weather and becomes a sticky, gooey mess in hot weather. A process called vulcanization changes the properties of rubber and allows it to remain flexible at a greater variety of temperatures. The natural rubber (C_5H_8) is combined with sulfur (S) and heat (Δ), which loosens its chemical bonds and makes the compound more elastic.

A Nation Runs on Tires

By the early 1900s, Henry Ford's Model T car was rolling off the assembly line at a rate of one per hour, and all those new cars needed rubber tires. Trees were taken from the Amazon rain forest and grown in crowded plantations. But these overcrowded trees developed diseases. Landowners needed thousands of additional laborers to find, cut, and collect the latex from wild trees deep in the forest. Eventually the great rubber plantations of the Amazon began to disappear.

World War I caused disruptions in international trade. Raw materials required for manufacturing often arrived late or not at all. American businessmen quickly realized that they could not rely on foreign sources for raw materials. When the war ended, they worried that the British and Dutch would monopolize, or control, the world's supply of rubber. Imported rubber was already expensive, and American industry demanded more tires for a growing economy.

In 1927, Henry Ford and Harvey Firestone asked the retired inventor Thomas Edison to find another source of rubber for use in automobile tires. Edison began to search for a homegrown plant that could yield rubber.

Edison planted hundreds of shrubs and trees from around the world at his home in Fort Myers, Florida. His wife, Mina, wrote, "Everything has turned to rubber in our family. We talk rubber, think rubber, dream rubber." Edison did find a type of goldenrod plant that could produce a rubber-like substance, but it was not economical[1] to produce. Edison was still working on these experiments when he died in 1931.

MAIN IDEA AND DETAILS What is the main idea of the section called "A Nation Runs on Tires"? Underline the details that support this main idea.

____

____

____

TEXT STRUCTURE Circle the words and phrases that show how this section is organized.

[1]**economical** operating with little waste; thrifty

CAUSE AND EFFECT What effect did World War II have on the availability of natural rubber? What other effects did this lead to?

____

____

____

GLOSSARY Which term from paragraph 15 would you most likely find in the glossary of a science textbook? Explain why.

____

____

VISUAL INFORMATION Use the labels and arrows in the diagram to identify the sequence of steps in the oxygen, carbon, and water cycles in the rain forest.

___ Leaves rot and release nutrients into the soil.

___ Tree roots take up water and nutrients.

___ Leaves take in carbon dioxide (CO_2) from the air and release oxygen (O) back into the air.

___ Moisture falls from heavy rains.

___ Water evaporates back into the air from the trees.

___ Dead leaves and branches fall to the forest floor.

15 Scientists never found an affordable natural replacement for rubber. Instead, by the mid-1930s, they developed a human-made rubber latex by mixing together petroleum and soap products. During World War II, all supplies of natural rubber to the United States were cut off. Synthetic rubber production became an important new industry to meet the wartime demand for tires and other rubber products.

Deforestation

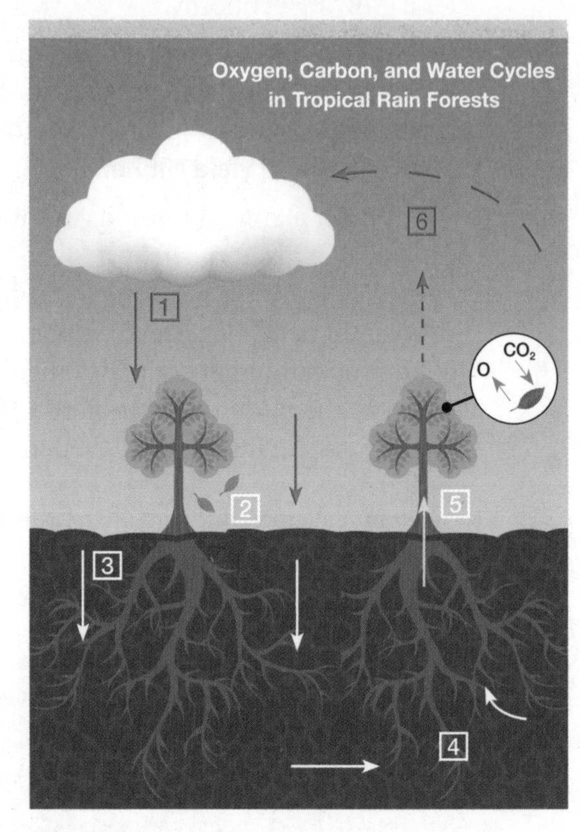

Every day, the smell of burning wood and the sounds of rumbling bulldozers break the quiet of the world's rain forests. People are destroying rain forests at an alarming rate. Today, almost 50 percent of the world's rain forests are gone. About one and a half acres of rain forest disappear every second. People slash and burn[2] these forests for three reasons: to make land for crops, to harvest lumber for wood products, and to make pasture land for livestock. These human behaviors not only destroy valuable plant and animal species that are unique to the rain forests, they also disturb the natural cycles that are necessary to sustain plant and animal life. This diagram illustrates the cycle of oxygen, carbon, and water in the rain forest.

Experts now advise governments, businesses, and landowners to use sustainable development. These methods provide a balance between using resources and conserving them for future generations. If deforestation continues at its present rate, tropical rain forests will disappear in our lifetimes.

[2]**slash and burn** a process of clearing forests in which trees are cut down and the land is burned to make it suitable for farming

Anchor Standard Discussion Questions

Discuss the following questions with your peer group. Then record your answers in the space provided.

1. The author of "Wealth in the Rain Forests" includes several references to rain-forest plants throughout the article. Do these references add up to a convincing argument that rain forests need greater protection? Citing evidence from the text, explain whether or not the author successfully convinces readers.

2. Evaluate the diagram on page 158. Does it support the argument presented in the "Deforestation" section of the article? Why or why not? Cite details from the text in your answer. Then suggest an idea for another diagram that would support the information presented in that section.

Comprehension Check

1. Identify the main idea of “Wealth in the Rain Forests.”

2. How does deforestation interrupt the oxygen, carbon, and water cycles in the rain forest?

3. Compare and contrast the content and structure of the articles “Let It Burn?” and “Wealth in the Rain Forests.”

Read On Your Own

Read another scientific and technical text, “A Fire-Friendly Tree,” independently. Apply what you learned in this lesson and check your understanding.

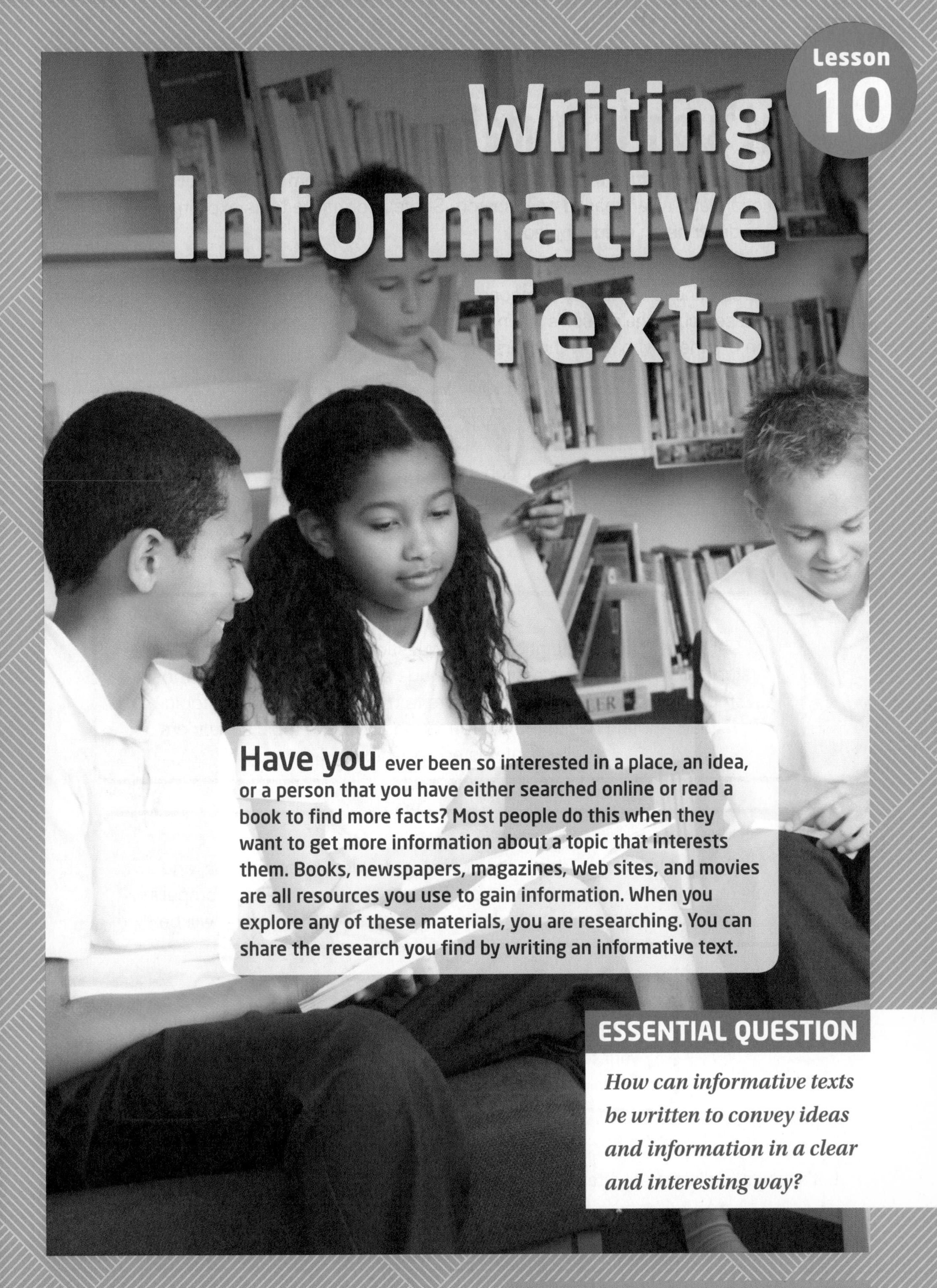

Lesson 10

Writing Informative Texts

Have you ever been so interested in a place, an idea, or a person that you have either searched online or read a book to find more facts? Most people do this when they want to get more information about a topic that interests them. Books, newspapers, magazines, Web sites, and movies are all resources you use to gain information. When you explore any of these materials, you are researching. You can share the research you find by writing an informative text.

ESSENTIAL QUESTION

How can informative texts be written to convey ideas and information in a clear and interesting way?

What's an Informative Text?

Informative texts either tell the reader something or explain something about a topic. All are nonfiction, and all are based on research. Some informative texts explain a scientific process or describe an event or place.

Biographies are some of the most popular informative texts. A biography tells about the life of a person and is written by someone else. To find information about the person, the writer researches the person's life in several ways. Sometimes the writer can interview the person or others who know the person. If the person is no longer living, the writer must read things written by or about the person, such as interviews, essays, articles, or historical texts.

An **informative text** presents information and supports it with facts, details, descriptions, examples, and explanations. Here are ways to present information effectively in an informative text.

Introduction

Catch the readers' attention with a question, an interesting fact, or a story for your opening statement. Include a thesis statement, the most important idea you want the readers to understand about the topic. Explain enough background information about the topic so readers will be interested and informed.

Supporting Details

Support your main idea with relevant facts, details, quotations, and examples drawn from your research. The more interesting and compelling the facts, details, and examples are, the stronger your writing will be.

Conclusion

Write a final paragraph that summarizes your topic and provides some final thoughts or information about the topic.

Let's look at an informative text.

Analyze a Mentor Text

This is an example of an effective informative text for an eighth grader. Read it and then complete the activities in the boxes as a class.

Man with a Camera

Ansel Adams, age fourteen, looked through a book about Yosemite Valley, which was located about 150 miles east of his San Francisco home. "That's where I want to go on vacation this year," he told his parents. So on June 1, 1916, the three of them set off for a month of exploring the majestic and awe-inspiring scenery of Yosemite. Soon after they arrived, Ansel's parents gave him a box camera. This photographic tool opened a whole new world to the young man. Eventually, Adams became one of the most well-known and respected photographers of his time.

The young Adams soon became absorbed in photography. Back in San Francisco, he worked doing odd jobs at a photo lab, where he learned how to develop and print photos. He was drawn to Yosemite, where he returned often to hike and take photographs. One spring day in 1927, Adams was hiking in Yosemite with his photographic equipment when he found himself high on a cliff with a view of a famous mountain. In those days, serious photographers used large, coated-glass plates instead of film to capture images, and Adams had just two unexposed plates remaining. With one of them, he took a typical shot of the mountain. Then he was inspired to do something different: "[T]hat was the first time I realized how the print was going to look—what I now call visualization—and was actually thinking about the emotional effect of the image . . . I began to visualize the black rock and deep sky. I really wanted to give it a monumental, dark quality. So I used the last plate I had with a . . . red filter . . . and got this exciting picture."

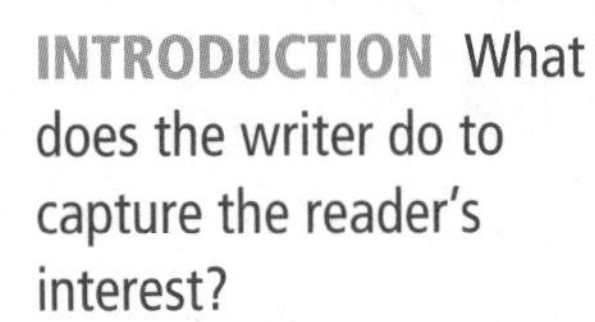

INTRODUCTION What does the writer do to capture the reader's interest?

MAIN IDEA The writer states the main idea in the form of a thesis statement. Draw a box around the thesis statement.

SUPPORTING DETAILS Writers use details, such as quotations, statistics, or facts, to support the thesis statement. What types of details does the writer use to show that Adams was inspired while hiking in Yosemite?

SUPPORTING DETAILS How does the writer use details to contrast the styles of Adams and earlier photographers? Underline the antonyms the writer uses to show contrast.

Ansel Adams's work set a precedent in early-twentieth-century photography, when he and some other photographers changed the way photography was done. Earlier photographers had tried to make their photographs look like paintings. They had employed a variety of methods such as using soft-focus lenses, applying brush strokes to negatives, and printing their images on soft-textured paper. But Adams and other photographers of his era developed a new style, known as "straight photography." This style used sharp focuses, and the images were printed on glossy paper, which made the subject of the photograph more vivid and visual.

Adams introduced the concept of visualization in his photography to capture emotion in his images. He liked to work with black-and-white images rather than color, because he felt that black and white focused the viewer on the emotional content of the scene, instead of on the external reality of what was being shown.

Throughout his life (1902–1984), Adams held a deep appreciation for the American West. He often took photographs of its natural beauty to satisfy his passion for it. He became closely involved with the Sierra Club, an organization devoted to the protection of wilderness areas. As a nature advocate, Adams frequently used his photographs to convey the message that the wilderness must be preserved. His photographs revealed to many people the true beauty of the land.

CONCLUSION The purpose of a conclusion is to sum up the main points that have been presented. Draw a box around the sentence that restates the main idea of the passage.

By the time he died, in 1984, Adams and his camera had become a permanent fixture in American photographic history. After his death, the U.S. Congress established the Ansel Adams Wilderness Area, southeast of Yosemite National Park. In 1985, a mountain on the southeast border of Yosemite was named Mount Ansel Adams in his honor.

Think About It ► What is the most important idea the author conveys in this informative text?

How does the writer inform the reader with strong facts, details, and examples?

Vocabulary Study: Word Roots and Affixes

Word parts can provide clues about the meaning of a word. A **root** is the part of a word that carries its core meaning. A **prefix** is a word part added to the beginning of a word. A **suffix** is a word part added to the end of a word. Prefixes and suffixes are called **affixes**.

When affixes are added to a word, they change its meaning. Many roots and affixes come from Greek and Latin words. When you know the meaning of these word parts, you can break down an unknown word to figure out its meaning. Here are some common roots, prefixes, and suffixes. Work with classmates or a partner to fill in the chart.

Word Parts and Meanings	Example	Meaning
Roots		
bio means "life"	biography	a story of a person's life
port means "to carry"	transport	
vis/vid means "to see"	visible	
Prefixes		
anti- means "against"	antigovernment	against government
post- means "after"	postdate	
semi- means "half" or "part"	semitransparent	
Suffixes		
-al means "relating to"	musical	relating to music
-ness means "a state or condition"	awareness	
-ous means "full of" or "having"	courageous	

Look back at the informative text about Ansel Adams on pages 163–164. Find one example of a word that uses a root, one word that uses a prefix, and one word that uses a suffix. Write each word and its meaning in the chart below.

	Meaning
Word with root:	
Word with prefix:	
Word with suffix:	

Writing Process

Now that you have read and analyzed an informative text, you are going to create your own informative text by following the steps of the writing process.

1. Get Ready: Take Notes on Research Select and evaluate the print and electronic resources you will use to investigate your topic. Take notes as you read, and cite the sources where you found the information.

2. Organize Use a graphic organizer to plan your informative text by arranging supporting facts, details, and examples.

3. Draft Create the first draft of your informational text.

4. Peer Review Work with a partner to evaluate and improve your draft.

5. Revise Use suggestions from your peer review to revise your informative text.

6. Edit Check your work carefully for errors in spelling, punctuation, and grammar.

7. Publish Create a final version of your informative text.

Writing Assignment

In this lesson, you will write your own informative text. As you create the piece, remember the elements of the mentor text that were most effective. Read the following assignment.

"Man with a Camera" is about a famous American photographer. Louis Sullivan has also made a great contribution to the world. State what that contribution is, support your idea with significant details from the research texts, and provide a conclusion.

1. Get Ready: Take Notes on Research

The writer of the mentor text wrote about the photographer Ansel Adams. Before she could write a draft, she researched her topic. Here is a paragraph from one of the articles she found.

In 1927, photographer and nature lover Ansel Adams went on a trip with the Sierra Club—a trip that started a lifelong relationship. Since 1892, the Sierra Club had been one of the most important environmental organizations in the United States. Soon Adams became more involved in the club. He worked with others to make proposals for protecting and improving wilderness and wildlife areas. For 37 years, he was on the board of directors of the Sierra Club. Adams often used his photography of wilderness areas to get support for programs that would protect these important areas.

The writer took notes on each of the articles she found. Here is the note card that she filled out for the text above. What kinds of information does she include?

Important Idea: In 1927, Adams went on a trip that started a long relationship with the Sierra Club.
Detail: The Sierra Club had been an important environmental organization in the U.S. since 1892.
Detail: Adams went on a trip with the Sierra Club.
Detail: He was on the board of directors of the Sierra Club for 37 years.
Detail: He used photography for the support of environmental programs.
Source: *A Photographer and a Club* by Kyle Wolf

MAIN IDEA On the first line, the writer includes an important idea from the passage that she is interested in using in her report.

DETAILS Next, she lists notes about details from the passage. Which details would be the most important to include in a report about Ansel Adams?

SOURCE Finally, she writes where she found the passage. What other source information should she provide?

Researching Text

Your topic is the American architect Louis Sullivan. Here is some information that you might use in your informative text. Read the article. Think about the important ideas in each paragraph. Also think about interesting details that would fit well in your informative text.

SOURCE Identify where the passage comes from. How would you document this source?

MAIN IDEA The first paragraph introduces Louis Sullivan's role as the "father of skyscrapers."

BIAS Bias in writing presents a one-sided opinion or judgment by the writer. Often, bias is used when a writer presents an opinion as a fact without evidence. Underline sentences that show bias.

DETAILS Which details do you find most interesting in the article? Which details would you use to write your informative piece?

from

Louis Sullivan: His Story

by Keith Gannett

The American architect Louis Sullivan (1856–1924) is often called the "father of skyscrapers" simply because he designed them at a time when buildings were far from reaching the sky. Before the late 1800s, buildings were supported by their outside walls, which were thick and often made of brick. The taller the building, the thicker the walls had to be. As a result, tall buildings were impractical. A building with more than six floors was considered very unusual.

The advent of steel changed the way that buildings would be constructed, and Sullivan took advantage of this revolutionary material. Mass production of steel began in the second half of the 1800s. Steel made it possible for buildings to be supported from the inside with intricate skeletons. Sullivan was instrumental in helping to imagine and implement something the world had never seen before—a tall building structured around a steel skeleton. This phenomenon became known as the "skyscraper." Sullivan was the best architect of the time. Through his many designs, Sullivan helped change modern architecture forever.

Try It! Record Your Notes

Use these note cards to take notes on the text about Louis Sullivan. Write the main idea and interesting details of each paragraph. Remember to document the source on each note card.

Important Idea:
Detail:
Detail:
Detail:
Source:

Important Idea:
Detail:
Detail:
Detail:
Source:

Researching Text, *continued*

Here is some more information that you might use in your informative text. Read the articles, and take notes on the important ideas and relevant details they contain.

RELEVANCE
Relevant details are the ones that are directly connected with your main idea. Which facts in this source are relevant?

from

American Architects

by Andrew Tambler

Louis Sullivan
Born: September 3, 1856 **Died:** April 14, 1924

Important Buildings:
- Auditorium Building (1889)
- Wainwright Building (1891)
- National Farmers' Bank (1908)
- The Bradley House (1910)

Bio: Louis Sullivan grew up in Boston, where at an early age he developed a love of architecture. He left high school early to study architecture at Massachusetts Institute of Technology. Sullivan began his career working for an architect in Philadelphia but soon moved to Chicago, where there were more opportunities. There, he worked with William LeBaron Jenney, architect of Chicago's first skyscraper, and partnered with Dankmar Adler. During their fifteen-year partnership, Sullivan and Adler would design about 180 buildings. He also became mentor to the budding architect Frank Lloyd Wright.

CREDIBILITY
Credible sources are believable ones that come from well-researched and knowledgeable sources. This source comes from a museum. What inferences can you make about its credibility?

Sky High: A New Exhibit

from the Chicago Museum of Architecture *Web site*

The Chicago Museum of Architecture is pleased to announce a special exhibit celebrating the life and work of architect Louis Sullivan. Sullivan designed Chicago's most recognized buildings, helping to establish the city as the center of innovative architecture. His work featured stunning ornamental work and what he called "the poetry of architecture."

Sullivan's brilliant steel-framed designs have greatly influenced modern architecture. This event will feature tours, lectures, and film screenings. We hope that you can join us for this not-to-be-missed exhibit!

Try It! Record Your Notes

Use these note cards to take notes on the texts about Louis Sullivan. Write the main idea and interesting details of each paragraph. Remember to document the source on each note card.

Important Idea:
Detail:
Detail:
Detail:
Source:

Important Idea:
Detail:
Detail:
Detail:
Source:

Researching Visual Information

When you research a topic, you will discover that information can be presented in a variety of ways. You may find photographs, diagrams, charts, and tables, all of which reveal information and show data. You can use note cards to record notes and information from these different formats.

The first example below shows a photograph, while the second example shows a graph. Think about how both of these resources could be useful to glean information, ideas, and details about Louis Sullivan and the development of skyscrapers.

PHOTOGRAPH
How does the photograph help you understand building methods after the mass production of steel?

Steel support beams allowed Louis Sullivan to build taller buildings, such as the Schlesinger & Mayer Department Store in Chicago.

Source: ***The Library of Congress***

GRAPHICS
How could this graph help you write about the contributions of Louis Sullivan?

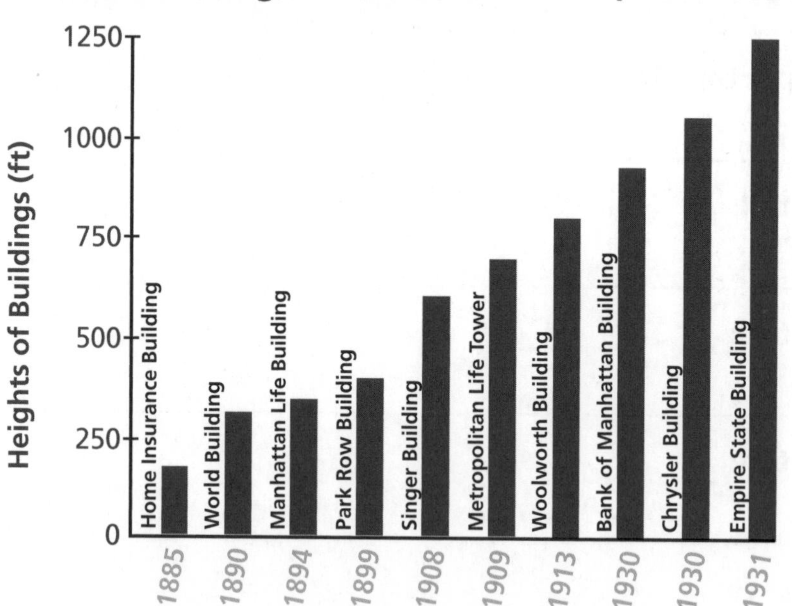

After steel was used in the construction of tall buildings, skyscrapers grew exponentially taller.

Source: ***Skyscrapers Through History*** **by Owen Hague**

Try It!

Record Your Notes

Use these note cards to take notes on the photograph and graph shown on the previous page. Use information from that page to help you.

Important Idea (Photograph):
Detail:
Detail:
Detail:
Source:

Important Idea (Graph):
Detail:
Detail:
Detail:
Source:

2. Organize

You are almost ready to begin a draft of your informative text. You can use a graphic organizer to help organize the facts, details, and examples that you gathered while researching. You can then refer to the graphic organizer as you work through the different parts of your draft. The writer of the mentor text completed this graphic organizer.

INTRODUCTION In the first paragraph, tell the topic of your informative text and include your thesis statement.

Introduction
Eventually, Ansel Adams became one of the most well-known and respected photographers of his time.

Idea 1 Adams became absorbed in photography.
- worked odd jobs at photo lab
- learned to develop and print photos
- tried new techniques

SUPPORTING PARAGRAPHS In subsequent paragraphs,
- give evidence that supports your thesis statement
- elaborate on the evidence with facts, details, and examples

Idea 2 Adams changed the way photography was done.
- information about the way it had been done
- developed "straight photography," which uses sharp focuses and images printed on glossy paper

Idea 3 Adams used photos to capture emotional reality.
- black-and-white images instead of color
- focused on emotional qualities rather than external reality

Idea 4 Adams combined his love of photography and the American West.
- took photos of natural beauty in the West
- became active in the Sierra Club

CONCLUSION In the final paragraph, summarize the ideas that have been presented.

Conclusion
By the time he died in 1984, Ansel Adams and his camera had become a permanent fixture in American photographic history.

Try It! Organize Your Informational Text

Now use the graphic organizer below to organize the supporting facts, details, and examples you have taken notes on. Try to include at least three of these to support each idea.

Introduction

Idea 1

Supporting facts, examples, or details:

Idea 2

Supporting facts, examples, or details:

Idea 3

Supporting facts, examples, or details:

Idea 4

Supporting facts, examples, or details:

Conclusion

3. Draft

Now it's time to write the first draft of your informative text. Remember, your draft does not have to be perfect! This is the time to use your notes, get your ideas down in an organized way, and experiment with different ways to convey your research. You will have time to revise your writing later. Start by drafting your informative text on a computer or on a separate sheet of paper. Explain who Louis Sullivan was and what his major contributions were. Then provide facts, details, and examples to support your thesis.

Writer's Craft: Using Transition Words and Phrases

Transition words and phrases connect the ideas within a piece of writing. They help the reader to understand how the writer is moving from one idea to the next. In informative texts, transitions can help readers understand time or sequence, cause-and-effect relationships, and comparisons and contrasts.

Transitions that show *sequence*	**first, then, next, after, later, while, finally, during, soon, eventually, meanwhile**
Transitions that show *cause-and-effect relationships*	**so, if, then, since, because, therefore, as a result, consequently**
Transitions that show *comparisons*	**like, as well as, similarly, in the same way, likewise**
Transitions that show *contrasts*	**but, however, in fact, on the other hand, while**

The author of the mentor text uses transition words and phrases in the paragraph below.

TRANSITIONS
Read this section of the mentor text. Circle the transition word or phrase that shows a cause-and-effect relationship. Underline any transitions that show time or sequence.

Ansel Adams, age fourteen, looked through a book about Yosemite Valley, which was located about 150 miles east of his San Francisco home. "That's where I want to go on vacation this year," he told his parents. So on June 1, 1916, the three of them set off for a month of exploring the majestic and awe-inspiring scenery of Yosemite. Soon after they arrived, Ansel's parents gave him a box camera. This photographic tool opened a whole new world to the young man. Eventually, Adams became one of the most well-known and respected photographers of his time.

Try It! Write Your First Draft

On a computer or a separate sheet of paper, create the draft of your response to the writing prompt. Remember to use words, phrases, and clauses that show clear relationships between ideas in your piece. Use this draft checklist to help you as you write.

- ✓ A good introduction captures your reader's attention. Keep your audience in mind. You can begin with a question, a quotation, an interesting or funny experience, or a statement to which readers can relate.
- ✓ Be sure to include your thesis statement in the first paragraph. Your thesis statement should reflect your purpose.
- ✓ Support your thesis with relevant facts, details, and examples from the research you've completed.
- ✓ Avoid showing bias against or in favor of the subject.
- ✓ Include quotations or excerpts that are related to your topic, as appropriate. Correctly cite the sources.
- ✓ Summarize your main idea in the conclusion. Write a memorable conclusion that gives your reader something to think about.

Tips for Writing Your First Draft

- Talk to others about your topic. These discussions may provide additional insight that you can use in your writing.
- Write down questions about your topic before you begin researching. This can help you find appropriate resources and look for interesting facts, quotations, and visuals.
- Review the information and the sources where you obtained it. Is the information accurate? Does the writer show bias by presenting opinions as facts?
- Use transition words to guide the reader through the text, from one idea to the next.

4. Peer Review

After you finish your draft, you can work with a partner to review each other's drafts. Here is an early draft of the mentor text. Read it with your partner. Together, answer the questions in the boxes. Then we'll see how the writer's classmate evaluated the draft.

INTRODUCTION In the draft, the writer does not state a thesis clearly. What does the author want to talk about *the most*? What is she saying about the significance and importance of Ansel Adams?

SUPPORTING PARAGRAPHS These paragraphs could use more details and examples to support the main idea. What details and information can be added?

CONCLUSION This conclusion only gives details about people's opinions of Adams's work. How would you improve it?

Man with a Camera

Ansel Adams, age fourteen, looked through a book about Yosemite Valley, located about 150 miles east of his San Francisco home. "That's where I want to go on vacation this year," he told his parents. So on June 1, 1916, the three of them set off for a month of exploring the majestic scenery of Yosemite. Soon after they arrived, Ansel's parents gave him a box camera. He really liked it a lot. He took a lot of photographs.

The young Adams soon became absorbed in photography. He learned about what to do with film, and a lot of different jobs related to photography were done by him. He took his own photographs and felt that he had a lot to contribute to the field of photography.

Adams used his photography to capture the emotional reality behind external scenes. He liked to work with black-and-white images, rather than color. He felt this focused the viewer on the emotional content of the scene, instead of on the external reality of what was being shown.

Throughout his life (1902–1984), Ansel Adams held a deep appreciation for the American West. What were some of the ways he did this? He often took photographs of its natural beauty. He became closely involved with the Sierra Club, an organization devoted to the protection of wilderness areas. Frequently, he used his photographs to convey the message that the wilderness must be preserved.

Ansel Adams died in 1984, which left a lot of people feeling sad that he would not be alive to continue taking photographs. The country was grateful for all that he had done.

An Example Peer Review Form

This peer review form gives an example of how a classmate evaluated the draft of the mentor text shown on the previous page.

Criteria	Feedback
The introduction states the topic in an interesting way. **The writer gives a clear, strong thesis statement.**	You did a good job of *telling the reader the topic.*
	You could improve your informative text by *writing a clearer thesis statement. The one you wrote is unclear.*
The writer supports the thesis statement with strong facts, details, or examples.	You did a good job of *giving facts, details, or examples.*
	You could improve your informative text by *adding facts, details, or examples to each paragraph to support your thesis statement.*
The writer uses words, clauses, and phrases to make the writing flow smoothly and to connect ideas.	You did a good job of *using the transition phrase "rather than" in paragraph 3 to show contrast.*
	You could improve your informative text by *using active-voice verbs rather than passive-voice verbs in paragraph 2.*
The writer restates the thesis statement in the conclusion.	You did a good job of *restating the contributions made by Ansel Adams.*
	You could improve your informative text by *adding an interesting detail or idea for the reader to ponder.*

Try It! Peer Review with a Partner

Now you are going to work with a partner to review each other's informative text drafts. You will use the peer review form below. If you need help, look back at the mentor text writer's peer review form for suggestions.

The introduction states the topic in an interesting way. The writer gives a clear, strong thesis statement.	You did a good job of You could improve your informative text by
The writer supports the thesis statement with strong facts, details, or examples.	You did a good job of You could improve your informative text by
The writer uses words, clauses, and phrases to make the writing flow smoothly and to connect ideas.	You did a good job of You could improve your informative text by
The writer restates the thesis statement in the conclusion.	You did a good job of You could improve your informative text by

Try It! Record Key Peer Review Comments

Now it's time for you and your partner to share your comments with each other. Listen to your partner's feedback, and write down the key comments that you hear in the left column. Then write some ideas for improving your draft in the right column.

My review says that my introduction	I will
My review says that my thesis statement	I will
My review says that my supporting details	I will
My review says that my transitions	I will
My review says that my conclusion	I will

Use the space below to write anything else you notice about your draft that you think you can improve.

5. Revise

In this step of the writing process, you work on parts of your draft that need improvement. Use the peer review form that your classmate completed. Also use your own ideas. This checklist includes some things to think about as you revise.

Revision Checklist

- ✔ Does my introduction catch the reader's interest? Do I state the topic and my thesis clearly?
- ✔ Are my details, facts, and examples important? Do they support my thesis?
- ✔ Is it clear where my facts, details, and examples come from?
- ✔ Is my conclusion interesting? Have I summarized my research effectively?
- ✔ Do I use words, phrases, and clauses to connect my ideas?
- ✔ Have I chosen words that are clear, powerful, and appropriate for my audience?

WORD CHOICE AND TONE A verb is in the active voice when the subject performs the action of the verb. Underline several of the verbs in the active voice in this paragraph. Why is it important that the sentence that begins "But Adams and other photographers" is written in the active voice?

____

____

____

Writer's Craft: Using Word Choice and Tone

Precise language, including powerful verbs, is important when writing an essay or a report. Use a formal and respectful tone to convey information. Avoid using passive voice. For example, instead of saying *The young man was encouraged by his math teacher,* say *The math teacher encouraged the young man*. Now look at this excerpt from the mentor text for examples of active voice.

> Earlier photographers had tried to make their photographs look like paintings. They had employed a variety of methods such as using soft-focus lenses, applying brush strokes to negatives, and printing their images on soft-textured paper. But Adams and other photographers of his era developed a new style, known as "straight photography." This style used sharp focuses, and the images were printed on glossy paper, which made the subject of the photograph more vivid and visual.

Try It! Revise Your Informative Text

Replacing passive-voice verbs with active-voice verbs is an important part of revising an informative text. Practice using active-voice verbs with the following paragraph. Several sentences have been written in the passive voice. Rewrite these sentences in the active voice on the lines below the paragraph.

(1) Contributions have been made to the well-being of our society by many Americans. (2) Some of those people are quite well known, like Ansel Adams and Louis Sullivan. (3) Quiet contributions through small deeds are often made by others. (4) Help is often given by neighbors when nobody else notices there's a need.

Sentence 1: ______________________________

Sentence 2: ______________________________

Sentence 3: ______________________________

Sentence 4: ______________________________

Writing Assignment

Now it's time to revise the draft of your informative text. Continue working on a computer or on a separate sheet of paper. Review the assignment, repeated below, and the checklist. Doing so will help you make sure that you have included everything you need.

"Man with a Camera" is about a famous American photographer. Louis Sullivan has also made a great contribution to the world. State what that contribution is, support your idea with significant details from the research texts, and provide a conclusion.

6. Edit

After revising your informative text, you will edit it. When you edit, you read very carefully to be sure to locate any mistakes in your writing. Here's a checklist of some things to watch for as you edit.

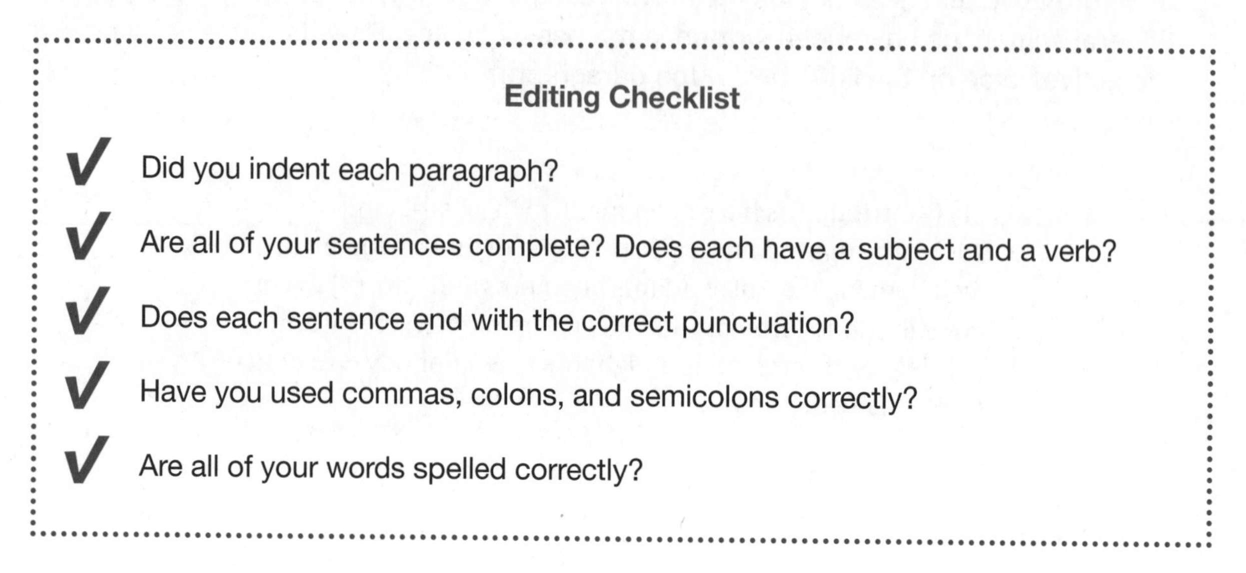

Editing Checklist

- ✔ Did you indent each paragraph?
- ✔ Are all of your sentences complete? Does each have a subject and a verb?
- ✔ Does each sentence end with the correct punctuation?
- ✔ Have you used commas, colons, and semicolons correctly?
- ✔ Are all of your words spelled correctly?

You can use these editing marks to mark any errors you find.

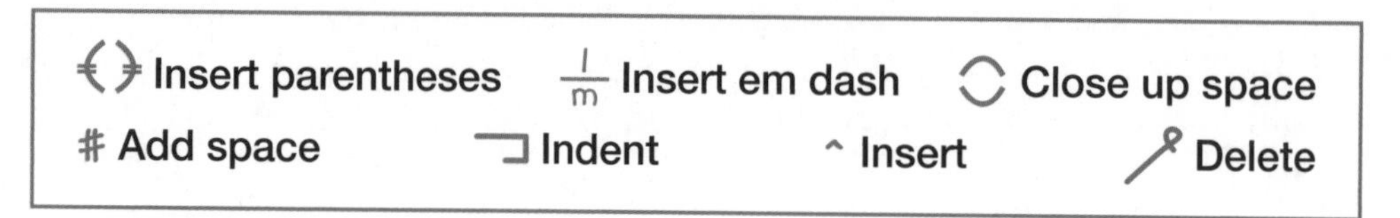

This paragraph from an early draft of the mentor text shows how to use editing marks.

Ansel Adams and ~~sum~~ some other photographers changed the way photography ~~were~~ was done. In theearly years of the twentieth century, photographers tried to make ~~there~~ their photographs look like paintings by using soft-focus lenses, applying brush strokes ~~two~~ to negatives, and printing their images on soft-textured paper.

Language Focus: Verb Mood

Verbs are one of your most powerful tools in writing. You can use **verb moods** to develop the voice and tone of a piece of writing.

Use the indicative mood to state a fact or express an opinion.

- Shantay departed the train station on her way to school yesterday.

Use the imperative mood to express a command or request.

- Leave for school early tomorrow morning.

Use the interrogative mood to ask a question.

- Did you leave for school early this morning?

Use the subjunctive mood to express something that is not factual.

- If you had left for school early, we would have been able to meet for breakfast.

It is important that you use verb moods correctly in your writing.

Throughout his life (1902–1984), Adams held a deep appreciation for the American West. He often took photographs of its natural beauty to satisfy his passion for it. He became closely involved with the Sierra Club, an organization devoted to the protection of wilderness areas. As a nature advocate, Adams frequently used his photographs to convey the message that the wilderness must be preserved. His photographs revealed to many people the true beauty of the land.

INDICATIVE MOOD Read this section of the mentor text. The indicative mood states a fact or expresses an opinion. Circle a sentence in the indicative mood in this paragraph.

Try It! Language and Editing Practice

For each sentence below, identify the verb mood of the sentence (indicative, imperative, interrogative, subjunctive).

1. Marquis, run three miles in thirty minutes.

   Verb mood: ______________________________

2. Marquis can run three miles in thirty minutes.

   Verb mood: ______________________________

3. If Marquis runs three miles in thirty minutes, he will break a school record.

   Verb mood: ______________________________

4. Can Marquis run three miles in thirty minutes?

   Verb mood: ______________________________

Now use editing marks to correct the errors in this paragraph.

If I known you were coming, I would have cleaned the house up. please give me some warning next time. I am quiet glad to see you, however, and I hope you can stay for lunch. What would you like to eat.

Try It! Edit Your Informative Text

Now edit your informative text. Use this checklist and the editing marks you have learned to correct any errors you find.

- [ ] Did you indent each paragraph?
- [ ] Are all of your sentences complete?
- [ ] Did you use correct punctuation and capitalization?
- [ ] Did you use the correct verb moods?
- [ ] Did you use precise language and transitions?
- [ ] Are all of your words spelled correctly?

Editing Tips

- Read your writing aloud. Ask yourself whether the text is clear and makes sense as written.
- Review the different types of verb moods. Reread your writing to make sure each has been used correctly.
- Read your writing over at a slow pace several times. Read it aloud, if possible. You may hear an error you otherwise would have skipped over while reading to yourself.

7. Publish

On a computer or a separate sheet of paper, create a neat final draft of your informative text. Correct all errors that you identified while editing your draft. Be sure to give your informative text an interesting title.

The final step is to publish your informative text. Here are some different ways you might choose to share your work.

- Create a poster featuring your informative text along with photos or illustrations.
- Read your informative text aloud to a small group of your classmates, and compare and contrast it with those of other students.
- Compile your informative text and those of other classmates into a booklet to share with a younger class.
- Read your informative text aloud to a family member. Ask the family member to list what he or she learned about Louis Sullivan after hearing your report.

Technology Suggestions

- **Upload your informative text onto a class or school blog.**
- **Create a digital presentation of your informative text and share it with the class.**

Lesson 11
Reading Persuasive Nonfiction

Look at this snow leopard, a member of an endangered species.
What emotional response do you think viewers are likely to have to this photo?

ESSENTIAL QUESTION

In what ways does persuasion appeal to our reason and our emotion?

Listen and Learn

Consider ▶ Do you think facts are stronger than opinions?

Can you think of a time when one might be a stronger persuasive factor than the other?

DAY OF INFAMY

Address to Congress
delivered by Franklin D. Roosevelt
December 8, 1941

ARGUMENT An author's claim and the evidence that supports the claim make up the author's argument. What is the author's argument in paragraph 1?

POINT OF VIEW Point of view is the author's perspective or feelings about the topic. What words in paragraph 1 reveal the writer's feelings?

MAKING JUDGMENTS A persuasive text is based on a particular point of view, so a reader must make judgments about whether the information is accurate and from a knowledgeable source. Which facts from the speech can be verified?

1 Yesterday, December 7, 1941—a date which will live in infamy—the United States of America was suddenly and deliberately attacked by naval and air forces of the Empire of Japan.

The United States was at peace with that Nation and, at the solicitation of Japan, was still in conversation with its Government and its Emperor looking toward the maintenance of peace in the Pacific. Indeed, one hour after Japanese air squadrons had commenced bombing in the American island of Oahu, the Japanese Ambassador to the United States and his colleague delivered to our Secretary of State a formal reply to a recent American message. While this reply stated that it seemed useless to continue the existing diplomatic negotiations, it contained no threat or hint of war or of armed attack.

It will be recorded that the distance of Hawaii from Japan makes it obvious that the attack was deliberately planned many days or even weeks ago. During the intervening time the Japanese Government has deliberately sought to deceive the United States by false statements and expressions of hope for continued peace.

The attack yesterday on the Hawaiian Islands has caused severe damage to American naval and military forces. I regret to tell you that very many American lives have been lost. In addition, American ships have been reported torpedoed on the high seas between San Francisco and Honolulu.

5 Yesterday the Japanese Government also launched an attack against Malaya.

Last night Japanese forces attacked Hong Kong.

Last night Japanese forces attacked Guam.

Last night Japanese forces attacked the Philippine Islands.

Last night the Japanese attacked Wake Island.

10 And this morning the Japanese attacked Midway Island.

OPPOSING CLAIMS
An effective persuasive text addresses opposing claims, or arguments that might be given against the author's argument. In paragraph 3, Roosevelt argues that Japan had been planning the attack while negotiating for peace. What evidence does he give against any claim that Japan was, in fact, pursuing peace?

INCOMPLETE INFORMATION
A persuasive text may sometimes neglect to include details about the topic that go against the claim. In his speech, Roosevelt does not mention any action the American military forces had taken against the attack. What effect does this have on Roosevelt's argument for declaring war?

EVIDENCE Persuasive texts may present evidence in the form of examples, research findings, statistics, expert opinions, or direct quotations. What type of evidence is in these paragraphs?

Japan has, therefore, undertaken a surprise offensive extending throughout the Pacific area. The facts of yesterday and today speak for themselves. The people of the United States have already formed their opinions and well understand the implications to the very life and safety of our Nation.

As Commander-in-Chief of the Army and Navy, I have directed that all measures be taken for our defense. But always will our whole nation remember the character of the onslaught against us.

No matter how long it may take us to overcome this premeditated invasion, the American people in their righteous might will win through to absolute victory.

I believe that I interpret the will of the Congress and of the people when I assert that we will not only defend ourselves to the uttermost but will make it very certain that this form of treachery shall never again endanger us.

EVALUATE EVIDENCE
A reader of a persuasive text must carefully consider all of the information provided. Is the evidence presented so far relevant and connected to the argument? Is it sufficient, or thorough and specific enough, to support the argument? Explain your reasoning.

PERSUASIVE TECHNIQUES
Authors may employ certain techniques to try to sway a person's opinion and gain support, often by appealing to a person's emotion rather than reason. One such technique is bandwagon appeal, which refers to the portrayal of an idea as gaining popularity. Others include name-calling, making generalizations, and stereotyping. Which technique is used in paragraphs 11 to 14? Identify examples to support your answer.

COMPARE AND CONTRAST
Reading several texts on the same subject and finding similarities and differences can provide a more complete understanding of a topic. The headline of the *New York World Telegram* on the day of the speech read "1500 Dead in Hawaii; Congress Votes War." What is the major difference between the speech and this headline in the way information is presented? What effect might each have on a reader?

15 Hostilities exist. There is no blinking at the fact that our people, our territory, and our interests are in grave danger.

With confidence in our armed forces, with the unbounding determination of our people, we will gain the inevitable triumph—so help us God.

I ask that the Congress declare that since the unprovoked and dastardly attack by Japan on Sunday, December 7th, 1941, a state of war has existed between the United States and the Japanese Empire.

Today there is a memorial at Pearl Harbor in Hawaii to remember those who perished on December 7, 1941.

BIAS Often a persuasive text can show the author's bias, a preconceived and often unfair feeling for or against something related to the topic. Read paragraphs 15–16. Does Roosevelt show a bias for or against any aspect of the topic? Explain your answer.

AUTHOR'S PURPOSE The purpose, or main reason, an author has for writing a text may be to inform, explain, persuade, entertain, or expresss emotion. What is Roosevelt's purpose for giving this speech?

PROPAGANDA Propaganda is an extreme persuasive technique that appeals to peoples' emotions to support a cause or belief. During World War II, many posters in the U.S. influenced people to show patriotism by buying war bonds, saving food and materials needed for the war effort, and encouraging women to work for industries in place of men who had enlisted to fight the war. What examples of propaganda could FDR have used to enhance his argument?

Comprehension Check

Look back at "Day of Infamy" and consider the persuasive techniques it employs to support the declaration of war against Japan. Use the T-chart below to differentiate between the facts and opinions in the speech.

Facts	Opinions

Now, write a statement that analyzes the way in which each column helps to support the author's persuasive purpose.

Vocabulary

Use the word map below to help you define and use one of the highlighted vocabulary words from the Share and Learn reading or another word your teacher assigns you.

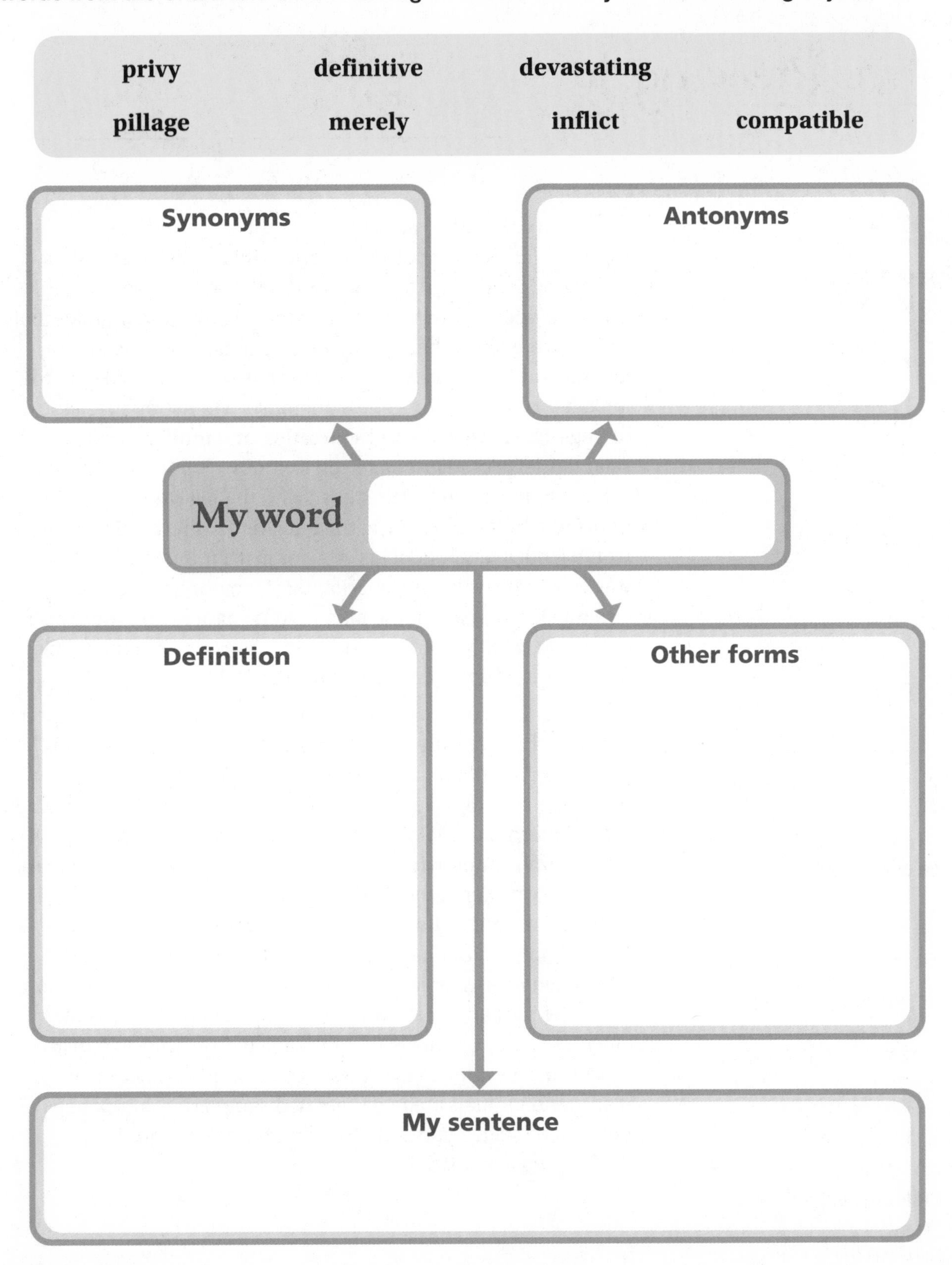

Share and Learn

Consider ▶ How does the author use facts to advance the argument?

What effect does word choice have on a reader?

Captive Breeding to Save a Species

FACT VS. OPINION Underline one fact and circle one opinion in paragraph 1.

BIAS Based on paragraph 1, do you think the author has a bias that might interfere with a fair presentation of the topic? Explain.

____

____

____

EVIDENCE Identify two different types of evidence presented in paragraph 2.

____

____

____

POINT OF VIEW Draw a box around the sentence in paragraph 2 that best demonstrates the author's point of view.

1 Were you excited about going to the zoo when you were a child? Many adolescents and adults look back on their childhoods and have fond memories of their zoo experiences. Zoos provided a glimpse at many amazing live wild animals that people were only otherwise privy to in books. Did you have a favorite animal or bird that you couldn't wait to see? Maybe you looked forward to the amphibian house, where tiny species of frogs, immense land and sea turtles, and multicolored salamanders could fascinate you for hours. Some of the most extraordinary exhibits were those with the big cats. I'd wait for hours just to sneak a peak at the enormous Siberian tiger that would slink in and out of his cave for just a minute, but it was worth the wait. The Siberian tiger is among the top-ten endangered species on the planet. And chances are, whichever of the zoo exhibits were your favorite, some types of the species from those exhibits are, have been, or will be endangered.

Although exact numbers are difficult to obtain, most experts estimate that there are more than five thousand endangered species on our planet at any given time. To be considered "endangered," a species must meet specific criteria as established by the International Union for Conservation of Nature (IUCN). This organization maintains a "Red List" of endangered species, which is considered the definitive source for endangered species data and is the basis for many conservation programs. For example, an update to the Red List in 2002 showed that 30 percent of amphibians were at risk for extinction. This report led to the formation of new conservation groups to focus their efforts on those species. But for people who are not scientists, the important thing to know is that thousands of species of plants and animals are in danger of disappearing completely, never to be seen again in a zoo or in the wild. It's quite devastating to consider.

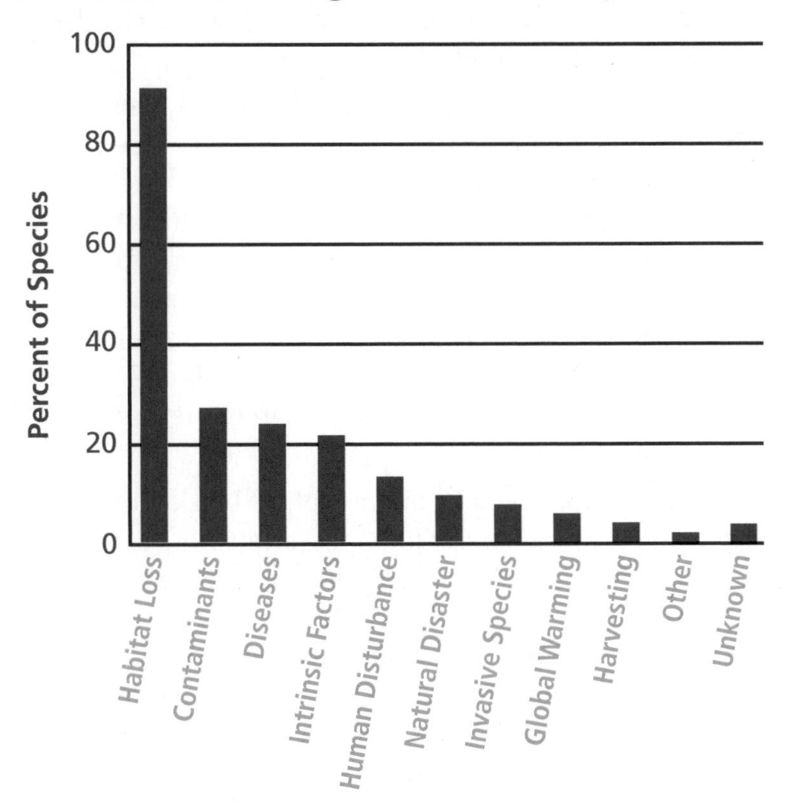

Many people who are interested in animals, whether they are animal scientists or animal lovers, are concerned about the issue of endangered species. Most experts agree that the major causes of species endangerment can be traced back to human behaviors that destroy animals' natural habitats.

- Humans steamroll over animal habitats to build houses, businesses, and shopping malls.
- Humans slash and burn the flora that make up animals' homes to build massive commercial farms.
- Humans pillage the mineral and biological resources of natural habitats for those resources' economic value.
- Humans impose their highways, railroads, and even airfields upon animals' habitats with no consideration for the effect on plant and animal populations.
- Humans upset the balance of animals' habitats by creating water pollution, air pollution, and global warming.
- Humans barge into animals' homes merely to satisfy their need for adventure or recreation.

VISUAL INFORMATION Based on the graph, what conclusion can you draw about the effect of human behavior on the threat of amphibian extinction?

____

____

COMPARE AND CONTRAST Look at the graph and paragraph 3. What is similar about the topic of each? How is the purpose of each type of text different?

____

____

WORD CHOICE What structural technique is the author using in paragraph 3? Why might this technique be effective? Circle words and phrases that were chosen for their specific meaning.

____

____

TONE What overall tone does the author create in this section?

____

____

AUTHOR'S PURPOSE Based on what you have read so far, what is the author's purpose?

____

____

____

ARGUMENT Identify the author's main argument in paragraphs 4 and 5.

____

____

____

INCOMPLETE INFORMATION Look carefully at the evidence presented in paragraph 6. Is the information thorough and clear, or is there more that the reader needs to know?

____

____

____

Sadly, the damage that humans inflict upon animals' natural habitats is irreversible. However, there is something humans can do to reverse the trend of disappearing animal species. Humans can establish captive breeding programs.

5 Captive breeding is the practice of mating a species in a controlled environment. The purpose of captive breeding is to create a population of the species that is large enough to include healthy individuals of a variety of ages—individuals that can eventually begin to reproduce themselves. Some captive breeding programs also have the goal of releasing the species back into the wild, where it can go on to increase its population naturally. Captive breeding can save thousands of threatened species on our planet and protect us all from the loss of such valuable biodiversity.

Consider, for example, the case of the black-footed ferret. Again, due to the actions of humans, ferrets were dying out because they had nothing to eat. Once considered extinct, a small population did resurface, although only eighteen were left! The U.S. Fish and Wildlife Service developed the Black-Footed Ferret Recovery Plan. Part of the plan was an analysis of each animal's DNA. Then the most compatible animals were bred. As a result, a large number of black-footed ferrets have been released into the wild, and about 250 now remain in captive breeding centers for future reproduction.

Black-footed ferret

Another extinct species that has been restored due to captive breeding is the oryx, whose natural habitat is in North Africa. There are still no oryx in the wild. However, the efforts of zoos in both North Africa and Europe have resulted in an explosion of captive oryx populations in these regions. The success of this program, along with the Black-Footed Ferret Recovery Plan, shows us that captive breeding can restore endangered animal populations in the wild as well.

The practice of captive breeding does have its opponents. Some people object to these programs because they take animals out of their natural habitats and place them in zoos or other artificial breeding facilities. However, the endangered species have already been driven out of their habitats, or their habitats have been destroyed. In other words, most endangered species no longer have a "natural habitat."

Another argument against captive breeding comes from within the field of animal science itself. Some zoologists argue that captive breeding is usually carried out with very small populations of the species, which brings about the risk of inbreeding and birth defects. However, as long as the scientists in charge of the program are careful, this risk can be avoided.

EVALUATE EVIDENCE How well does the author use facts and details to support the argument in paragraphs 7–9?

____

____

____

OPPOSING CLAIMS In paragraphs 8–9, underline the opposing claims that the author addresses.

MAKING JUDGMENTS Is the author's response to opposing claims effective? Explain why or why not.

____

____

____

PROPAGANDA Is this passage an example of propaganda? Explain.

____

____

____

PERSUASIVE TECHNIQUES Which persuasive techniques do you notice in paragraph 10? What effect do these techniques have on the author's argument?

______

______

______

PRIMARY VS. SECONDARY SOURCES There is a direct quotation in paragraph 10. Does that make this text a primary or a secondary source? How can you tell?

______

______

______

10 In conclusion, do not forget how much you loved zoo visits when you were a child. Many animals have been driven to the brink of extinction because human behavior has destroyed their habitats. Thus, it is only fair that humans should find a way to make up for the destruction they have caused. Captive breeding may be our last chance to restore the damage we have inflicted on our planet's biodiversity. In the words of Jean-Christophe Vié, deputy director of IUCN's Global Species Programme, "[I]f we do not act now, future generations may not know what a Chinese water fir or a bizarre-nosed chameleon look like." I, for one, do not want my children to grow up in such a world. Do you?

The giant panda, tiger, and snow leopard are all species facing extinction.

Anchor Standard Discussion Questions

Discuss the following questions with your peer group. Then record your answers in the space provided.

1. The authors of "Day of Infamy" and "Captive Breeding to Save a Species" try to persuade readers to agree with their solutions to certain injustices. Do you think emotional and biased language strengthens or weakens their arguments? Support your answer with examples from both texts.

2. If the author of "Captive Breeding to Save a Species" had written the article purely to inform readers about captive breeding, how might the style of the article have been different? Support your answer with details from the text.

Comprehension Check

1. What evidence could the writer have added to "Captive Breeding to Save a Species" to better support the claim that human action resulted in the near extinction of black-footed ferrets?

2. Summarize the major differences between "Captive Breeding to Save a Species" and "Day of Infamy" in terms of their methods of persuasion.

3. Which persuasive techniques in "Captive Breeding to Save a Species" are the most effective in influencing the reader?

Read On Your Own

Read another persuasive nonfiction text, "Voting at Sixteen," independently. Apply what you learned in this lesson and check your understanding.

Lesson 12

Writing Opinion Pieces

In 1972, the U.S. government passed a law to ensure that boys and girls have equal opportunities to participate in athletic activities in public schools. Some people think that gender equality in school sports is a good idea, while others do not. What athletic opportunities are available to the students in your school? Do males and females have equal opportunities to participate in the same sports? Do you think that some activities *should* be reserved for only males or only females? You can share your thinking about gender equality in athletics by writing an opinion piece.

ESSENTIAL QUESTION

How can persuasive writing be used to influence and challenge the opinions of others?

What's an Opinion Piece?

Many laws have been passed in the United States regarding how students are educated in public schools. There are laws about the number of days students must attend school each year, the number of years students must attend school, and the types of courses that are required for students to earn a diploma. There are laws about the equal treatment of male and female students in school. People have different opinions about these and other education issues.

In an **opinion piece**, you tell how you think about an issue. You use clear reasons and relevant evidence to support your argument and to persuade others to agree with you. Read the ways to present your opinion effectively in writing.

Introduction

Make a general statement about the topic you will address in your essay. Then make a statement of opinion, in which you state your claim about the issue clearly. The statement should tell your readers what argument you plan to make about the topic.

Support

Explain and elaborate on your opinion with clear reasons and relevant evidence. A reason is the basis for a claim or opinion. The stronger the reasons and the more accurate the evidence you can provide, the stronger your argument will be.

Conclusion

Make a final statement that summarizes and supports the argument presented.

Let's look at an opinion piece.

Analyze a Mentor Text

This is an example of an effective opinion piece. Read it and then complete the activities in the boxes as a class.

Athletics for All!

In today's society, we consider an active lifestyle an important key to good health and a full life. Many public schools offer a variety of athletic activities for students to choose from. For a long time, options for athletic activities were limited for girls. In 1972, a law called Title IX was passed in the United States. This law stated that "No person in the United States shall, on the basis of sex, be excluded from participation in, be denied the benefits of, or be subjected to discrimination under any education program or activity receiving Federal financial assistance. . . ." This law changed the way schools had to plan their athletic programs. I agree with this law. Girls and boys should have equal opportunities to participate in school sports.

There are many benefits both girls and boys can gain from participating in school sports. One important benefit is improved physical fitness. Getting regular exercise is a good habit to start before adulthood. Regular exercise helps students stay mentally sharp. It also helps students get better sleep at night. Students need to be rested and ready to learn in order to be successful in school.

It used to be that a few sports were considered appropriate for girls, while most were reserved for boys. Many people thought that some sports were too rough for girls. For example, it was unusual for a school to have a girls' basketball team. Many strong-willed girls proved those people wrong. Today, girls and boys enjoy many of the same sports. Not all girls want to play only tennis, and not all boys want to play basketball, for example. It is important to offer a wide variety of sports for students to choose from. If there is a girls' tennis team, there should be a team for boys. If there is a boys' basketball team, there should be a team for girls.

CLAIM The writer states a claim, or an opinion, in the introduction. It tells what the rest of the opinion piece will support. Draw a box around the writer's claim.

SUPPORT The writer supports a claim by giving clear reasons for the claim. What is one reason given in paragraph 2?

OPPOSING CLAIM
A claim that makes the opposite argument of the claim in an essay is an opposing one. The writer shares an opposing claim, or counterclaim, in paragraph 3 to show that he or she has considered another side of the argument. Circle the opposing claim.

TRANSITIONS A writer can use words, phrases, or clauses to show relationships between a claim and a reason for the claim. Circle the phrase that connects a claim and a reason.

CONCLUSION The purpose of a conclusion is to restate the writer's opinion and wrap up the main points of the argument. Draw a box around the opinion statement in the last paragraph.

Sometimes it isn't realistic to offer the same sports for girls and boys. It may be hard for a school to find enough players for a girls' football team, for example. However, I think that girls should be able to try out for the school's football team and play on the team if they have the talent. There should be equal opportunities for boys as well. Many schools now have male cheerleaders. Both cheerleading and football provide great exercise for students.

Another reason for having gender equality in school sports programs is that both boys and girls benefit from being part of a team. They learn to work with others to achieve a common goal. If sports teams are reserved for only one gender, then the other gender misses out on a terrific opportunity to be part of a group and to meet new people with common interests. I asked one student about her experiences as a member of the school volleyball team. She responded, "I enjoy being on the team. . . . I have learned a lot about cooperation and have made new friends."

In addition to the immediate benefits of equality in school sports, many colleges and universities offer athletic scholarships. If one gender is excluded from school sports in high school, they are also excluded from the opportunity to get an athletic scholarship to help pay for college. Even if a student does not get a scholarship, being involved in school sports looks good on a college application. It shows that the person is willing to work hard and be part of a team.

In conclusion, it is imperative that girls and boys have equal opportunities when it comes to school sports. Students should not be excluded from an athletic activity based on their gender. Athletic activities give students many opportunities—for physical activity, teamwork, and developing new interests—that are important for their growth as human beings. Girls and boys should have an equal opportunity to participate in school sports.

Think About It ► Whom do you think the author was attempting to persuade with this opinion piece?

Did the writer support his or her argument with valid reasons and relevant evidence?

Vocabulary Study: Connotation and Denotation

Denotation is the definition of a word that can be found in a dictionary. **Connotation** is the emotion, or feeling, that people get when they read or hear a word. Writers must consider the emotional effects, or connotations, that their word choices will have on their readers. The chart below shows some examples of how the connotation of a word can change the meaning of a sentence. Work with your class or a partner to replace the underlined word in each sentence to change the connotative meaning.

Example	Denotative Meaning	New Word or Phrase	Connotative Meaning of New Word
Welcome to our house!	A building in which people live	home	A place where people feel safe and loved
Angelina took charge when she joined the group.	acted as the leader		
The cook made a fabulous meal.	A person who prepares food		
Daniel was surprised by the low score he received on his test.	Having a sudden reaction to something that happened unexpectedly		
My brother moved down the street on his skateboard.	Went from one place to another		

Look back at the opinion piece on gender equality in school sports on pages 205–206. Choose two sentences, and rewrite them in the left column below. Choose a word in each sentence that has either a positive or a negative connotation. Rewrite the word. Identify it as positive or negative.

Mentor Text Sentence	Word	Positive or Negative Connotation

Writing Process

Now that you have read and analyzed an opinion piece, you are going to create your own by following these steps of the writing process.

1. Get Ready: Brainstorm List several topics you might want to write about. Choose the topic that you have the strongest opinion about. Brainstorm more about your topic. Think of reasons that support the way you feel about the topic. Choose the strongest reasons to include in your opinion piece.

2. Organize Use a graphic organizer to organize supporting details and plan your opinion piece.

3. Draft Create the first draft of your opinion piece. Don't worry too much about making mistakes. Get your ideas down.

4. Peer Review Work with a partner to evaluate and improve your draft.

5. Revise Use suggestions from your peer review to revise your opinion piece.

6. Edit Check your work carefully for spelling, punctuation, and grammar errors.

7. Publish Create a final version of your opinion piece.

Writing Assignment

In this chapter, you will write your own opinion piece. As you create this piece, remember the elements of the mentor text that were most effective. Read the following assignment.

Some studies have shown that boys and girls learn in different ways. Should classrooms be separated based on gender?

Write at least five paragraphs telling your opinion about separating classrooms based on gender. Clearly state your argument, and support your claim with strong evidence.

1. Get Ready: Brainstorm a Topic

When writing an opinion piece about a topic that has been given to you, it is important to give careful consideration to the claim that you will make. You should look at the topic from all possible angles. For each possible claim, you should think about the positive and negative aspects before making a decision.

Here's how the author of the mentor opinion piece brainstormed topics.

Claim	Positive Aspects	Negative Aspects
There should be gender equality in school sports.	All students will have an equal opportunity to be part of a team.	Schools may not have the money to provide sports teams for both genders.
There should not be gender equality in school sports.	Students who are not good at sports can focus on other activities.	Students who want to play sports might not get the opportunity to do it outside of school.

Try It! Use a Brainstorming Graphic Organizer

Now use the chart below to help brainstorm topics for you own opinion piece. Choose the claim you feel most strongly about.

Claim	Positive Aspects	Negative Aspects

Brainstorm Ideas for Your Topic

You can use a graphic organizer to help brainstorm ideas and details for your opinion piece. Here is how the author of the mentor text used the graphic organizer.

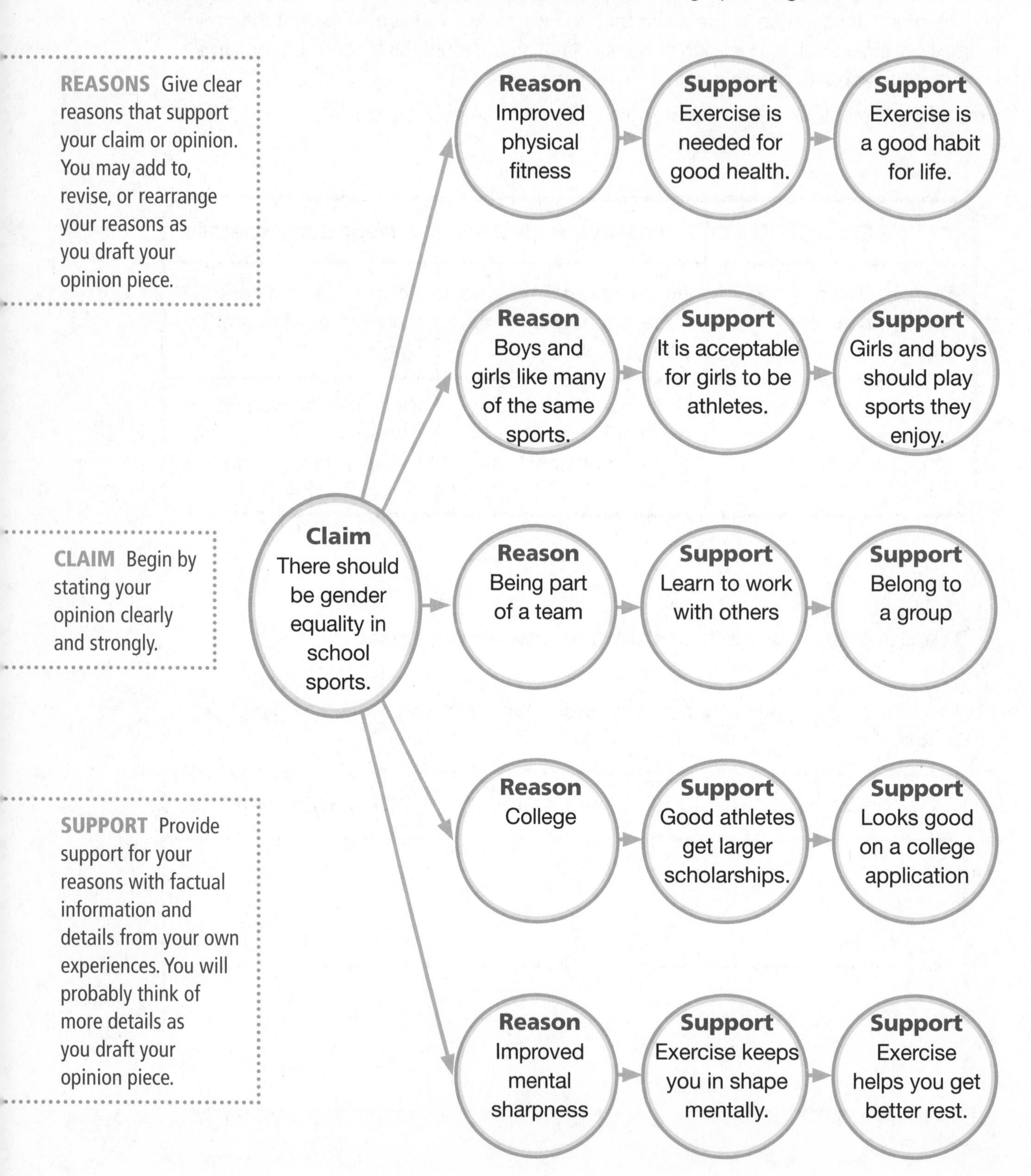
REASONS Give clear reasons that support your claim or opinion. You may add to, revise, or rearrange your reasons as you draft your opinion piece.
CLAIM Begin by stating your opinion clearly and strongly.
SUPPORT Provide support for your reasons with factual information and details from your own experiences. You will probably think of more details as you draft your opinion piece.
Claim There should be gender equality in school sports.
Reason Improved physical fitness
Support Exercise is needed for good health.
Support Exercise is a good habit for life.
Reason Boys and girls like many of the same sports.
Support It is acceptable for girls to be athletes.
Support Girls and boys should play sports they enjoy.
Reason Being part of a team
Support Learn to work with others
Support Belong to a group
Reason College
Support Good athletes get larger scholarships.
Support Looks good on a college application
Reason Improved mental sharpness
Support Exercise keeps you in shape mentally.
Support Exercise helps you get better rest.

Try It! Use a Graphic Organizer for Brainstorming

Now use the opinion map below to brainstorm your opinion, reasons, and support for your own opinion piece.

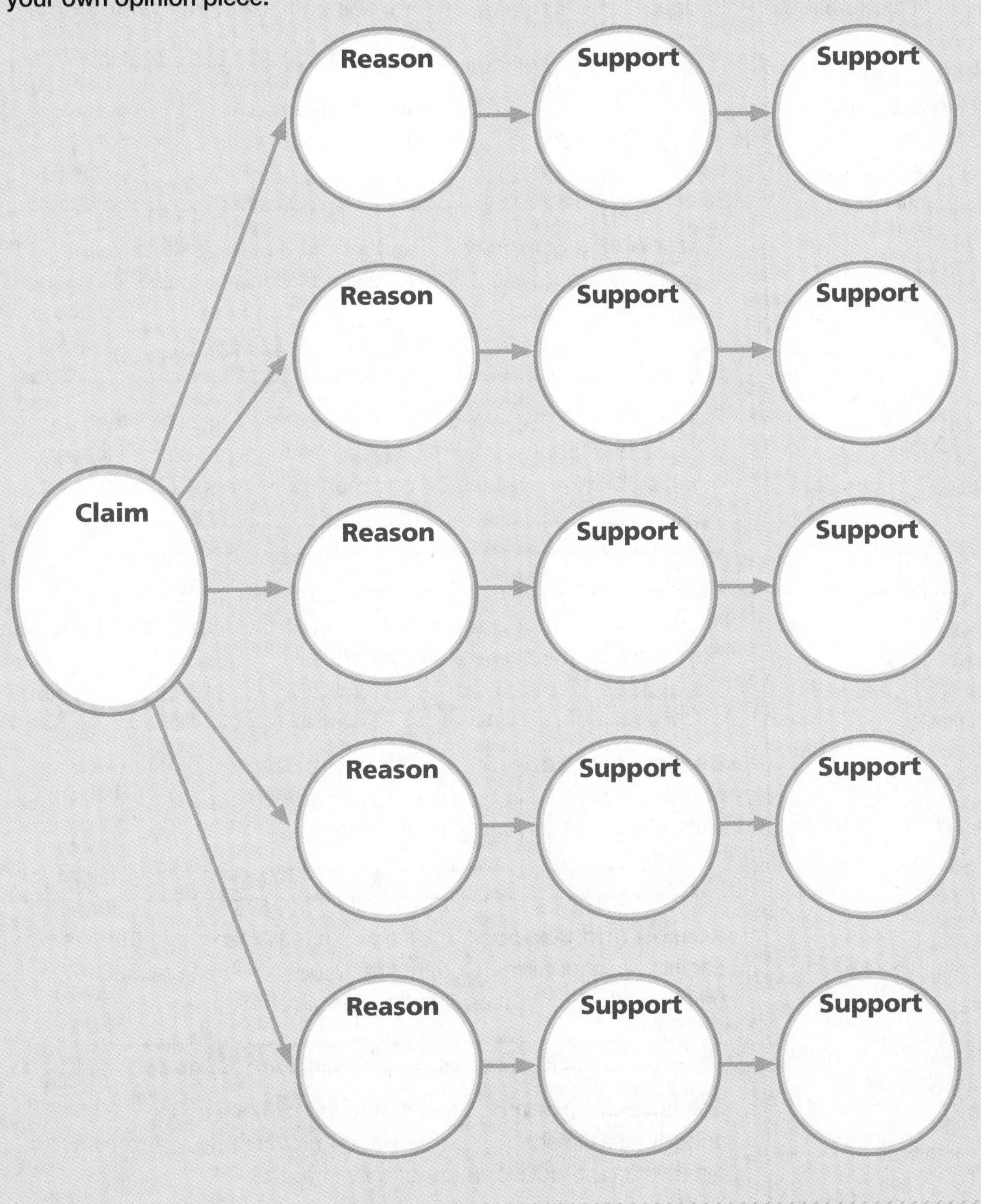

2. Organize

You are almost ready to begin a draft of your opinion piece. You can use a graphic organizer to help organize the reasons and support for your claim that you gathered during brainstorming. You can then refer to the graphic organizer as you work through the different parts of your draft. The writer of the mentor text completed this graphic organizer.

INTRODUCTION
In the first paragraph, you tell the topic of your opinion piece and state your claim about the topic.

SUPPORT
In subsequent paragraphs, you:

- give reasons that support your claim
- elaborate on the reasons with relevant facts, clear details, and experiences

CONCLUSION
In the final paragraph, you:

- restate your claim
- summarize your reasons
- appeal to your reader

Claim/Opinion
There should be gender equality in school sports.

Reason and Support 1 Students who participate in sports have improved physical fitness. Getting regular exercise is a good habit to have.

Reason and Support 2 Regular exercise improves mental sharpness. Students who get regular exercise get better sleep at night, so they are well rested and ready to learn at school.

Reason and Support 3 Boys and girls like many of the same sports. Some girls want to play basketball or football, and some boys want to do cheerleading or dance.

Reason and Support 4 Both boys and girls benefit from being part of a team. Being on a team gives students a chance to work with others and be part of a group.

Reason and Support 5 Being on a team can help students get into college. Some students get athletic scholarships. Being on a team looks good on a college application.

Conclusion It is imperative that students have equal opportunities in school sports. Sports provide physical activity, teamwork, and development of new interests.

Try It! Organize Your Opinion Piece

Now use the graphic organizer below to organize the ideas and details you want to use in the different paragraphs of your draft.

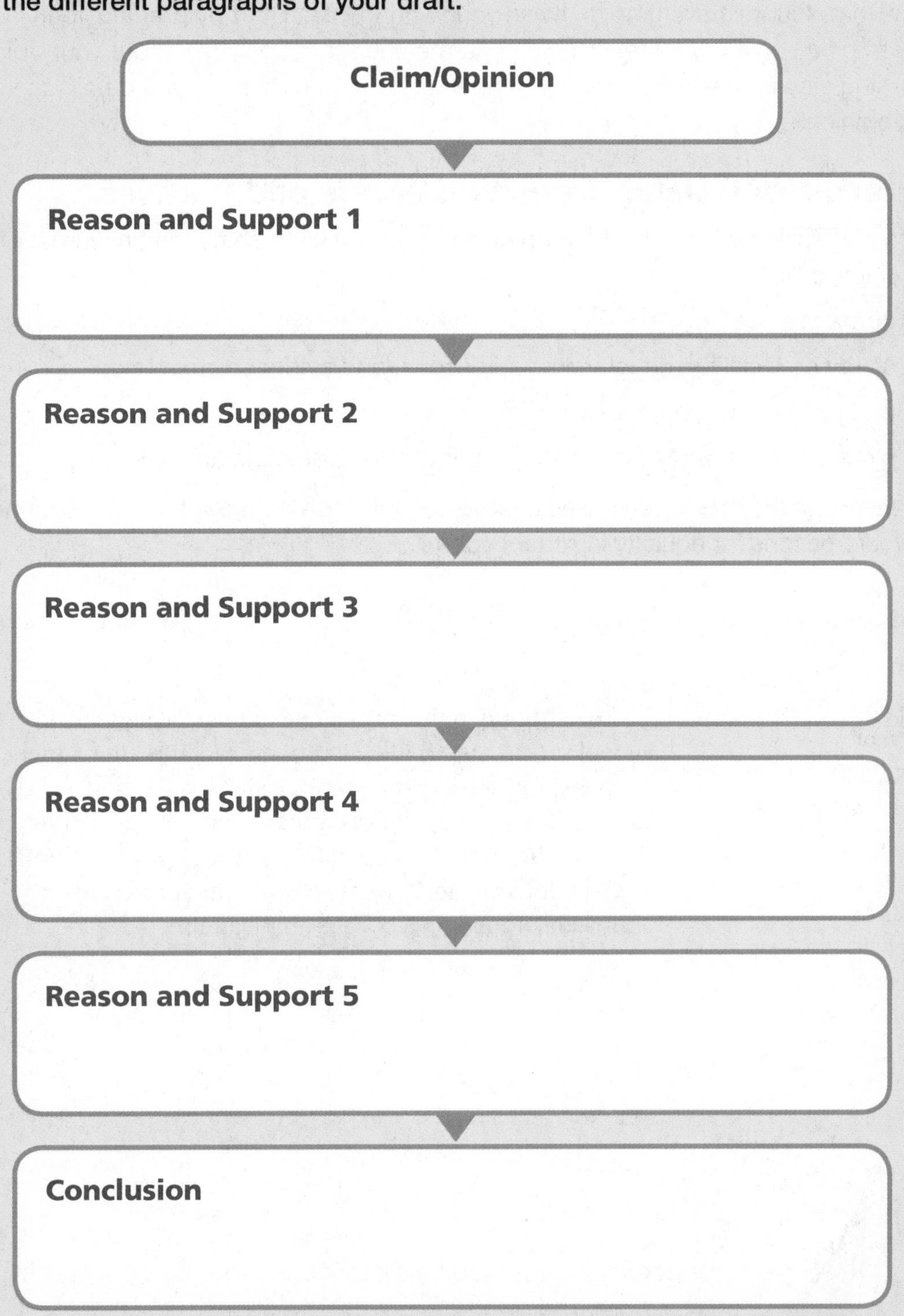

3. Draft

Now it is time to write the first draft of your opinion piece. Remember, your draft does not have to be perfect! This is the time to use your notes, get your ideas down in an organized way, and experiment with different ways to present your argument effectively. You will have time to revise your writing later. Start by drafting your opinion piece on a computer or on a separate sheet of paper. Tell about your opinion regarding classrooms separated by gender, and provide reasons and details to support your opinion.

Writer's Craft: Using Transition Words and Phrases

When supporting your claim in an opinion piece, you can use transition words, phrases, and clauses to

- connect ideas
- clarify how claims, counterclaims, reasons, and evidence are related
- provide clear writing that is well organized
- write a piece in a style that is appropriate and interesting for the reader

The author of the mentor text uses a phrase in the sixth paragraph to show connections between reasons for equality in school sports.

TRANSITIONS
Read this section of the mentor text. Circle the transition phrase that connects one reason supporting equality in sports to another reason that was stated earlier in the paragraph.

In addition to the immediate benefits of equality in school sports, many colleges and universities offer athletic scholarships. If one gender is excluded from school sports in high school, they are also excluded from the opportunity to get an athletic scholarship to help pay for college. Even if a student does not get a scholarship, being involved in school sports looks good on a college application.

Try It! Write Your First Draft

On a computer or a separate sheet of paper, create the draft of your response to the writing prompt. Remember to use words, phrases, and clauses that show clear relationships among ideas in your piece. Use this draft checklist to help you as you write.

- ✓ A good introduction gets your reader's attention. You can begin with a question, a quotation, an interesting or funny experience, or a statement that the reader can relate to.
- ✓ Be sure to state your claim in the first paragraph.
- ✓ Write a topic sentence that clearly states the reason in each supporting paragraph.
- ✓ Use the reasons and support you came up with in Step 1: Brainstorm and Step 2: Organize.
- ✓ In each supporting paragraph, include sentences with details, facts, and experiences.
- ✓ Summarize your argument in the conclusion. Try to write a memorable conclusion.

Tips for Writing Your First Draft

- Talk to others about your topic. These discussions may lead to a new reason to support your claim that you had not thought of yourself.
- Write down key phrases and ideas before you begin writing. Sometimes this is a great warm-up to get you started!
- Write each supporting paragraph on an index card first. This makes it easier to move paragraphs around to determine the best order for supporting ideas.

4. Peer Review

After you finish your draft, you can work with a partner to review each other's drafts. Here is an early draft of the mentor text. Read it with your partner. Together, answer the questions in the boxes. Then we'll see how the writer's classmate evaluated the draft.

INTRODUCTION In the draft, the writer does not state his claim clearly. Should boys and girls have *some* opportunity to participate in school sports or an *equal* opportunity? What did Title IX require schools to do?

SUPPORT All of the supporting paragraphs could use more details and examples to support the claim the writer is trying to make. What details can be added to paragraph 3? What information can be added to paragraph 5?

CONCLUSION This conclusion does not restate the writer's argument clearly or sum up the writer's reasons for that claim. How would you improve the conclusion?

Athletics for All!

In today's society, we consider an active lifestyle an important key to good health and a long life. Many public schools offer athletic activities for students. For a long time, options for athletic activities were limited for girls. In 1972, a law called Title IX was passed in the U.S. This law changed the way schools had to plan their athletic programs. I think that girls and boys should participate in school sports.

There are many benefits both girls and boys can gain from participating in sports. They have improved physical fitness. Regular exercise helps students stay sharp. It also helps them sleep at night.

It used to be that a few sports were considered appropriate for girls, while most were reserved for boys. Many strong-willed girls proved those people wrong. Girls and boys enjoy many of the same sports. It is important to offer a variety of sports for students to choose from. Sometimes it may be hard for a school to offer equal opportunities.

Another reason is that both boys and girls benefit from being part of a team. If sports teams are reserved for only one gender, the other gender misses out on an opportunity. I asked one student about her experiences being part of the school volleyball team. She responded, "I enjoy being on the team. . . . I have learned a lot."

In addition, many colleges and universities offer athletic scholarships. Even if one does not get a scholarship, being involved in school sports looks good on a college application.

In conclusion, school sports are important to boys and girls. Athletic activities give students many opportunities that are incredibly important for their growth.

An Example Peer Review Form

This peer review form gives an example of how a classmate evaluated the draft of the mentor text shown on the last page.

The introduction states the topic in an interesting way. **The writer makes a clear, strong claim.**	You did a good job of telling the reader the topic. You could improve your opinion piece by writing a clearer opinion. The one you wrote is confusing.
The writer supports the claim with at least three strong reasons. **The writer uses interesting details and relevant support to explain the reasons.**	You did a good job of giving more than three reasons. You could improve your opinion piece by adding some details or examples to each paragraph to support your reasons.
The writer uses words, clauses, and phrases to make the writing flow smoothly and to connect ideas.	You did a good job of using "in conclusion" in the last paragraph. You could improve your opinion piece by adding transition phrases to show how your reasons and support for your claim are connected.
The writer appeals to the reader. **The conclusion sums up the argument.**	You did a good job of stating the importance of sports to boys and girls. You could improve your opinion piece by adding a sentence that sums up your reasons for your argument.

Try It!

Peer Review with a Partner

Now you are going to work with a partner to review each other's opinion piece drafts. You will use the peer review form below. If you need help, look back at the mentor text writer's peer review form for suggestions.

The introduction states the topic in an interesting way. **The writer gives a clear, strong claim.**	You did a good job of You could improve your opinion piece by
The writer supports the claim with at least three strong reasons. **The writer uses interesting details and relevant support to explain the reasons.**	You did a good job of You could improve your opinion piece by
The writer uses words, clauses, and phrases to make the writing flow smoothly and to connect ideas.	You did a good job of You could improve your opinion piece by
The writer appeals to the reader. **The conclusion sums up the argument.**	You did a good job of You could improve your opinion piece by

Try It! Record Key Peer Review Comments

Now it's time for you and your partner to share your comments with each other. Listen to your partner's feedback, and write down the key comments that you hear in the left column. Then write some ideas for improving your draft in the right column.

My review says that my introduction	I will
My review says that my claim	I will
My review says that my supporting reasons	I will
My review says that my use of relevant details	I will
My review says that my transitions	I will
My review says that my conclusion	I will

Use the space below to write anything else you notice about your draft that you think you can improve.

5. Revise

In this step of the writing process, you will work on parts of your draft that need improvement. Use the peer review form that your classmate completed to help you. You will also use your own ideas about how to improve each part of your opinion piece. This checklist includes some things to think about as you get ready to revise.

Revision Checklist

- ✓ Does my introduction get the reader's interest? Do I state my claim clearly?
- ✓ Are all of my reasons important? Do they support my claim in a strong way?
- ✓ Do I use details, facts, and experiences to make my reasons clear and strong?
- ✓ Is my conclusion interesting? Have I summed up my reasons well?
- ✓ Do I use words, phrases, and clauses to connect my ideas and make the writing flow smoothly?
- ✓ Do I use formal language that is appropriate for an opinion piece?

FORMAL LANGUAGE
Formal language is a style of writing used for reports and essays. Underline formal language used in this paragraph. In the first sentence, would *students of both genders benefit* be more or less formal than *both boys and girls benefit*? Why?

____

____

Writer's Craft: Using Formal Language

Using formal language is important when writing an essay or a report. It makes your opinion piece appear more polished and professional. Avoid slang words or casual-sounding words. Use *student* instead of *kid*. Use full words rather than abbreviations. Look at the mentor text for examples of formal language.

Another reason for having gender equality in school sports programs is that both boys and girls benefit from being part of a team. They learn to work with others to achieve a common goal. If sports teams are reserved for only one gender, then the other gender misses out on a terrific opportunity to be part of a group and to meet new people with common interests. I asked one student about her experiences as a member of the school volleyball team. She responded, "I enjoy being on the team. . . . I have learned a lot about cooperation and have made new friends."

Try It! Revise Your Opinion Piece

Replacing informal language with formal language is an important part of revising an opinion piece. This should not be limited to nouns. Choosing the appropriate verb or adjective can also make your writing more formal. Practice using formal language with the following paragraph. Replace each underlined word or phrase with a formal word or phrase. Write your answers on the lines below the paragraph.

Eating a good breakfast is important. It helps kids focus in school. It helps stop people from overeating later in the day because they're not as hungry. Guys and gals should eat a healthy breakfast every day. Remember, you are what you eat!

Replace *kids* with ______________________________

Replace *stop* with ______________________________

Replace *they're* with ______________________________

Replace *Guys and gals* with ______________________________

Replace *you are what you eat* with ______________________________

Writing Assignment

Now it's time to revise the draft of your opinion piece. Continue working on a computer or on a separate sheet of paper. Review the assignment and the checklist.

Some studies have shown that boys and girls learn in different ways. Should classrooms be separated based on gender?

Write at least five paragraphs telling your opinion about separating classrooms based on gender. Clearly state your argument, and support your claim with strong evidence.

6. Edit

After revising your opinion piece, you will edit it. When you edit, you read very carefully to identify any mistakes in your writing. Here's a checklist of some things to look for as you edit.

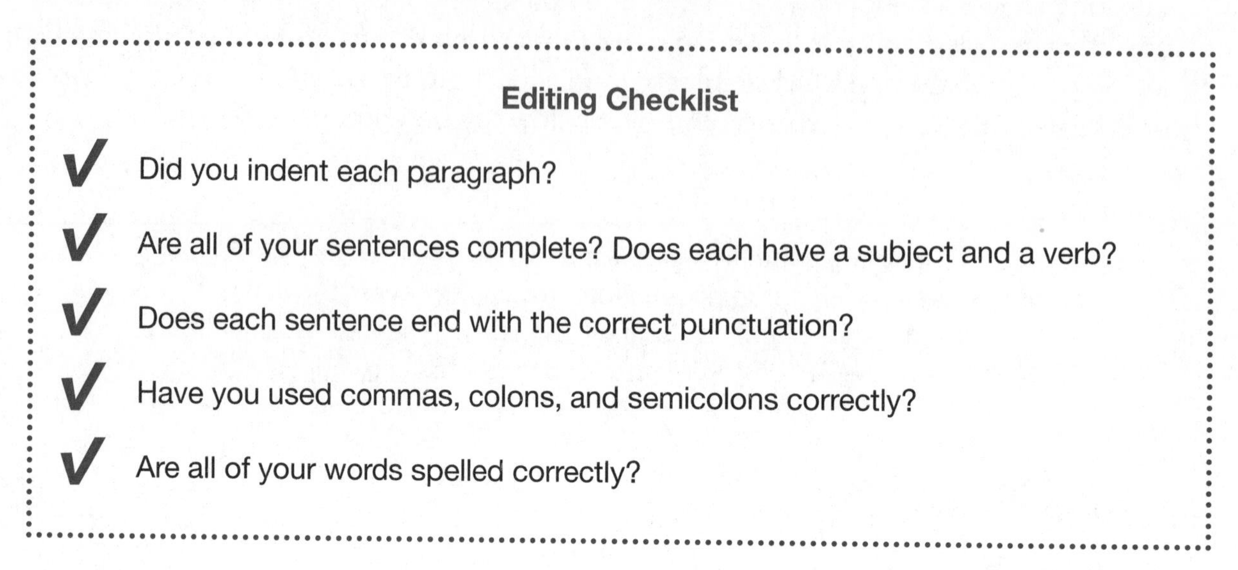

Editing Checklist

- ✔ Did you indent each paragraph?
- ✔ Are all of your sentences complete? Does each have a subject and a verb?
- ✔ Does each sentence end with the correct punctuation?
- ✔ Have you used commas, colons, and semicolons correctly?
- ✔ Are all of your words spelled correctly?

You can use these editing marks to mark any errors you find.

Indent	Add hyphen	Delete
Close up space	Insert	Reverse order

This paragraph from an early draft of the mentor text shows how to use editing marks.

It used to be that a few spo rts were considered appropriate for girls, while most were reservde for boys. Many strongwilled girls proved those people wrong. Grils and boys enjoy many of the same sports. It is important to offer a variety of sports for students to choose chose from.

Language Focus:
Using Punctuation to Indicate Breaks in Text

There are many ways to indicate breaks in text using punctuation. **End punctuation** is used to show the end of a question (?), statement (.), or exclamation (!). Other punctuation can be used to indicate different breaks or pauses in text.

Use an **ellipsis** (. . .) to indicate that a section of the original text was omitted, or left out of the text.

Use a **comma** (,) to indicate where to pause in a sentence. Commas are used to separate three or more items in a list, between parts in a compound sentence, and to set quotations apart from the rest of the text.

Use an **em dash** (—) to show a change in direction when the text is still connected to the original thought of the sentence.

Here are some examples of punctuation used to show breaks in text:

"To get to school, first I make a left on Elm Street. . . . Finally I make a right on Waterford Lane and walk to the main entrance."

On Saturday I played tennis, walked the dog, and rode my bike.

Mom said, "You can go to the mall with your friends, but you need to finish your homework first."

I cleaned my room—which is not my idea of a fun activity—on Sunday.

COMMAS Commas are used in compound sentences, to separate items in a list, and to separate a quotation from other text. In the paragraphs below, circle the commas used in compound sentences. Draw a square around commas in a list. Underline commas that separate a quotation from other text.

If sports teams are reserved for only one gender, then the other gender misses out on a terrific opportunity to be part of a group and meet new people with common interests. I asked one student about her experiences as a member of the school volleyball team. She responded, "I enjoy being on the team. . . . I have learned a lot about cooperation and have made new friends."

ELLIPSES Read this section of the mentor text. Ellipses are used to show breaks in the text. Circle the ellipsis in this paragraph.

In conclusion, it is imperative that girls and boys have equal opportunities when it comes to school sports. Students should not be excluded from an athletic activity based on their gender. Athletic activities give students many opportunities—for physical activity, teamwork, and developing new interests—that are important for their growth as human beings.

EM DASHES Em dashes show a break in thought that is still related to the surrounding text. Circle the em dashes and underline the thought that is a break from the rest of the sentence.

Try It! Language and Editing Practice

Choose the proper punctuation for each sentence. Rewrite each sentence using commas, ellipses, and em dashes as needed.

1. Valerie bought milk broccoli apples and bananas at the store.

   ____

2. This book which I borrowed from you is very interesting.

   ____

3. Tuesday the day I was sick was a boring one.

   ____

4. I'm going to the library where I can read my book.

   ____

Now use editing marks to correct the errors in this paragraph.

Last Saturday my family and I went to the state park. There were a variety of animal species to see. We saw squirrels rabbits deer and even a skunk! My sister she's three years old tried to hop after the rabbits. My mom spent a lot of time frantically chasing her and she had to hold on to the dog's leash. I think my mom was frazzled by the end of the day! I was intrigued by the moss growing on the trees. I studied it I looked it up on the Internet when I got home. I enjoy studying plants, so this was the perfect family day for me!

Try It! Edit Your Opinion Piece

Now edit your opinion piece. Use this checklist and the editing marks you have learned to correct any errors you find.

- [ ] Did you indent each paragraph?
- [ ] Are all of your sentences complete? Does each have a subject and a verb?
- [ ] Are transition words and phrases used effectively to connect ideas?
- [ ] Does each sentence end with the correct punctuation?
- [ ] Have you used commas, colons, and semicolons correctly?
- [ ] Have you used ellipses and em dashes correctly?
- [ ] Are all of your words spelled correctly?
- [ ] Have you used formal language?

Editing Tips

- Read your writing aloud. Add any missing words, and correct any awkwardly constructed sentences. Ask yourself, "Does that sound right?"
- Review when it is appropriate to use commas, ellipses, and em dashes to show breaks in text. Reread your writing to make sure each has been used correctly.
- Read your writing over at a slow pace several times. Each time you read, focus on something different. For example, focus on punctuation in one reading and spelling in another reading.

7. Publish

On a computer or a separate sheet of paper, create a neat final draft of your opinion piece. Correct all errors that you identified while editing your draft. Be sure to give your opinion piece an interesting title.

The final step is to publish your opinion piece. Here are some different ways you might choose to share your work.

- Create a poster using your opinion piece and an advertisement that you design to capture a reader's attention.
- Display your opinion piece on a bulletin board in your school.
- Read your opinion piece aloud to your class, and use it to lead a discussion on the topic you wrote about.
- Send your opinion piece to your school newspaper as a letter to the editor.
- Read your opinion piece to a classmate who has a different opinion from yours about the topic. Explain your claim, and try to persuade the classmate to see your point of view.

Technology Suggestions

- **Upload your opinion piece onto your class or school blog.**
- **Create a digital presentation of your opinion piece, and share it with the class.**

Writing Handbook

A Guide to Functional Texts

Functional texts are things you read and write to help you in your day-to-day life. If you need to cook something, you read the recipe first. If you are going to a special event, you read the invitation to find out when and where the event will be. If you invite a friend to your house, you may need to write directions and include a map. In this section, you will find examples of different functional texts and labels that show you the important features of each text. If you are asked to read or write one of these functional texts, use the sample in this handbook as a model to follow.

Models

Envelope

Write the sender's name and address in the upper-left corner. Be sure to include the city, state, and zip code.

Stamps go in the upper-right corner.

Sender's name
Street Address
City, State Zip code

Recipient's Name
Street Address
City, State Zip code

The name and address of the person getting the letter should be in the center. Be sure to include the city, state, and zip code.

Scott Mester
12 White Knoll Drive
Pleasantville, NY 12345

Carolyn Long
34 Church Road
Old Bridge, Michigan 45678

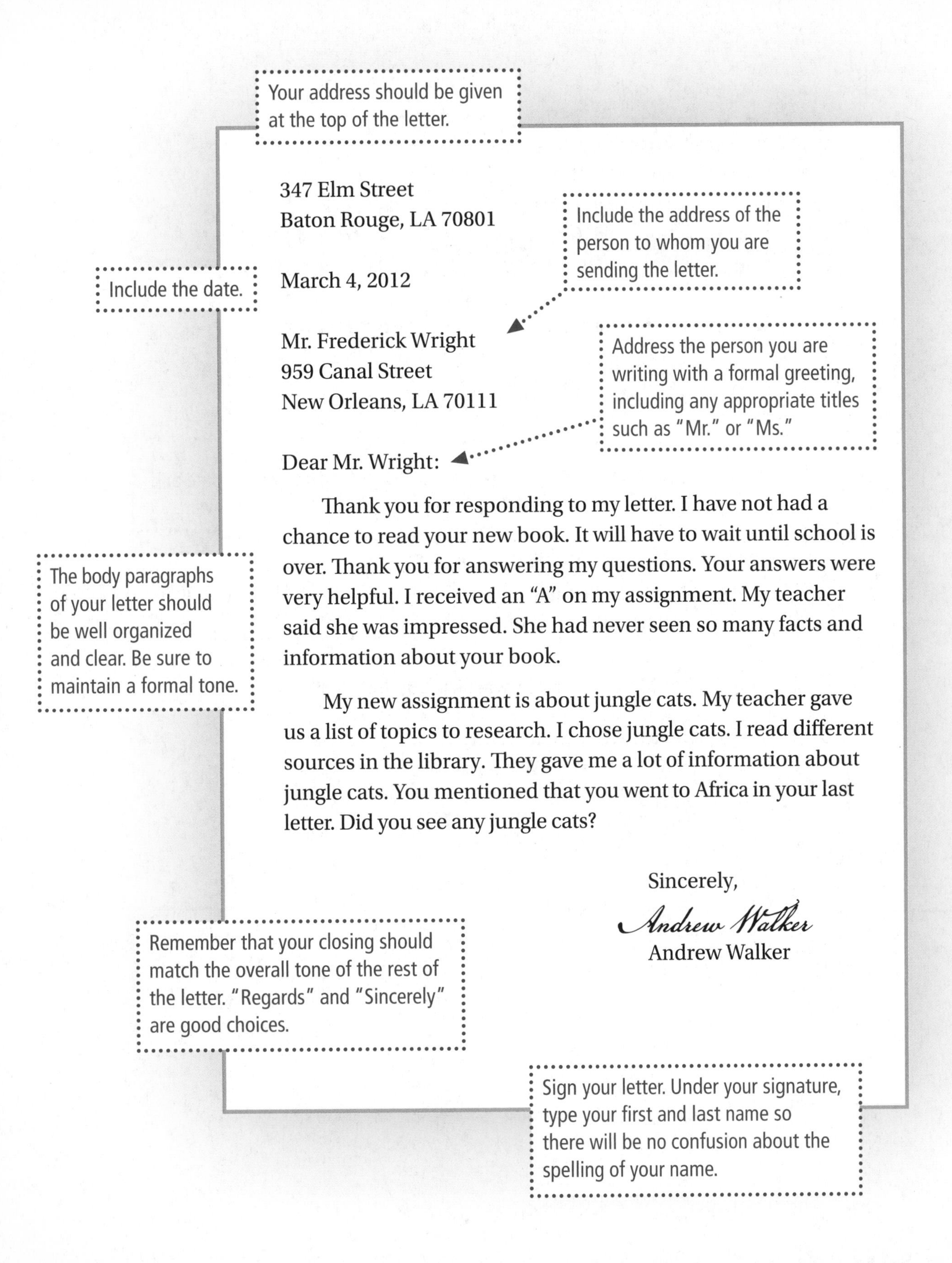

Your address should be given at the top of the letter.

347 Elm Street
Baton Rouge, LA 70801

Include the address of the person to whom you are sending the letter.

Include the date.

March 4, 2012

Mr. Frederick Wright
959 Canal Street
New Orleans, LA 70111

Address the person you are writing with a formal greeting, including any appropriate titles such as "Mr." or "Ms."

Dear Mr. Wright:

Thank you for responding to my letter. I have not had a chance to read your new book. It will have to wait until school is over. Thank you for answering my questions. Your answers were very helpful. I received an "A" on my assignment. My teacher said she was impressed. She had never seen so many facts and information about your book.

The body paragraphs of your letter should be well organized and clear. Be sure to maintain a formal tone.

My new assignment is about jungle cats. My teacher gave us a list of topics to research. I chose jungle cats. I read different sources in the library. They gave me a lot of information about jungle cats. You mentioned that you went to Africa in your last letter. Did you see any jungle cats?

Sincerely,

Andrew Walker

Andrew Walker

Remember that your closing should match the overall tone of the rest of the letter. "Regards" and "Sincerely" are good choices.

Sign your letter. Under your signature, type your first and last name so there will be no confusion about the spelling of your name.

Start by giving the reason for the event and inviting your guests to attend.

Brooke Edwards is celebrating her thirteenth birthday!

* 13 *

Join us as we celebrate on
Saturday, May 19, 2012 at 5:00 p.m.

Include the date and time of the event.

Northern Ice Skating Rink
123 N. Sunrise Highway
Middletown, Virginia

Provide the location's name and address.

Regrets only to Mr. and Mrs. Edwards (123) 456-7890.

Provide a way for your guests to respond to the invitation.

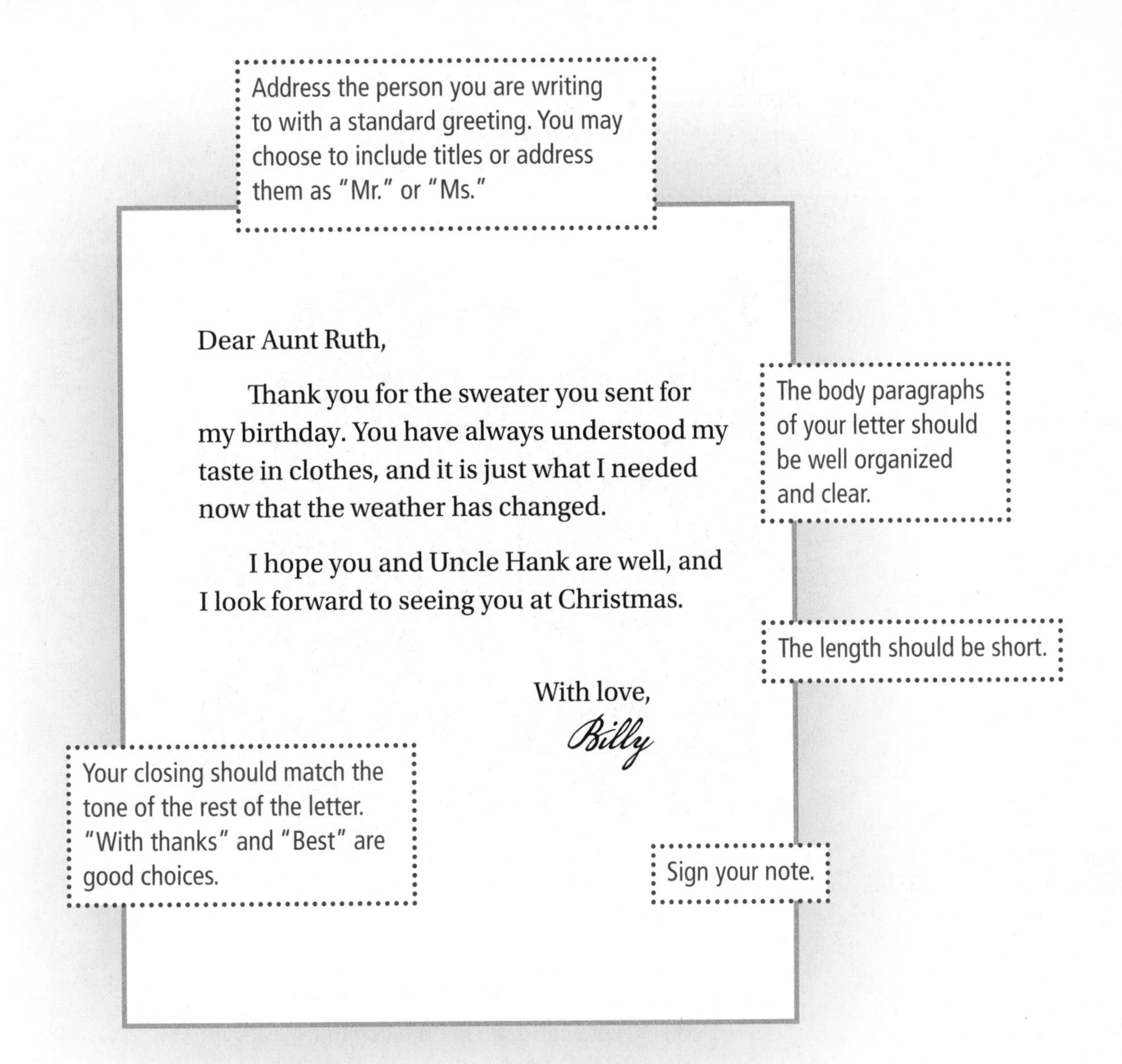
Address the person you are writing to with a standard greeting. You may choose to include titles or address them as "Mr." or "Ms."

Dear Aunt Ruth,

Thank you for the sweater you sent for my birthday. You have always understood my taste in clothes, and it is just what I needed now that the weather has changed.

I hope you and Uncle Hank are well, and I look forward to seeing you at Christmas.

With love,

Billy

The body paragraphs of your letter should be well organized and clear.

The length should be short.

Your closing should match the tone of the rest of the letter. "With thanks" and "Best" are good choices.

Sign your note.

Place a photo in your report or presentation. Use a photo that shows something your readers might not have seen before.

The caption should be directly below the photo.

Buffalo are usually brown. White buffalo are very rare and are considered sacred by some Native American groups.

Be sure to say exactly what is in the photo. You may provide extra information that relates to the report.

Decide what information you want to show and divide the chart into columns.

A heading should be at the top of each column.

Context Clue Type	Example
Definition	We can learn about dinosaurs through *paleontology, the study of fossils*.
Synonym	In many ways, early *littoral* settlements in Ireland resembled the *coastal* villages there today.
Contrast	We expected the hotel to be *opulent*, but instead we found *cracked ceilings, leaky faucets*, and *cramped, run-down rooms*.
Association	Betsey's bedroom was in complete *chaos*. *Piles of clothes* lay *all over the floor, books and papers* were *spilling off the desk*, and a *half-eaten pizza* poked out from *under the bed*.

List items under the first column so they start their own row.

Items in the next column should relate to the heading and the item at the left in that row.

Diagram

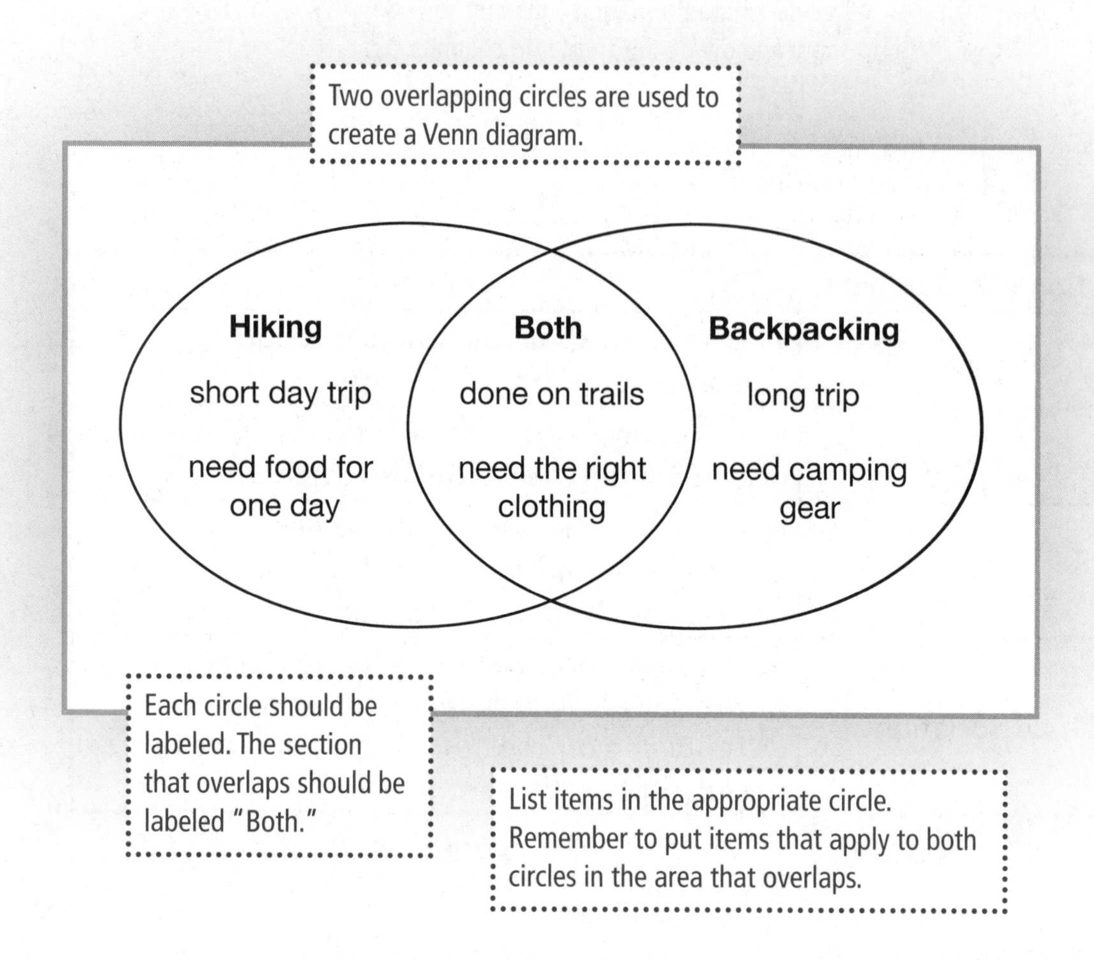
Two overlapping circles are used to create a Venn diagram.
Hiking
short day trip
need food for one day
Both
done on trails
need the right clothing
Backpacking
long trip
need camping gear
Each circle should be labeled. The section that overlaps should be labeled "Both."
List items in the appropriate circle. Remember to put items that apply to both circles in the area that overlaps.

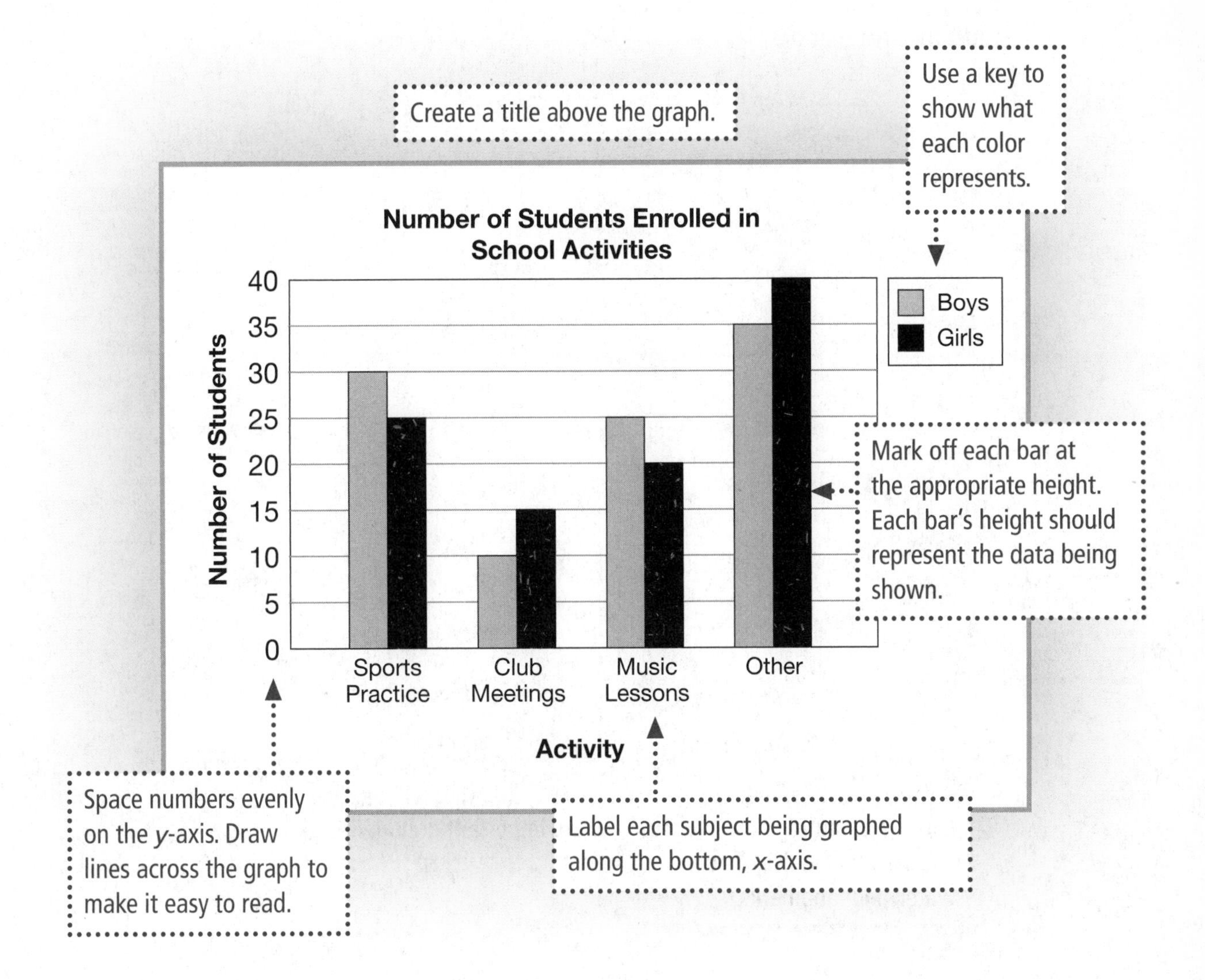
Create a title above the graph.
Use a key to show what each color represents.
Number of Students Enrolled in School Activities
Number of Students
40
35
30
25
20
15
10
5
0
Boys
Girls
Sports Practice
Club Meetings
Music Lessons
Other
Activity
Mark off each bar at the appropriate height. Each bar's height should represent the data being shown.
Space numbers evenly on the y-axis. Draw lines across the graph to make it easy to read.
Label each subject being graphed along the bottom, x-axis.

Label the area that the map represents.

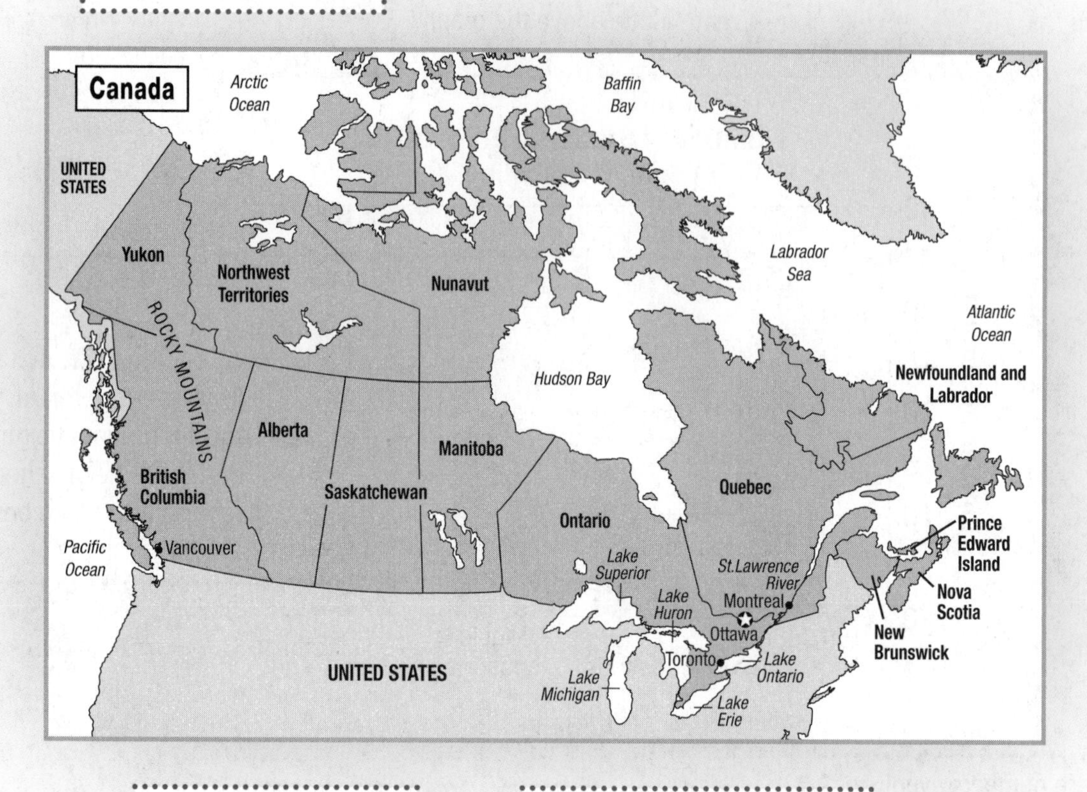

Label relevant regions, cities, rivers, bodies of water, and landmarks.

Show important boundaries.

Texas Chili

Ingredients:

The name of the dish should be given at the top of the page.

- 1 lb beef, cubed
- ½ cup beef broth
- ½ cup chicken broth
- 1 cup chopped tomatoes
- 3 serrano peppers
- 1 tsp onion powder
- 1 tsp garlic powder
- 1½ Tbsp chili powder
- salt

List all the ingredients needed for the recipe.

Include measurements of ingredients.

Directions should be listed and numbered.

Directions:

1. Brown the beef in a pan over medium heat.
2. Drain the beef, and set it aside.
3. Bring the beef broth, chicken broth, and tomatoes to a boil in a pot.
4. Add the serrano peppers, onion powder, garlic powder, chili powder, and a pinch of salt.
5. Add the beef, and simmer for about 60 minutes over medium-low heat.

Instructions should be written clearly. Be sure they explain all the steps necessary to make the dish.

Be sure to provide cooking time.

Title the procedure.

How to Make a Bolo Tie

Supplies

- leather strip (30 to 40 inches long)
- strong safety pin
- something decorative but not too large, such as a wooden button or an old belt buckle
- beads
- strong glue
- scissors

List all the materials needed.

Instructions

Step 1: Place the leather strip around your neck. Ask yourself: Is the strip the length I want it to be? If the strip (or cord) is too long for your liking, use the scissors to trim it.

Step 2: Decorate both ends of the leather strip with beads. If your beads have large enough holes, slide them over each end, and tie the ends of the strip to keep the beads in place. If your beads are too small, dip each end of the leather strip into glue. Then dip the ends into a pile of the tiny beads so that the ends are covered in beads.

Procedure steps should be numbered.

Step 3: Hang the strip in a place where the glue can dry. Be sure the ends of the strip do not touch as they dry.

Step 4: Now make the decorative clasp. Your decoration can be a wooden button, an old belt buckle, a plastic flower, or anything you like. Glue the safety pin to the back of the decoration.

Step 5: When the leather strip and clasp are both dry, put the strip back around your neck. Carefully guide both pieces of the strip into the safety pin and close the pin. Now you have your own fashionable bolo tie!

Instructions should be written clearly. Be sure they explain exactly what steps must be done and how to complete them.

Title the experiment.

List all the materials needed for the experiment.

Procedure steps should be numbered.

Static Electricity Experiment

Materials:

- a hard rubber or plastic comb
- thread
- pieces of dry, O-shaped cereal

Procedure:

1. Tie one piece of cereal to the end of a foot-long piece of thread. You may use any kind of knot you choose.
2. Attach the other end of the thread to something that is not close to anything else so that the piece of cereal is hanging freely.
3. Next, clean the comb well and dry it.

Instructions should be written clearly. Be sure they explain exactly how to perform the experiment and do not contain unnecessary information.

4. Run the comb through long, dry hair a couple of times or rub the comb on a rug.

5. Gently and slowly, pass the comb near the cereal. It should move toward the comb to touch it. Hold the comb still until the cereal moves away on its own.

6. Try to touch the comb to the cereal again. It should move away as the comb comes near.

Read a title at the top of the label.

List all items separately.

If more information is needed, use an asterisk (*) and provide the additional information later.

Remember to keep wording short. Space is limited, so only use the words needed.

Nutrition Facts
Serving Size 8 oz
Servings Per Container About 3

Amount Per Serving

Calories 180	Calories from Fat 60
	% Daily Value*
Total Fat 6g	10%
Saturated Fat 1g	5%
Trans Fat	0%
Cholesterol 5mg	2%
Sodium 75mg	3%
Total Carbohydrate 26g	9%
Dietary Fiber 5g	19%
Sugars 11g	
Protein 8g	

Vitamin A 60%	Vitamin C 70%
Calcium 8%	Iron 10%

*Percent Daily Values are based on a 2,000 calorie diet. Your daily values may be higher or lower depending on your calorie needs.

	Calories	2,000	2,500
Total Fat	Less than	65g	80g
Sat Fat	Less than	20g	25g
Cholesterol	Less than	300mg	300mg
Sodium	Less than	2,400mg	2,400mg
Total Carbohydrate	300m	375g	
Dietary Fiber	25g	30g	

Calories per gram:

Fat 9 Carbohydrate 4 Protein 4

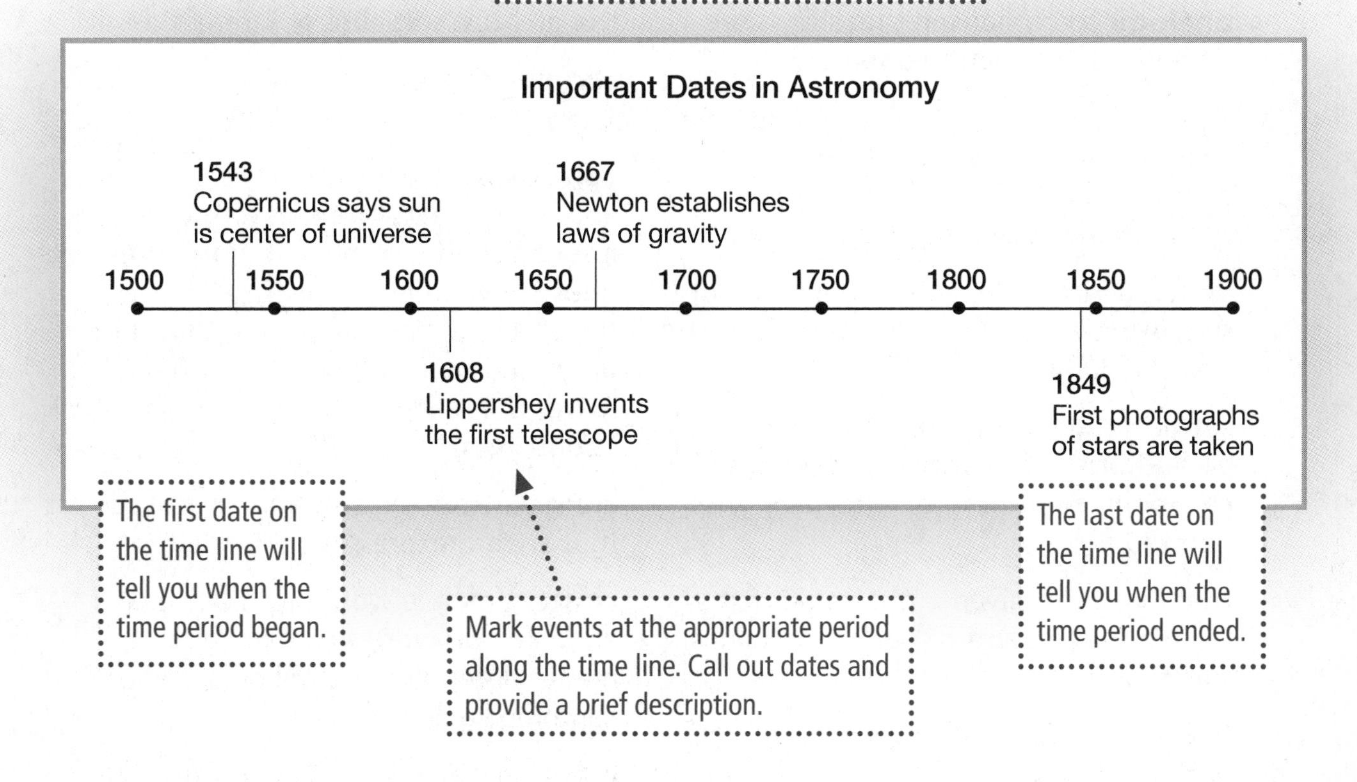
The title of a time line will tell you what subject the time line is explaining.
Important Dates in Astronomy
1543
Copernicus says sun is center of universe
1667
Newton establishes laws of gravity
1500
1550
1600
1650
1700
1750
1800
1850
1900
1608
Lippershey invents the first telescope
1849
First photographs of stars are taken
The first date on the time line will tell you when the time period began.
Mark events at the appropriate period along the time line. Call out dates and provide a brief description.
The last date on the time line will tell you when the time period ended.

Glossary

allusion a reference to a person, place, or event from literature or history (Lessons 1, 3, 7)

analogy a comparison that shows the similarities between two things (Lessons 1, 3)

archetype a character who follows a specific pattern of behavior that is common in literature (Lessons 1, 7)

argument a statement of opinion that is supported by evidence; see also *claim* and *point of view* (Lesson 11)

author's purpose the main reason an author has for writing a text, most commonly to inform, to entertain, or to persuade (Lesson 11)

bias a preconceived and often unfair feeling that an author has for or against something (Lessons 10, 11)

body paragraph see *supporting paragraph*

cause something that brings about an effect or a result (Lesson 9)

character a person, an animal, or an object that takes part in the action of a text (Lesson 1)

characterization the way a writer reveals a character's personality—through the character's words and behavior, descriptions of the character's appearance, descriptions of the character's thoughts and feelings, and comments made about the character by others in the story (Lessons 1, 6)

claim a statement of opinion (Lessons 11, 12)

climax the point in a story that creates the greatest suspense or interest (Lesson 8)

compare to look for similarities (Lessons 1, 3, 5, 6, 7, 9, 11)

conclusion a decision the reader makes about all or part of a passage, based on information from the text, inferences, and prior knowledge (Lessons 3, 5, 9); the end of a piece of writing that sums up the text's main points and often leaves the reader with something to think about (Lessons 2, 4, 10, 12)

connotation the emotion or attitude that a word expresses (Lessons 3, 6, 12)

context clue a word or phrase near an unknown word that can help the reader determine the unknown word's meaning (Lessons 3, 4)

contrast to look for differences (Lessons 1, 3, 5, 6, 7, 9, 11)

denotation the dictionary definition of a word (Lessons 3, 6, 12)

descriptive detail a piece of information that tells about a character, scene, or idea (Lesson 4)

details see *supporting details*

dialogue the words that characters speak in a text; a conversation between characters in a text (Lessons 1, 4, 6, 8)

domain-specific vocabulary a word or phrase that has a specific meaning within a subject area (Lessons 5, 9)

dramatic irony a situation in which the reader or audience knows something that the characters in the text do not (Lesson 6)

dramatic structure the way in which a play is organized, including acts, scenes, and stage directions (Lesson 6)

effect an outcome (Lesson 9)

ellipsis (. . .) a punctuation mark used to show that words have been omitted from quoted material (Lesson 12)

em dash (—) a punctuation mark that sets off an abrupt break in thought in a sentence (Lesson 12)

evaluate evidence to assess an author's arguments to see if they are relevant and sufficient (Lesson 11)

evidence information an author provides to support the main idea of a text, including examples, research and survey results, statistics, case studies, anecdotes, expert opinions, and direct quotations (Lessons 9, 11, 12)

fact something that can be observed or proved true (Lessons 5, 9, 11)

figurative language a word or phrase that means something other than its dictionary definition, such as a simile, an idiom, or a pun (Lessons 3, 6, 7)

figure of speech see *figurative language*

formal language see *formal style*

formal style an approach to writing that uses sophisticated language and avoids slang in order to convey a professional image; often used in reports and essays (Lessons 2, 12)

gerund a verb form ending in *-ing* that is used as a noun (Lesson 4)

glossary a collection of specialized terms with their meanings, often found at the end of informational references (Lesson 9)

humor the amusing elements of a text, included to maintain the reader's interest (Lesson 1)

idiom a figurative expression with a commonly understood meaning that is different from its literal meaning (Lesson 8)

imagery a word or phrase that appeals to the senses; see also *sensory language* (Lesson 7)

imperative mood the verb form used to state a command or request (Lesson 10)

incomplete information situations in which an author does not provide all of the facts or details related to an argument (Lesson 11)

indicative mood the verb form used to state a fact or express an opinion (Lesson 10)

inference a guess about a text based on evidence and prior knowledge (Lessons 1, 3, 7)

infinitive a verb form that can be used as a noun, an adjective, or an adverb that names an action without specifying the subject; usually preceded by the word *to* (Lesson 4)

informal style a type of writing that uses casual, everyday language (Lesson 2)

interrogative mood the verb form used to ask a question (Lesson 10)

introduction the beginning of a piece of writing that captures the reader's attention and presents the text's thesis, or main idea statement (Lessons 2, 4, 8, 10, 12)

literal language a word or phrase that means the same as its dictionary definition (Lessons 3, 6, 7)

main idea what a text is mostly about (Lessons 3, 6, 10)

make judgments to analyze the way in which an author presents and interprets information (Lesson 11)

mood the overall atmosphere or feeling that an author creates for the reader (Lesson 7)

opinion a view that someone takes on a certain issue based on a personal judgment (Lessons 5, 11)

opposing claim the opposite argument or viewpoint of the one given in a text (Lessons 11, 12)

participle a verb form that acts as an adjective and ends in *-ing*, *-ed*, or *-en* (Lesson 4)

persuasive techniques the ways in which an author tries to influence the reader's opinion, including bandwagon appeal, name-calling, snob appeal, and stereotyping (Lesson 11)

plot the series of related events that make up a story (Lessons 1, 6, 8)

poetry structure the way a poem is organized into lines and stanzas (Lesson 7)

point of view the perspective from which a story is told, most commonly first person or third person (Lessons 1, 4, 7); how an author feels about a particular topic or idea (Lesson 11)

precise language words that indicate exactly what the author wishes to convey, bringing images in a text to life (Lesson 4)

primary source a document, speech, image, or other piece of evidence created by someone who was present when an event happened (Lessons 5, 11)

propelling action an event or detail in a text that drives the story forward (Lesson 6)

pun a play on the multiple meanings of a word or on two words that sound alike but have different meanings, generally used for humorous effect (Lesson 8)

reason the basis for a claim or an opinion (Lesson 12)

reasoned judgment a personal view that is based on facts, logic, and reason (Lessons 5, 9)

resolution the part of the plot that takes place after the climax, bringing the story to a close (Lesson 8)

rhyme scheme the pattern of end rhymes in a poem that is represented by a string of letters, such as *ababcdcd* (Lesson 7)

scientific symbol a unit of measure, chemical formula, or other object used to present data and information in science and technical texts (Lesson 9)

secondary source something created or written about an event by a person who was not present when the event took place (Lessons 5, 11)

sensory language words that appeal to a reader's sense of sight, hearing, touch, smell, and taste (Lessons 4, 8)

setting the time and place in which a story occurs (Lessons 1, 6)

simile a type of figurative language that compares two things or ideas using *like* or *as* (Lesson 8)

situational irony a situation in which the outcome of an event is the opposite of what is expected; used by writers for effect (Lesson 1)

source a book, person, Web site, etc., that provides information (Lessons 2, 10)

speculation a conclusion based on incomplete evidence (Lesson 9)

steps in a process an organizational pattern in which information in a text is presented in sequence (Lessons 5, 9)

subjunctive mood the form of a verb used to express an idea that is hypothetical, or not based in fact, such as thoughts and wishes (Lesson 10)

summary the most important ideas of a text, expressed in a few sentences (Lessons 1, 3, 6)

support see *supporting details*

supporting details facts, statistics, explanations, data, and other evidence that help to convey the main idea of a text (Lessons 2, 3, 4, 10, 12)

supporting paragraphs groups of sentences that provide more information about the main idea (Lessons 2, 4, 10, 12)

suspense a state of uncertainty an author creates for the reader in order to maintain the reader's interest (Lesson 1)

symbol an object or action that represents a larger idea or stands for something else (Lesson 7)

text structure how a text is organized, such as by chronological order, cause and effect, or problem and solution (Lessons 3, 5, 9)

theme the central message of a text, usually a general idea about life (Lessons 1, 6, 7)

thesis a statement that presents the main argument of a piece of writing, usually found in the introduction of the text (Lesson 2)

tone the author's feelings and attitude toward the subject of a text (Lessons 3, 7, 10, 11)

topic what a piece of writing is mostly about (Lesson 4)

transition a word or phrase that indicates a sequence of events or connects ideas (Lessons 4, 10, 12)

varying sentence structure the use of different types of sentences to make the text interesting (Lesson 2)

verb voice the form a verb takes to indicate whether the subject of the verb performs the action (active voice) or receives the action (passive voice) (Lesson 8)

verbal a noun, adjective, or adverb formed from a verb (Lesson 4)

verbal irony a situation in which a character's or narrator's words do not match what is really meant; used by writers for effect (Lesson 1)

visual information a chart, graph, map, photograph, illustration, or diagram that expands on information provided in a text or gives new information in a clear, concise format (Lessons 9, 10, 11)

word choice the words or phrases selected by an author to convey his or her meaning (Lessons 3, 10, 11)

Acknowledgments

Picture Credits 5 Thinkstock.com; 21 Thinkstock.com; 23 Thinkstock.com; 48 (c) Thinkstock.com; 48 (br) Library of Congress; 49 (cr) Thinkstock.com; 54 Thinkstock.com; 57 Thinkstock.com; 58 Thinkstock.com; 61 Thinkstock.com; 63 Thinkstock.com; 64 Thinkstock.com; 85 Thinkstock.com; 86 (l, r) National Park Service; 86 (bkgrd) Thinkstock.com; 87 Library of Congress; 88 Library of Congress; 89 (bl, c, br) Thinkstock.com; 92 Thinkstock.com; 97 Thinkstock.com; 98 Thinkstock.com; 99 Library of Congress; 100 Library of Congress; 101 Library of Congress; 104 Library of Congress; 106 Library of Congress; 107 Library of Congress; 108 (t, b) Library of Congress; 111 Thinkstock.com; 123 Thinkstock.com; 125 Thinkstock.com; 126 Thinkstock.com; 147 Thinkstock.com; 148–149 (b) Thinkstock.com; 149 (bkgrd) Thinkstock.com; 150–151 (b) Thinkstock.com; 150 (cr) Thinkstock.com; 155 (bl, br) Thinkstock.com; 156 (l, c, r) Thinkstock.com; 157 Library of Congress; 158 Thinkstock.com; 161 Thinkstock.com; 163 Library of Congress; 164 Library of Congress; 172 Library of Congress; 189 Thinkstock.com; 190 Library of Congress; 191 Library of Congress; 192 Library of Congress; 193 Thinkstock.com; 198 National Park Service; 199 National Park Service; 200 (t, bl, br) Thinkstock.com; 203 Thinkstock.com; 205 Thinkstock.com; 206 Thinkstock.com.

Illustrations Cover Jing Jing Tsong; 6–11 Chris Gall; 14–18 Marcia Adams; 112–113 Bats Langley; 117–118 Peter Ferguson.